Babel to Byzantium

Babel to Byzantium

POETS & POETRY NOW

James Dickey

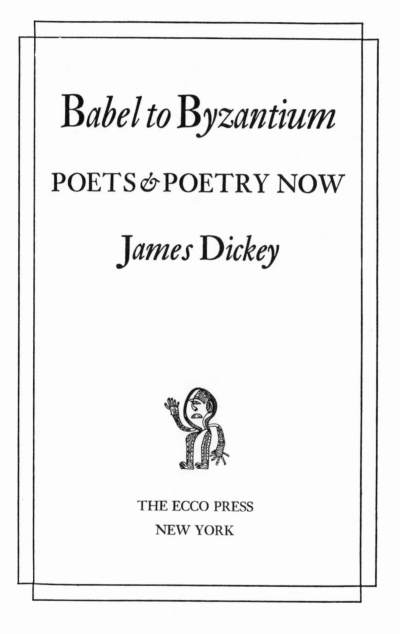

THE ECCO PRESS

NEW YORK

Grateful acknowledgment is made to the editors of *The American Scholar*, *The Atlantic Monthly*, *The Hudson Review*, *The New York Times Book Review*, *Poetry*, *The Sewanee Review*, and *The Virginia Quarterly Review*, in whose pages some of these essays were originally published.

"Edwin Arlington Robinson" is reprinted, with the permission of The Macmillan Company, from *Selected Poems of Edwin Arlington Robinson*, edited by Morton Dauwen Zabel, introduction by James Dickey (Copyright © The Macmillan Company 1965). "Notes on the Decline of Outrage" was first published in *South: Modern Southern Literature in Its Cultural Setting*, Copyright © 1961 by Louis D. Rubin, Jr., and Robert D. Jacobs (Doubleday & Company, Inc.). "The Poet Turns on Himself" was first published in *Poets on Poetry*, edited by Howard Nemerov, © 1966 by Howard Nemerov (Basic Books, Inc.). The essays in Part II, "Five Poets," were first published in *Master Poems of the English Language*, edited by Oscar Williams, Copyright © 1966 by Trident Press; reprinted by permission of Trident Press. "The Lifeguard," Copyright © 1961 by James Dickey, is reprinted from *Drowning with Others* and originally appeared in *The New Yorker;* "The Firebombing," Copyright © 1964 by James Dickey, is reprinted from *Buckdancer's Choice* and originally appeared in *Poetry;* "Sleeping Out at Easter," Copyright © 1960 by James Dickey, is reprinted from *Poems 1957–1967*—all by permission of Wesleyan University Press. The poem *Harp Music* appeared originally in *The New Yorker*.

to my wife Maxine,

the critic's critic, but with love

PREFACE

A BOOK such as this one seems to be obligated to carry with it the notion that the critic has a System of Evaluation that he can defend not only in its practical and local instances but in its broader theoretical and philosophical implications as well. If the critic is myself, he knows beyond any doubt that he cannot do these things at all. He knows that any reasonably good teacher of aesthetics could tear his "ideas" apart with no trouble; he lives in constant dread of falling into the hands of the neighborhood community college's Socrates. But even should this not befall him, he is still inordinately bothered by the number of quite obvious contradictions that occur throughout the book, some of them on the same page. He certainly cannot claim consistency, although he secretly thinks he has it, in some intuitive, mysterious, and perhaps subliminal way. Nevertheless, despite all his misgivings, he has at one time or another *had* these opinions. And now he has collected them, and is consequently obliged to believe that there is some value in doing so.

Though I have been made aware by my whole education of the necessity of internally consistent thinking and judgment, it appears to me that, where poetry is concerned, there are more important things than judgment involved, and that foremost among these is participation. More often than not, our kind of education is likely to take us the other way, into systems of ranking poets and poems, into the now-familiar myopia of close-reading, into the sociology and history and psychology that surrounds poems, if you insist on looking at them in these particular ways, instead of into the bodily and often purely irrational personal experience of the poem. At any rate, it should be clear that responses depend very largely not only on who is responding but on the mental and physical circumstances under which the responses are taking place. This is unlikely to make for completely coherent judgment, but complete participation is always possible, depending on how much we are "up" (in the athletic sense) for the poem.

Like Leslie Fiedler, I abjure the full-scale critical performance, the huge exegetical tome that quite literally *uses up* the creative work it purports to discuss and leaves little for the less thorough and professional reader to participate in, the critic having made all possible responses to the work *official:* that is, sanctioned by criticism. I am very much against this approach, and very much in favor of any kind of reading that will make *living* the poem— at a definite time and in a definite place—possible. I am for the individual's reaction, whatever extraneous material it includes, and against all critical officialdoms. As a critic I hope to hold on to my amateur standing, and to write but little more unless moved to it by works that allow me no choice.

J. D.

February 1968

CONTENTS

Contents

II. Five Poems

III.   *The Poet Turns on Himself*

I

Poets & Poetry Now

IN THE PRESENCE
OF ANTHOLOGIES

THERE are four or five main ways of reacting to poems, and they all matter. In ascending order of importance they are (a) "This probably isn't so, and even if it were I couldn't care less," (b) "This may be true enough as far as it goes, but, well . . . so what?" (c) "This is true, or at least convincing, and therefore I respond to it differently than I do to poems in the first two categories," and (d) "This is true with a kind of truth at which I could never have arrived by myself, but its truth is better than the one I had believed." The first two classifications are useful because they are what we feel about bad poems, very bad ones in (a) and half-bad or unsuccessfully realized ones in (b). In (c) are most of the poems we like well enough to call "good" in reviews and to which we may want to return occasionally, and in (d) are those we continue to call great when conversing only with ourselves, and which we would hope to die hearing or remembering. Almost all writers of verse aspire simply to reside in (c), and many a solid reputation—such as that of Robert Graves —has been founded on just such a semi-permanent residence, which is by no means as easy of attainment as I may make it seem. Even those whom we call "major" poets catch only a few glimpses of the world I have designated (d), or at most stand for a handful of moments in that bewildering light, in the certainty that they are bringing about an entirely new kind of human communication compounded of about equal parts of the commonality of all mankind and the unique particularity of the poet's vision and his language. The achievement of even a small but steadily authentic flame is immensely difficult, as we all know, and requires, as well as a great deal of luck, a lifelong attention to those means by which we might best hope to feed it. With each poem, the difficulties come at us from all sides anew. How far, the poet thinks, should I entrust my poem to the flux of images and memories that are its only hope? The stream of consciousness (and unconsciousness) is the source of all good things, but it is also the source of all bad things. If I inhibit it with too many rules, it is likely to give me nothing, and I will end up writing a poetry of the pure will, like Lee Anderson's (true, Paul Valéry insisted that he wrote this kind, but if so his will was a better imagination than my imagination). The opposite thing to do is to let everything out, and for a brief dazzling moment which some poets never outlive this looks like the answer, the philosopher's stone, the Comstock Lode of poetry. Abandoned to that stream, and with all kinds of subterranean creatures thrusting words into your mouth by the bucketful, it is hard not to ride thus forever, singing and shouting whatever comes to mind. If someone were to tell you that your "song" was only a kind of monstrousness that has to be understood and ordered according to some principle to be meaningful, you might be likely to bring up in refutation what the French refer to as the Surrealist Breakthrough, and the marvelous poems of Éluard and Desnos, which (these poets assure us at great length) could not have come forth in any other way. And if you are young, and if you get the proper kind of encouragement from your elders, men like Kenneth Rexroth and Charles Olson, you can coast downstream forever, perfectly mindless and jubilant. This is, I think, a fair description of the writers in Mr. Donald Allen's anthology.* And to an era weary of overrefined, univer-

* *The New American Poetry 1945–1960* edited by Donald M. Allen. New York, Grove Press.

sity-pale subtleties, they look interesting; at least they look *different*. Nothing on God's earth can shut them up, and the fact that a good many of their own kind and a few curio-seekers from other walks of life listen to them bellow in coffeehouses convinces those who wish to be convinced that they are "bringing poetry back to the public," restoring it to its true role, making it prophetic, and so on. Meanwhile their mentors keep telling the genteel, mildly interested middle-brow public that this is a *real* movement: that, as Mr. Rexroth said recently in *The New York Times Book Review*, these writers are aware of their "unchanging responsibility to poetry's most ancient utterances," that this one is "unquestionably the best" of the lot and that that one is a "rough, startlingly honest poet," and so on, as if these estimates were indeed of some value, much as if I were to say that a grade-school sprinter displays "startling leg drive" or is "explosive off the blocks," and said nothing at all of what would happen to him if he were to line up on the same track with Dave Sime or Bob Hayes. The fact is that few of those who fill up the 454 pages of *The New American Poetry* can write a lick. These few are occasionally good in some of the ways in which it matters to be good, but put against a really intelligent and *resourceful* poet like Howard Nemerov, even they show up pretty drably. The fact that a reasonably large segment of the reading public might now be persuaded that the "New Poets" are "real" and that poets like Nemerov are only "mandarin" writers (as Rexroth, using Cyril Connolly's term, says) indicates as nothing else has done for a long time how little we really care about poetry, how little we love it for what it is to *us* (and not for what we have been told it is), and above all how little we have learned about it.

Perhaps poetry is by nature a realm where only extremes and things of more than life size, more than life intensity, are valid. But there is a vast difference between the extremes of Rimbaud, a genius who screamed, and Allen Ginsberg, an ordinary and somewhat pretentious man who screams. It may be, too, that the answer deserved by the sober constipation of the Yvor Winters school and the chatty, knowledgeable aesthetic elegance of the likes of Anthony Hecht and George Starbuck is the aggressive gabble of the "Beats" and the other and similar poets whom Mr. Allen puts before us. And perhaps, again, what we really want (or perhaps I had better say what *I* really want) has very little to do with either.

When I stop to examine them, as I frequently do these days, I find that my tastes in poetry are actually quite simple. I wish merely to be able to feel and see and respond to what the poet is saying, and with as much strength and depth as possible. The difficulty is that much contemporary (and other) poetry is made up of a number of totally unconvincing postures and induces a kind of disbelief in the reader completely different from that cited by Coleridge. It is a disbelief which refuses to be suspended either willingly or unwillingly, for it is occasioned by a growing certainty that the writer has wilfully betrayed his own experience. The most unconvincing of these postures—all so remarkably alike that they posit a new poetic conformity-in-anarchy which may well presage the death of all authentic expression in this generation—are to be found in Mr. Allen's collection. If the first blow is dealt the reader's belief in the poem by any hint of insincerity, this belief is simply annihilated by such yowling for attention (not in order to communicate anything, but merely to be noticed, to be discovered saying something ostensibly poetic and /or philosophical) as this "line" from Michael McClure: OH BEAUTY BEAUTY BEAUTY BEAUTY BEAUTY BEAUTY IS HIDEOUS. I think this is not an unfair sample of Mr. McClure's approach, if such it may be called. Mr. Ginsberg's is similar, though even less interesting, despite the fact that some of it has to do with narcotics and homosexuality. Ginsberg's comic abilities, which I still enjoy, are not much in evidence here, which is a shame. But then Mr. Ginsberg's poems are not the best in this anthology, either, though certainly the most publicized, and so my regret over the omission of his poem about the luggage room at the Greyhound bus station is balanced by some work by other writers in which there are certain glimmers of talent which may eventually lead to better poetry than these poets are able to come up with at present. Of these, Gary Snyder comes closest to valid expression. The example of Pound has helped him, and that probably explains his superiority to the others. I think, too, that Robert Duncan is quite imaginative, though somewhat pretentious, and that there are some good passages in the selections from Charles Olson, Paul Blackburn, Robert Creeley, Paul Carroll, Larry Eigner, Jonathan Williams, and Denise Levertov. The rest, as far as I am concerned, are a complete and dead loss, and must bore even their authors.

Both the public and "critical" (or Rexrothian) success and the actual failure of these people (or the majority of them, at any rate) can be traced to the absence in each of them of what W. H. Auden calls "the censor": the faculty or indwelling being which determines what shall and what shall not come into a poem, and which has the final say as to how the admitted material shall be used. It is basically the same as Coleridge's "architectonic" faculty: that which builds the good details into coherent wholes. But if everything we come out with is called "good," what basis is there for the *selection* of the real good? Much less the ordering of authentic materials into significant communicative structures? If I feel a little guilty about using this kind of academic language I do so with some defiance, for I recognize that even academism, much as I have inveighed against it in the past, is (as Dr. Winters tells us) a defense of the mind, and so of the only way in which permanently valuable poetry may be written. It is quite true—and has been amply demonstrated over the last twenty years—that the censor can censor you to death, and can cut off the life-stream of the unconscious entirely, or poison it in subtle and sterilizing ways. To make matters even more complicated, the censor can even write poems out of virtually nothing, much as if a man were to build a house only of nails, or as if a poem were to fancy itself the subject of Roy Campbell's justly celebrated quatrain about the South African novelists, using "the snaffle and the curb" on a nonexistent horse. And this is not good, either. But when the stream of images is rich and full and the censor is at his best: when he (or it) knows what to look for and seize on and what to do with it when it appears, poetry has its only legitimate chance to come into being. It is precisely this chance that the "Beats" are systematically denying themselves, with the help of (again) Mr. Rexroth, William Carlos Williams, Charles Olson, and editors like Donald Allen, who has the temerity to label his book *The New American Poetry*. What he has given us, instead, is an enormous amount of fairly low-grade whale fat, at least part of which might, with the help of the censor, render down into usable oil. But this is something we are unlikely ever to see happen. There is too much encouragement given it to remain what it is: "natural."

[1961]

.   .

.

In a sense, every poem of every new book is presided over and judged by an imminent Anthology. Anthologies are perhaps the most important harbingers of lastingness that a writer's work may know during his lifetime; thus they have come to seem a kind of trial immortality for all good poems. In them, poets look for their names and their best or most typical poems, or their atypical, one-shot successes with fear, pride, satisfaction, and awe: in the presence of anthologies the mighty tremble; the lesser know fantastic hope, and the plainly unworthy are exalted. Doubts are many, on the part of the anthologist no less than on that of the poets, for what type of book is more open to attack? Anyone who reviews or even reads it is almost certain to use it merely to throw out in favor of the one *he* would edit, if he could ever get round to it, or if he were ever asked. Into the presence of this celestial and awesome Book all others come at their own risk, and are withered in the impossible light of Heaven. Reading earthly collections *does*, however, lead one to certain conclusions about the function of the *genre*, which is not at all what we sometimes suppose it to be. The *raison d'être* of the anthology is only secondarily to indicate trends, groups, schools, and periods, or to show what the young are writing, or what the old have written at different times, under different cultural conditions, or to demonstrate what Oscar Williams considers to be *A Treasury of Great Poems*. It is not to present a reflection of "the sensibility of an era" as seen in the eyes of its editors, or, more fragmentarily, in those of its poets. It is to lead readers to the poets on their home ground, their own books, where they present their worlds as fully and deeply as they are able. Such, especially, is the value of a book like *The New Poets of England and America*,* since only a few of these writers are at all well known. Reading through *New Poets*, I found myself, after a first, freewheeling, and very enjoyable game of "Put-in, Take-out," objecting less and less to the selections, for the book is superbly edited, and, though its inclusions and exclusions are questionable in many cases, most of these poets have every right to admission, being as well as any others representative of a generation that has as yet exhibited very little passion, urgency, or imagination. I am still disturbed at not seeing John Logan, Wilfred Watson, Claire McAllister, and Ernest Sandeen, from this side of the Atlantic. From among the English poets, I miss Burns Singer, Christopher Logue, the brilliant Hilary Corke, and, most of all, Robert Conquest, editor of the important *New Lines* collection, and certainly superior to seven-tenths of these writers. The editors promise subsequent editions, however, and it may be that one day we shall have them all, and shall then be able to construct our ideal Anthology merely by exclusion.

* *The New Poets of England and America* edited by Donald Hall, Robert Pack, and Louis Simpson. Cleveland, Meridian Books, The World Publishing Company.

The main English *bloc* here is formed of the so-called "Movement" poets, and the American, less well defined but still quite identifiable, of the university-taught, New-Criticism-oriented writers whom I am tempted to label collectively the "School of Charm." Though assuredly not of great moment, the "Movement" poets are considerably more interesting than ours. In their work, an uneasy alliance has been joined between Auden and Empson, and fitted with a special Outlook best exemplified in the poems of John Wain (not represented here) and Kingsley Amis. There are the familiar "lists" from Auden ("The . . . the . . . the . . . / The . . . the . . . the . . . the . . .") and many waggish instances of *zeugma* (". . . tickled up with ghosts / That brandish warnings or an abstract noun"). There are the terse, laconic statements learned from Empson ("For one month afterwards the eye stays true . . ."). But these devices are only background for the Outlook, which may be defined as a mutually understood helplessness, in the face of which, much as Hemingway's hero displays "grace," the poet must show wit. I am reminded by the Outlook of nothing so much as of T. E. Hulme's statement that "philosophical syntheses and ethical systems are possible only in arm-chair movements. They are seen to be meaningless as soon as we get into a bus with a dirty baby and a crowd." Amis, particularly, is so strongly in sympathy with the man happy to forget his "philosophical syntheses" under such circumstances that he appears continually to be half apologizing for writing at all. Reading Amis's own book, *A Case of Samples*,* one sees that his real *theme* is this embarrassment about writing: his assumption, which he expects us to share, that it is amusingly futile at best: he not only believes, but must *confess* he believes his poems bear not the slightest *real* relation to the tiresome, routine, scrubby existences that people live. Yet Amis is not empty; only thin, bright, and somewhat brittle. He is amusing, and should make his contribution to light verse,

* *A Case of Samples* by Kingsley Amis. New York, Harcourt, Brace and World.

wherein he is perfectly assured, quite funny, and certainly in fashion.

Of the other "Movement" writers included in *New Poets*, only Philip Larkin is worth considering. He is said to exemplify the best of the group's work, and I am inclined to agree with the judgment. He is assuredly a great deal more interesting than Thom Gunn, John Holloway, or Donald Davie, all of whom seem to me derivative, cautious, and nearly profitless. Unlike these, Larkin is in a continuously right and meaningful relation to his material. Without straining in the least, he gets a little more out of each subject than one would have thought likely; one understands at last that this small, characteristic difference between his poems and the quite ordinary ones he might have written stems simply from his warm, penetrating way of seeing his subjects and of thinking clearly about them. He has an easy, conversational voice that strikes me as being very nearly flawless in pitch, and a tender gravity I find most attractive.

In keeping with my earlier pronouncement about the "true function" of anthologies, I want to mention two young English writers whom I had not previously known, in hopes that the reader will be led to seek out their other publications, as I intend to do. Geoffrey Hill and Jon Silkin are both under thirty, and promise much. Hill's "Genesis" is one of the few very fine poems in *New Poets*. I can think of no better compliment to pay Hill than to say I was all but persuaded that, were God a very talented young poet, the six days of the Creation might very well have been as the poem says they were.

Silkin is a strange, breathless, visionary yet energetic poet who deals with the world largely in terms of the deaths of birds, insects, and animals, viewing these not only as portents of human death and perhaps of universal dissolution, but as happenings in themselves unfathomable: terrible, unforgivable. His work brings home to us again the fact that the poet must, inevitably, be *obsessed:* that it is his obsession that gives urgency and point to his use of the craft, being the thing that the words must at all costs embody. Beside Silkin's pathetic and passionate writing one is eager to forget the *New Poets'* pages and pages of neatly worked-up situations, such as "Or let me think I pause beside a door / And see you in a bodice by Vermeer . . ." and the countless other wearisome rehearsals of known, usable qualities that seem mostly the property of the American contingent, here.

Aside from Robert Lowell, represented only by his first and best work, *New Poets* shows only a few American writers who could not be exchanged one for the other without appreciable loss. Two of the editors, Hall and Simpson, are good; Hall is tasteful and delicate, with a generous sense of humor and a nice understanding of structural balance; Simpson is agreeable and sharp, using history lightly and imaginatively in "The Green Shepherd," and building an enveloping and moving dreamwork in "I Dreamed that in a City Dark as Paris." I also liked poems by Howard Nemerov, William Jay Smith, Howard Moss, William Meredith, and Reed Whittemore. The rest all seem to be each other.

The fault of most of this poetry—and perhaps of most poetry—is that one simply doesn't *believe* it. One longs in vain for some standard by which to measure the capacity of works of art to reach us "where we live": to be able to say something definitive about the mysterious enlightening conjunction between the good poem and the inner life of the beholder, without which poetry is an exercise differing from any other linguistic usage only in format. It is easy enough to like the poems in *New Poets;* they fulfill many of our notions of what poems should be; they are by turns clever (Amis), elegant (Anthony Hecht and Richard Wilbur), learned (Donald Davie and Thom Gunn), humbly aspiring (Robert Pack and Donald Justice), funny (Charles Causley and Reed Whittemore), ingenious (Henri Coulette), and sardonic (Donald Finkel), but never any of these things in a way that matters very much. It is easy to like them, but difficult to *care* about them. Most of these are *occasional* poets;

most have been schooled or have learned to pick up pretty nearly any scene or object from memory and make acceptable poetic currency of it. Yet this wider field of choice actually reduces the chances for an absolute and personal *fatality* of viewpoint to occur: the Inevitable tends to get blurred, obscured, and finally swallowed up by the imploring crowd of pretty and quite serviceable Possibles. Facility is not alone at fault; we have given a charming and deliberate smallness far more than its due. There are many poets here who may eventually emerge as significant, but at present, as this excellent selection makes clear, most of them are exemplars of the thing they must overthrow in order to do so.

[1958]

RANDALL JARRELL

A. Why are we Two?

B. I find that my opinions of Randall Jarrell's poetry are so violent that I have summoned you, or created you, out of niggling and Opposing Winds, to furnish me with arguments against which my own will stand forth even stronger, which I should like them to do.

A. I am glad you have created me. I think it good for writers to have the most violent possible arguments brought into play against them. Even unfair arguments. If the work is strong enough, all these will be overcome. Now, I was moved by Jarrell's poems even when I was Wind. Now that I am a Voice therefrom, I find I am moved even more, for I am nearer the human things he writes about.

B. I take it, then, that I have brought forth a satisfactory Opposing Self, for you seem to like Jarrell's poems.

A. I do. I think his book* is, or should certainly be, the occasion of a Triumph. He has been writing for twenty years now, and this book contains a fair portion of all he will do as a writer: that is, the book is a monument, if not to Jarrell *in toto,* then at least to his "early phase," no matter what he may do later.

B. And why is the book a Triumph, may I ask?

A. Because it is the work of an honest, witty, intelligent, and deeply gifted man, a man who knows more about poetry, and knows it in better, more human ways, than any other of our time. If you add to these other things that he has a rare *poetic* intelligence which works, not for itself, but totally in the service of human beings, in compassion and love, then you will have an idea of the kind of Triumph I'm talking about. All you can do about a book like this, as Herbert Read said of Dylan Thomas's *Deaths and Entrances,* is to praise it.

B. I must tell you, then, that to me the book is dull beyond all dullness of stupefaction or petrifaction; that when I read it from end to end I know more of boredom than the dead do. "In plain American that dogs and cats can read," the poems are the most untalentedly sentimental, self-indulgent, and insensitive writings that I can remember; when I read them I cry and laugh helplessly all night, over the reputation that has come out of such stuff.

A. I would say, in answer, that you have missed the entire point of Jarrell's contribution, which is that of writing about real things, rather than playing games with words. He is set like a kind of laughing death against the technique-on-principle people that fill the quarterlies. His world is *the* World, and People, and not the cultivated island of books, theories, and schools. Can't you see that?

* *Selected Poems* by Randall Jarrell. New York, Alfred A. Knopf.

B. Would you give me an example of this attitude at work in one of Jarrell's poems?

A. I'll just pick up a random sample. This is from "The Night before the Night before Christmas." He speaks of "the big old houses, the small new houses." Don't you see. . . .

B. That's real enough, all right, if that's what you mean by real. That is, there *are* big old houses and small new houses, and perhaps this observation tells us something about the economic and social changes that have taken place in the time between the building of the two types of houses. But isn't the statement pretty much of a commonplace? After all, we don't need a poet to point *this* out to us. Am I to believe that you and Jarrell think that comment of this rather tame and obvious kind constitutes Triumphal Poetry? I should be sorry to think so.

A. You certainly *are* to believe it. It is, for instance, far more important than surrealist poems, or those of García Lorca's *Poet in New York*, or any other poetry that uses objects as counters to whirl into and out of bizarre images, simply for the sake of the images, and the bizarreness. Jarrell's poems are far too respectful of experience, of life as it is lived by people, for that to happen. Their world is *our* world.

B. Now this word "real." Hadn't we better examine it a little more closely? Is it actually as important as you say to Jarrell's writing?

A. It *is* his writing. He writes about the things we know; that is, he writes about cats, common soldiers, about the dilemmas of children, and . . . and the small man, the man "things are done to," usually by the State, to the man's almost willing detriment and slow consternation.

B. "Reality," though, is what, exactly? The philosophers have gone into cold graves, for ages, still arguing about the nature of Reality, and probably will do so forever. Do you mean to tell me that if I read Jarrell's poems "in the right spirit" I will have the answer to all these vexing questions the Ages have turned back from with only provisional, unsatisfactory solutions?

A. Yes; in a sense, you will. Like any poet's, Jarrell's is an experiential reality. I believe that, without becoming entangled in metaphysics, we can assume that his reality is "the common ground of experience" of twentieth-century man, especially the American, but not confined to him. Through poems about what has happened to this man (or to his child) in this time, we get, in an extremely detailed, moving, and "true" way, the experience of our time defined. And that is Reality enough.

B. "Reality," then, is what everybody knows and feels it is, since we all have roughly the same experiences as human beings living under (approximately) the same conditions. When there is a war, for instance, we all react to it.

A. That's right.

B. And you think that it's important that Jarrell appeals to others' participation in this common ground of experience: that his poems draw their strength at least in part from this appeal?

A. I do. Can you deny that you have undergone many of the things he writes about?

B. No. I have undergone them. But so have newspapers, mediocre movies, soap operas, and bad poems. So has my old Aunt Virgie, on television. It is not enough that the poet's world be that of "all of us." Of course he must begin there, but that fact doesn't make him a poet, or his writings valuable.

A. Nobody is asserting anything of *that* kind. You oversimplify much too drastically.

B. Jarrell himself seems to assume something of this nature, though. In his criticism he speaks frequently, even obsessively, of a poet's evoking not "a" but "the" real world; he says of Whitman's world that it "so plainly *is* the world" (italics Jarrell's), and so on.

A. You are still missing the point. The poet must evoke a world that is realer than real: his work must result in an intensification of qualities, you might say, that we have all observed and lived, but the poet has observed and lived most deeply of all. This world is so real that the experienced world is transfigured and intensified, through the poem, into itself, a deeper *itself*, a more characteristic *itself*. If a man can make words do this, he is a poet. Only men who can do this *are* poets.

B. Isn't it, though, what all poets are trying to do? Or at least half of them, anyway. There are some poets who are on the side of the World against Art, like Jarrell, and there are others, like the surrealists, Mallarmé, and Valéry, who are for Art against the World. Nietzsche said that no true artist would tolerate for an instant the world as it is. Some artists want to characterize the world, and some to change it and make use of it in their own ways. Assuming for the moment that I, like you and Jarrell, think that the world ought to be characterized, let me ask you an important question: does Jarrell's work in fact *do* this intensifying and typifying you claim for it?

A. You bet it does. His realm is one of pity and terror, of a kind of nonunderstanding understanding (which I'll explain later), and above all of helplessness. All his people, the wounded soldiers, the children, the cancer patients, all these are people in predicaments that happen all the time. They are the things that our situation as human beings can't help bringing to bear on us. It is through the kind of compulsion that these things force up in us that Jarrell writes his poems. He is saying, in almost every poem, "There is no explanation for what is happening to you. *I* don't understand why it is; I can tell you nothing. But I know how it must be for you." The poems are moving in the way life is, when these things happen in it. And there is the compassion of a *man* in them, a man who knows that his helpless pity won't do any good, won't change anything, but who keeps pouring it out anyway because he can't help it. There is your real helplessness, and there is your poet Jarrell. And if you read him in a little less cynical manner than you have done, you would know this; you would become fully Human.

B. But these are *poems* he is trying to write. If you ignore that, you substitute sentimentality and special pleading (admirable though it be) for the poet's true work, which is to put down words in a certain order. You get, in fact, *my* Jarrell. Tell me, my Compassionate friend, with all these fine things that happen to you when you read a Jarrell poem, can you honestly tell me that you think Jarrell has a good ear, or is very perceptive or even accurate in his use of *language?*

A. Yes, I think he has, and is, in an unexceptional, unobtrusive way.

B. (reads)

> The yaks groaning with tea, the burlaps
> Lapping and lapping each stunned universe

Now, how about those "burlaps / Lapping and lapping"? What put *that* one past him if not laxity and not-hearing? Come, now; has he really the poet's deep, instinctive feel for language, the sense of language as a *mode* of experience?

A. He has, but he has a more important commitment, which is to humanity. And that is better.

B. Not in poetry, it isn't. Language and experience have got to be interactive at a deeper (or higher) level to make poetry happen. Deeper or higher than Jarrell commands, I mean. I maintain that Jarrell doesn't have in more than the slightest and rather synthetic and predictable degree this kind of grasp on language. He has a good sense of the poetically profitable situation, which by itself is by no means enough. It won't do, when you write a bad poem, a poem that doesn't "raise to consciousness" (to paraphrase Collingwood) a given segment of experience, to say, "Well, the World told me to say it that way. I looked at the Thing, the War, the Child, the Wounded Man, and it looked back, and the World told me, 'Son, what you see, *is*.' And so I put it down without Artifice, or with only a little, and I felt Compassion for the subject, and I had a poem. And that's what poetry is, by gum." No; that won't wash. Let Jarrell write a single phrase that has the harnessed *verbal* energy of Valéry's "*La mer, la mer, toujours recommencée*" and I'll begin to see him as a poet. And let me add that that line, as far as I'm concerned, has more of "the World" in it than all of Jarrell's; it has because the poet has *put* it there.

A. Do you think that Jarrell's criticism operates from the same assumptions as the poetry?

B. Yes, and these assumptions are infinitely more valuable to him there. He says, in effect, that the poet has to get into *rapport* with his world, which, if he is a real poet, will turn out to be part of Jarrell's definitional (but nowhere defined) World.

A. I believe him.

B. Well, the first part, yes. When he says of Marianne Moore that she has "the poet's immemorial power to make the things of this world seen and felt and living in words," I rejoice. When he says of Richard Wilbur (himself a far better poet than Jarrell) that a certain passage was "only an excuse for some poetry," I can see the justice of the remark, applied not so much to Wilbur, but to other poets Wilbur's age or a little younger: Anthony Hecht, James Merrill, W. S. Merwin. But when we turn to Jarrell's own poems to see what exemplifies, necessarily most centrally in attempt, if not in performance, these principles of writing about "real things," we sense immediately that something is gravely wrong. In reading them you have a feeling of great and self-satisfied relief in thinking, "Is *that* all there is to it? Me for Reality." For the "Real World" is far too often merely called on, and not created at all, by descriptions that would not be remarkable in an ordinary naturalistic short story or novel. This is in part the case, I suppose, because Jarrell evidently considers it a particular virtue, in his espousal of the "real," to cling like death to the commonplace, as though the Real were only the Ordinary, after all, and the solution that artists have sought for centuries were resolved in that recognition. But when García Lorca says, "Your belly is a battle of roots," is that Ordinary?

A. Jarrell might not admit it as poetry.

B. I can't judge as to that. But *I* admit it. Furthermore, it seems to me to be almost fearfully "real," Jarrell be damned. It comes down to this: I don't think you can impose your own notion of "reality" as everyone's, no matter how much you assume and take for granted that everyone is like you, or should be like you. You can't legitimately offer your *personal* interpretation of "reality" *as though it were* universally acceptable, and write criticism and poetry out of an agreement with yourself that this is the case.

A. But that is what you *have* to do, *especially* in your own work.

B. There is a difference between offering *a* view and attempting to impose *the* view.

A. I don't think that is arguable, really.

B. Perhaps not, but think of what I have said, anyway, the next time Jarrell says to you, "Surely everyone will want to read . . ." or "Anyone knows that . . ." or "Nowadays we all learn from . . ."

A. I suppose I am at liberty to believe in Jarrell's as a real world, as a world that is probably as near as a poet can bring me to *the* World, whatever that is (but I *feel* it!).

B. You are. Realer, though, than Dylan Thomas's?

A. Well, yes. Not so good, though, as poetry. But Jarrell's world is nearer what I know.

B. How about what Thomas knows? You appear to be willing to accept this business of Ordinariness as Reality. Tell me, then, why you believe Thomas's to be the better poetry?

A. He does something, well, something *else* to the world. Changes it, maybe.

B. Yes; birds fly through water, stars burst out of bearing mothers' ears (this from the prose), hunchbacks turn into tall young women, and so on. He plays pretty fast and loose with your Ordinary Reality, doesn't he?

A. Yes, I guess so. But what you're saying is that *anyone* who plays fast and loose with things is *thereby* a poet, which is just as untrue as any of the assumptions you say Jarrell makes.

B. I don't intend that inference at all. Would you admit that

Thomas's successes depend at least in part on these qualities of changing and shaping?

A. Yes, and so would Jarrell, probably. He says of Whitman that he is "the rashest, the most inexplicable and unlikely—the most impossible, one wants to say—of poets." Doesn't that knock out almost everything you've said?

B. Not at all. Consider the kinds of individualities he thinks *relevant* to poetry. All, or almost all the poets he likes, Frost, Williams, Elizabeth Bishop, Robert Lowell, Corbière, even poets mentioned, as it were, in passing, like Adam Drinan and Niccolo degli Albizzi, have what qualities in common?

A. I should say (except possibly of Lowell) that they use simple diction, different kinds of unpoetical offhandness, and are preoccupied largely with . . .

B. Everyday objects, scenes, and so on: brooms, cats, garbage cans, broccoli patches, chickens, squirrels, rabbit hutches, socks, boxes. If someone has a simile comparing defeated soldiers to ". . . barrels rolling, jolting," Jarrell will be more likely to approve it than if the soldiers were likened to dispossessed kings, unless the kings were homey ones. But mightn't kings be more effective, in some conceivable instances?

A. Aren't you just assuming all this?

B. I don't think I am, entirely. Most of the metaphors Jarrell cites as good are of this type. Almost all of his own are. "His raft's hot-water-bottle weight," for instance. There are hundreds. If you make a metaphor, Jarrell seems to be telling you, the second term of it, the thing the first term is being compared *to*, must be something homey, something ordinary, or else you are not dealing with "reality" and therefore not writing poetry.

A. Are you asserting that poetry shouldn't or can't be made with these things?

B. Of course not. Only that it can be made with other things as well.

A. Tell me, do you think these objections hold true of the war poems?

B. Yes, more even than of the others, if that is possible. They have all the attitudes that most people think ought to be shown by poets during wars. Can you imagine a poet loving war, or not pitying the individual soldiers?

A. Does that prevent Jarrell from *really* pitying them?

B. No, and he does pity them. I am disturbed, though, that despite all the pity he shows, none of it is actually brought to bear on any*one*. Did Jarrell never love any *person* in the service with him? Did he just pity himself and all the Others, in a kind of monstrous, abstract, complacent, and inhuman Compassion? I don't think there are really any *people* in the war poems. There are only The Ball Turret Gunner, A Pilot from the Carrier, The Wingman, and assorted faceless types in uniform. They are just collective Objects, or Attitudes, or Killable Puppets. You care very little what happens to them, and that is terrible.

A. It seems to me that Jarrell is writing mostly *about* the impersonal side of war: about the fact that wars are fought, now, almost entirely by machines, and that men suffer more or less as an irrelevant afterthought of the machines.

B. Yes, but men, not Man, suffer. You do get, however, in Jarrell's war poems, some sense of this vast and impersonal aspect of modern warfare, but little of it is realized dramatically. Most of the stuff about aircraft carriers, for instance, is like watching a good film on the subject, like *The Fighting Lady*. If I had to choose between the film and the poems, I would choose the film. I can think of no film I would prefer to Thomas's "Ceremony After a Fire Raid." Jarrell's second-hand Reality simply does not do enough.

A. So far you've been doing most of the talking. Just let me have the floor for a few minutes and I'll explain all this to you, so that you'll see Jarrell for what he is: a serious, important poet, with a great deal to say, a style of his own, and all the rest.

B. Go ahead.

A. In the first place, I think you've been seduced (although maybe that's not the word) by Jarrell's criticism.

B. I think it informs the poetry. Or perhaps the criticism and the poetry are two manifestations of the same attitude. Therefore I assume there is some point in connecting them.

A. No, let me go on. My belief is that there is an honest fellow under the smart-aleck, the fashionable, giggled-over-in-seminars trickster who can quote anything to his purpose much as the devil must be able to quote Scripture. From the evidence of the poems he is an honest, responsible human being and, as in every poet's essential way, innocent. Let me read you something.

(Reads "The Truth")

B. Well?

A. You mean you're not *moved* by that? Now, goddamn it, B., if that doesn't move you, you ought to be boiled down for soap. Look here; there's this little boy whose father and sister have been killed in a bombing raid on London. . . .

B. I understand all that. Perhaps that "slow, grave, choking voice" you read it in is supposed to do part or all of the poem's work. But the thing seems to me to be as sentimental as Eugene Field; after all, he wrote about death and children, too, if you remember. Jarrell certainly doesn't need me to be embarrassed for him, but I am anyway when I hear what you've just read.

A. It takes *courage* to be sentimental nowadays. Besides, the real things are *like* that.

B. Not like *that*. That is just sophisticated journalism; it is craft, in Collingwood's definition: working up a predictable emotion, and damned poor metrically, too. In these later poems, do you suppose Jarrell cares, any more, that poetry is supposed to display at least some degree of rhythmic concentration?

A. He is *beyond* those considerations. He is not Yvor Winters, you know. He is not your mechanical stress-monger. He is a Man, as he says in the last line of the book. He has broken away from all that petty finger-and-toe-counting, those neat, rectangular stanzas. He is past being concerned with those mechanics. He has attained a realm "where only necessary things are done, / With that supreme and grave dexterity that ignores technique" (though I may be misquoting from Kirkup here, in a word or two).

B. You say he's "broken through" these things, that he knows enough, now, not to have to worry about technical matters. Yet it seems to me that he hasn't really reached them at all, in any significant way, or has fallen progressively away from the very slight acquaintance with them evidenced in his first book. The unstated and insistent principle underlying the later poems is "The situation is enough." But, as I keep saying, he has not the power, or the genius, or the talent, or the inclination, or whatever, to make experience rise to its own most intense, concentrated, and meaningful level, a level impossible without *that* poet's having caught it in *those* words. And there the matter rests, as far as I'm concerned.

A. I can see that there's no arguing with you. But I believe that Randall Jarrell will have something to say to people for a very long time to come, especially as the world tries increasingly to survive by inhumanity (assuming you agree with me on this). The poems give you the feel of a time, our time, as no other poetry of our century does, or could, even. They put on your face, nearer than any of your own looks, more irrevocably than your skin, the uncomprehending stare of the individual caught in the State's machinery: in an impersonal, invisible, man-made, and uncontrollable Force. They show in front of you a child's slow, horrified, magnificently un-understanding and growing loss of innocence in which we all share and can't help: which we can neither understand nor help in ourselves in the hands of the State any more than can the children in *our* hands. The poems are one long look, through this expression, into a child's face, as the Things of modern life happen around it, happen to it, so that you see the expressions change, and even feel the breath change over you, and you come to be aware that you are staring back in perfect and centered blindness, in which everything to pity is clear as death, and none of the reasons for any of it. Now *that* is our time. It is humanity in the twentieth century. Or whatever is good, worth saving, there. And that is your poet Randall Jarrell, to stand against any objections, even legitimate ones. He gives you, as all great or good writers do, a foothold in a realm where literature itself is inessential, where your own world is more yours than you could ever have thought, or even felt, but is one you have always known.

[1956]

DAVID IGNATOW

DAVID IGNATOW writes a flat near-prose which sometimes helps his poems toward the kind of innocence and legendary strangeness they try for. The ultimate effect of its use, however, is numbing. Through repetition, understatement loses the sense of the deliberately left-out or held-down that should enhance the suggestiveness of the individual poem, and the poems tend to blur and run together.

The best pieces in *The Gentle Weight Lifter** might be called "Secret Histories." Oedipus, Aeneas, Achilles, King David are seen moving confidently and unsuspectingly through their familiar roles, to become resigned and incredulous at the end results. The reader, too, thinks, "Why, anyone could have made that mistake, and now look what's come of it." The perfectly human actions of these people have somehow been chosen to

* *The Gentle Weight Lifter* by David Ignatow. New York, The Morris Gallery.

become fabulized and "illustrative," but Ignatow's interest and sympathy lie with the human beings who must, unknowingly, act out the myths, and suffer as men their final point. His is a kind of parable-poetry, emphasizing the individual act and its effect on the participant rather than the generalizing or transcendent power of the episode.

> At Colonus Oedipus complained;
> Antigone attended him. He thought
> the sun too hot, she shielded him;
> his enemies too strong, she fought
> for him; his life bitter, she soothed him;
> and hope gone, like all things.
> His blinded eyes pained him, she bathed them;
> and when he left, by decree forced to,
> she went with him, her arm supporting him;
> and where he lay at the end of his strength,
> stretched out upon the forest floor,
> his head pillowed in her lap,
> his arms at his sides trembling,
> she thought surely some cover
> could be found for him.

Aside from the flatness, which is only in a very rudimentary sense a technique, Ignatow does almost completely without the traditional skills of English versification. He makes no effort to assure his lines rhetorical effectiveness; the import of each poem is thus far too dependent upon *what* is said, given in a low, gentle, spell-breaking murmur. At his best, however, Ignatow often seems a real primitive, with the small, serene vision of the Douanier Rousseau or of Bombois. His narrative gift appears to me to be worthy of encouragement, and I look forward, queerly, since concision and concentration are integral to Mr. Ignatow's successes here, to longer work.

[1956]

•   •

•

I have liked David Ignatow's work for a very long time, ever
since his *Gentle Weight Lifter*, and have watched the poems in
the present book* come out in various places, with the growing
conviction that they would make a superb showing when they
were collected. They do. This is one of the three or four best
books—with James Wright's *Saint Judas*, Robert Francis's *The
Orb Weaver*, and Louis Simpson's *A Dream of Governors*—that
Wesleyan has brought out, and these four titles alone give that
house the most exciting poetry list in current American publishing. Ignatow's poems are in no sense inferior to the best of
Wright's or Francis's, which is to say that they rank with the
most authentic now being written. What gives them their unique
power is a kind of strange, myth-dreaming vision of modern city
life, and the ability to infuse the décor of the contemporary city
with the ageless Old Testament fatality of death and judgment:
to make the traditional moral issues of the race *count* in an environment where seemingly they have ceased to, and to give
them a fitting dramaturgy of symbol and image which not only
brings the reader into the situations Ignatow writes about, but
makes him subject to the same unchangeable laws: judges him,
doesn't let him get away untouched. There is no obvious brilliance of language; in Mr. Ignatow's use, words are merely a
vehicle for recounting what happened: what happens. The
dramatic impact of each poem hits you foursquare, always con-
vincingly, and the whole thing, the incident, the judgment, is
what you remember. Mr. Ignatow's is a "total poetry" in a different sense from that in which the term is ordinarily used; not
like that, say, of Hopkins or Dylan Thomas or Mallarmé. Rather
than being word-oriented, it is an inspired and brilliantly success-

* *Say Pardon* by David Ignatow. Middletown, Connecticut, Wesleyan
University Press.

ful metaphysical reportage, with an "I-was-the-man" authority that shakes the involved beholder to his bones.

> Someone approaches to say his life is ruined
> and to fall down at your feet
> and pound his head upon the sidewalk.
> Blood spreads in a puddle.
> And you, in a weak voice, plead
> with those nearby for help;
> your life takes on his desperation.
> He keeps pounding his head.
> It is you who are fated;
> and you fall down beside him.
> It is then you are awakened,
> the body gone, the blood washed from the ground,
> the stores lit up with their goods.

[1961]

KENNETH BURKE

"OUR moods do not believe in each other," Emerson says on the title page of Kenneth Burke's *Book of Moments*.* The reviewer thinks a moment, agrees, and formulates a Reply: "In poetry it is not necessary that they should; it is sufficient that they believe in themselves." Though the judgment is much too easy, it sounds

* *Book of Moments* by Kenneth Burke. Los Altos, California, Hermes Publications.

irresistibly concise and final, and you decide to turn it to account in an examination of the poems. "Do Burke's poems believe in themselves?" you ask. If you read first "The Conspirators" you decide that they do.

> Beyond earshot of others, furtively,
> He whispered, "You best"; she, "You above all."
> It was a deal. They did conspire together,
> Using the legalities, planning for preferment.
>
> Going into the market, they got tables,
> Chairs, and other properties from the public
> Stock-pile, taking absolute possession
> For them alone. These things, all no one else's,
> They thought, plotting further to increase
> Their store. To have, to hold, to love—theirs only.
>
> And after dark, behind drawn blinds, with doors locked,
> And lights off, wordless in wedded privacy,
> They went and got out the family jewels,
> Put his and hers together, playing treasure.

When you read the other poems, however, you are less sure. You remember that Burke's familiar, deft, heavy Machinery has been working away in the Preface to evolve a Theory of the Lyric, and that all the poems must have been at least touched by the Five Master Terms. You become a little restive over the possibility that these simple-seeming and innocuous poems might have, threaded into them in God knows what ways, the whole corpus of human thought.

"In one's moments, one is absolute," the Foreword tells us; we come to want from the poems, then, an Absolute Burke: a highly individualized consciousness calling on language to realize, indispensably, given moments of insight and control. But for the most part this is just what we are not given; Burke's moments do not really get into the poems, unless we are willing to take on faith that they do so. That Burke has a distinguished mind is not to be doubted; that verse is the best, or even an adequate vehicle for its expression is, to my mind, dubious, though I would not want to do without "The Conspirators," and would wish Burke to persevere, in the hope of producing other poems as cleanly, secretly good. In the main, nevertheless, a great, theorizing blight has fallen over *Book of Moments*. In his attempt to hold himself to the use of his "shifting personalities" notion of the poet's role, Burke has deprived his work of a central core of feeling, of a uniting and coordinating sensibility which might have given the poems a kind of collective power, a power of realizing to some extent the mind of the author, as Herbert Read's poetry does, rather than that of creating authentic works of art. He has not, on the other hand, been able to give the single poems autonomy; the book resembles a kind of sketchbook for future poems; there are many prosy passages which look as if they were intended to preserve the train of thought until the author could find adequate poetic equivalents for them. There is therefore an air of fragmentariness about *Book of Moments;* most of the best things in it, in fact, *are* fragments, like the proposed poem on Roosevelt (which I should like to see completed, by Burke or someone). Further, you get the feeling that dialectical cleverness is being given too much of the burden of expression: though Burke can link any number of things with at least a tentative cord of reason, he is much less successful in fusing perceptions in an urgency of feeling. There is little sense of *necessity* in his figures; instead, there is that of ingenuity, manipulation. Ideas of considerable complexity are taken into a poem seemingly only to bury the original impulse, the "moment," which often promises a good deal; the poet is prevented from hitting straight back at the world, which of all things a lyric poet ought to be able to do.

As a poet Burke is an amateur, at his infrequent best a good one, and it is a kind of irony Burke himself would appreciate that we look to him for the amateur's virtues: naïveté, deep-felt

passion flashing out through clumsy, imitative passages, prosodic awkwardness, building-better-than-he-knows-in-a-way-
that-may-turn-up-something. But because of his long acquaintance with poetry he must *simulate* at least some of these qualities,
and is not really given a fair chance at the spontaneity and raw-
ness of perception that the gifted sometime practitioner must rely
on for his successes. He has not, save in a few rare instances, the
poet's *feel* of words, but knows, instead, their accepted poetic
usages. Some of the aphorisms in the curious "Flowerishes" are
good, very good indeed, and show Burke's real distinction in
succinct, allusive statement, which does not need in any significant way the appurtenances of verse, and often seems embarrassed by them.

[1956]

GENE DERWOOD

READING Gene Derwood's poems,* one feels a rising anger and
dismay at her determined cultivation of artificiality; between the
reader and some of the loveliest and simplest perceptions in recent poetry rises a dead, light, glittering wall of Poetic Effect
through which one must stare and stare, strength ebbing, in
search of the few things that the poet has intermittently, but
deeply, created. Somehow Miss Derwood's virtues, as a poet, are
not harsh enough, nor ruthless enough enemies of her generous
and overnourished failings. Her human figures, for example, the

* *The Poems of Gene Derwood.* New York, Clarke and Way.

drowned boys and other dead, are gigantesque, self-indulgent
Creations stylized into poetical attitudes, rather than beings
penetrated and understood. This heavy cast of poeticizing, the
working-up of a situation until it seems to plead to be given a
chance for itself against the language, draws a disturbing veil of
falsity about subjects that are moving and serious of their own
weight.

> Spun on a lucky wave, O early boy!
> Now ocean's fish you are
> As heretofore.
> Perhaps you had sweet mercy's tenderness
> To win so soon largesse of choice
> That you, by grace, went gayly to the wave
> And all our mourning should be to rejoice.

Reading this, we think, almost inevitably, that what is said of the
boy's death is said in service to a poetic mode, to the conventions
of poetic antithesis, rather than to the personal conditions of
death and grief. Miss Derwood's poems seldom give the sustained illusion that, reached through language, the matter realized by the poem has made language itself irrelevant; the poems
often sink into a gyrating verbosity akin to the worst writings of
George Barker and to nearly all those of Dunstan Thompson; in
these poems it is almost impossible to see past the determined
surface-flash of language to what the poet is really getting at; in
most cases (to change the metaphor) the pouring weather of the
Word neither releases, nor withdraws enough to disclose, nor
creates a livable world. After all, you can't have much interest in
"mountains of dove-tailed pebbles and words wordened." The
paucity of objects cleanly focused, the prevalence of the
swotted-up, the World-seen-as-Complexity-Roiling-Its-Words
make you very happy to come on a line like "There must be
something wrong with being wise," but this judgment is constantly being denied in most of the poems, the poet instead striking out *à la* Edith Sitwell against "our uranium sin" and in favor

of "love" and "imagination." Most of the poems contrive to give you the impression that, instead of being compelled by an inescapable urgency or necessity, the poet has, merely as a matter of course, *taken it upon herself* to write, to write *something*, and must consequently simulate these absent qualities of personal involvement and emotion by agitating the language, inflating the subject, puffing it up with words. Too, she has a liking for hyphenated word combinations, which tend to jag the meter up, keep it lumpish, busily uninteresting.

> The leaves hang steady though the airs unwind.
> Not so impervious dancers radio-blown
> On the substitute estate of Country Club
> Where the pseudo-peasant soles pound, rebound,
> To pseudo-savage beats of music. Brown
> Mat-dull skins wound in pseudo-royal white
> Flirt license through the hours of rub-a-dub.

All this is too bad, for Gene Derwood's poems are of a magnificent potential.

> Beneath a leaf one night-soul tuned a fife;
> Ants drove their buffalo, the aphids snorted;
> Under the wavy earth the youngest beet turned red;
> The shells upon the sea's edge housed soft life;
> The earthworm worked and served; deported
> Men dredged for new character; the hid sun led
> The seasons on the hinder side of tipping earth;
> Some small creatures, not yet human, kept their mirth.

This stanza, worked out in a quieter, more intense *statement* than most of her lines, makes us begin to see the kind of poet we have lost in Gene Derwood; there is the sterile and meaningless proof of our sense of deprivation in our attempt to invent "solutions" that might have enabled her to write thus more often: if she had not spent the time she did on feeble and graceless diatribes against science, if she had clung out of urgency to a simpler idiom, if the beauty of phrases like "stairs the diaphragm would like to climb by stealth," "words broken leave long soughs," "I breathe his dream's excess," "earth's saint-blue edge," and the wonderful "sing with all windows open," had taken root as they should have, and helped the other poems, if she had paid less attention to poets like George Barker. . . . Time after time as you go through the book, flashing hot and slowly turning cold, you feel that *here* the real thing has taken hold, yes, here certainly: isn't she saying "I'll talk of things as plain as this deal table"? But when you run, in a few lines, onto "Conceive I vector but it is twin you are able / As victor over vector matter's hold to splice through," you are forced to decide that she *prefers* this kind of thing, or, worse, that she thinks she *ought* to prefer it. Hers is a common assumption among poets, many of whom conceive of intensity as proceeding from or inherent in a complex busyness of line and figure, and as in deliberate and somewhat militant opposition to point-to-point statement. This tendency is evidence of a fear of the verbal commonplace which in many cases comes to infect the poet's relationship with the commonplaces of experience, from which in fact some of the best poetry (that of Elizabeth Bishop and William Carlos Williams, say) derives, technique being used in these instances to distill a more selective and profound commonplaceness. Gene Derwood's talent is capable of insights of this kind, superior ones. Her essential gift is characterized by Joseph Bennett, in his informative and moving introduction, as innocent. That seems to me to be the case, and the observation does her the kind of justice her best lines merit. Her truest vein is a little like that of Elizabeth Bishop, whose best lines are nothing like as good as Gene Derwood's, though her poems are more successful. Miss Derwood's is a talent that called (at least I hope it did) strongly and natively on deep simplicities, only to heave and strain at them with poetic mannerism. In most of her poems language feeds complacently on language, in a self-nourishing, succubal hermeticism, and works toward mediocrity, with a good deal of effort, what is certainly as pure a vision as we have had since Emily Dickinson's. Some of her stanzas, however, and a good number of her lines make you want to be an entire public, which, like the real one, will surely keep them alive.

[1956]

HOWARD NEMEROV

HOWARD NEMEROV is a fine poet in the process, here,* of becoming a finer one. His is a tough-minded, learned, subtle, and ironic lyricism, determined at all times not to let the world bring in anything poetic form can't handle. There is not a really bad poem in his book. What you do miss, though, is a sense of the poems speaking themselves out, or ever thinking that they ought to speak themselves out, beyond the poet's assured and confident and somewhat predictable idiom into their own uniqueness and necessity. In these tight, nervously offhand stanzas, the means are too obviously well satisfied at being "adequate"; there is not enough evidence of the exploratory, the big-thing-just-missed, or got-hold-of-in-part, that we feel we can legitimately expect of a talent as promising as his.

You are inclined to think of Nemerov as a "resourceful" poet, and he is, very. The resources are those you might imagine: Auden, Eliot, and, more pronouncedly, Yeats, but more especially yet, those of a kind of climate of "modern poetry" that these earlier figures have distilled. This weather of custom makes it

* *The Salt Garden* by Howard Nemerov. Boston, Atlantic-Little, Brown.

possible for one to pick his structures and even his attitudes
from the air, and it is doubly nice, considering the ease with
which this may be done, to be told that one is "in the tradition":
that one is "consolidating" (or even "improving") what one's
predecessors have but indicated. But the "tradition," considered
in this sense, makes a very real danger of "adequacy," or idio-
matic acceptability: makes it, in fact, a species of shallow and
expectant deathbed of originality, of the personal and individu-
ating reaction to things which in large part determines the value
of the poet's work. I don't mean to offer Nemerov as a sacrifice
to this (perhaps dubious) conjectural machinery, for he is too
gifted a poet to be a perfect or even a particularly good example
of the tendency I describe. Nevertheless, it seems to me that he
would do well to watch himself closely, or abandon himself less
shrewdly, perhaps, for the next few years, when he writes.

Nemerov is a very easy poet to read; you like him immediately. He always gives you "something to think about," even in
the lighter poems, the *New Yorker*ish ones, and you are inclined
to waive the feeling that you have thought about it before, with
more vital connections between you and the world, in the work
of Yeats and Auden. Despite the uneasy suspicion that many of
the poems are better exercises than poems, you do feel, when
you have finished the book, that Nemerov is beginning to limit
and perfect his own thing, or two things, rather: the satiric song
with learned overtones, the resigned, knowing, intellectual lyric,
and, on the other hand, the casual-serious meditation from nature, in which the schooled modern intelligence looks through
or past its burden of knowledge into the brute Fact of an aspect
of the surrounding world.

> these trees were here, are here,
> Before King Hannibal had elephants
> Or Frederick grew his red beard through the table
> Or Mordecai hung Haman at the gate.
> The other Ahasuerus has not spat

Nor walked nor cobbled any shoe, nor Joseph
So much as dreamed that he will found the Corn
Exchange Bank in the baked country of Egypt.
Not even those burnt beauties are hawked out,
By the angry Beginner, on Chaos floor
Where they build Pandemonium the Palace
Back in the high old times. Most probably
Nothing will happen. Even the Fall of Man
Is waiting, here, for someone to grow apples;
And the snake, speckled as sunlight on the rock
In the deep woods, still sleeps with a whole head
And has not begun to grow a manly smile.

The poetry of the present age in America, the forties and fifties, has its examplar in Nemerov, I think. He is in my opinion
the best poet under forty that we have, with the possible exception of Richard Wilbur. I should like to see him break out a
little, though, write a few bad poems, even, and then come at the
thing another way, through more "Deep Woods" and "Sanctu-
aries," keeping one hand on what he has won in the "Dialectical
Songs." It may be that the long sequence "The Scales of the
Eyes" is the poem I am wishing for him. Certainly it contains
many impressive things. It is concerned with spiritual definition:
with the Why of belonging anywhere, and with the especial and
far more mysterious Why of belonging "here," at *this* place and
time rather than another. Nemerov's "here" is between the city
and the sea, between process and permanence, between the fact
and the symbol. The interplay of figures, the star and the pool,
the vine, the bloodvessel, the snowfall, the waiting animal, the
spider's web, the bird, seems at first a little discursive, but each
of these entities comes to hold, through quiet, skillful shading, a
powerful and unique particularity.

The low sky was mute and white
And the sun a white hole in the sky

That morning when it came on to snow;
The hushed flakes fell all day.

The hills were hidden in a white air
And every bearing went away,
Landmarks being but white and white
For anyone going anywhere.

All lines were lost, a noon bell
I heard sunk in a sullen pool
Miles off. And yet this patient snow,
When later I walked out in it,

Had lodged itself in tips of grass
And made its mantle bridging so
It lay upon the air and not the earth
So light it hardly bent a blade.

Yet, despite its impressiveness, the poem misses a total, felt unity (though I should not be prepared to argue this with Mr. Kenneth Burke, whose reading of the poem draws on sources of interpretation to which I can pretend no knowledge at all). The individual poems seem to me to achieve more by themselves than the sequence does; the poem is somehow split and portioned out among its symbols and approaches instead of being concentrated, drawn in upon them.

I hope I am not ungrateful to Nemerov in this summary. He is a poet who rouses your fears that he will spend a great deal of time sewing himself a uniform which fits part of him perfectly, provided he exorcises the Fire-Bringer, who is harder to measure. I should like to see Nemerov a Power Among Us, not written off as a "careful minor artisan." The good poems here, "The Sanctuary," most of "The Scales of the Eyes," "Deep Woods," "The Priest's Curse on Dancing" (though when will someone point out that in the much-praised "I Only Am Escaped Alone to Tell Thee," the plaintive "But all that whalebone came from whales" is not really adequate, structurally, to bind the two parts of the central metaphor?), make this by far the poet's best book. It is better, I assume, to say a few hard things of it, hoping they will help the poet even if he sends them off to Hell, than cheerful half-truths, "the nice things one could say" if one looked the book over with an eye toward determining what they might be.

[1956]

                                    •   •

                                         •

I am of Howard Nemerov's generation, in age about midway between him and W. S. Merwin. I have never had great hopes for the poets of my time, since it has seemed for years that the writers who came to maturity just before, during, and immediately after the second war were to survive only as human beings, settling into the genteel, face-saving poverty and sterility of academic life and having their poems published simply because they were the only poets there were, and that they (or we) were never to count as poets at all, except as a kind of Georgian era that would be annihilated by some new revolution of the word, much as Pound and Eliot blew the literary world apart around 1912. After reading Mr. Nemerov's *New and Selected Poems,** however, and after noting that James Wright, Jon Silkin, Geoffrey Hill, and W. S. Graham are of the same generation: after noting, too, that those poets whose early work I most deplored for its neatness, correctness, and deadness—poets like Merwin and James Merrill—have not died as artists but developed toward other and better modes of expression: after reading the work of the "Beat" poets of the ilk of Ginsberg, Corso, and Ferlinghetti (surely the most ludicrously bad of them all) and

* *New and Selected Poems* by Howard Nemerov. Chicago, University of Chicago Press.

the defenses of same by the older Beats like Rexroth, none of whom is fit to appear on the same page (or platform) with Nemerov, Wright or any of the others I have mentioned: after all these things I begin to see my generation somewhat differently than before, and am a great deal more encouraged over its possibilities than I have ever been. That a new poetry of some kind is coming I have no doubt. But it will not be the anarchic collectivism of the Beats, nor will it be based on the sentimental eroticism of Rexroth or the bookish pastiche of Olson. It will not be the airless aestheticism of the forties, either. I cannot of course make any sure prediction as to what its outlines might be like, but if it is to prove of any value at all it will have to find a way to use the intelligence at full stretch, and to turn it into an instrument of liberation rather than constriction: a means by which the intellect can function without inhibiting whatever personal vision and imagination the writer may possess. The operation of such an essentially *poetic* intelligence can be seen in the work of Howard Nemerov, and in great and heartening abundance. Nemerov is one of the few poets I have ever encountered who can turn the sometimes rather grim business of reading through the poems of a book into a profoundly enjoyable experience without sacrificing a jot of intensity. He is one of the wittiest and funniest poets we have, and there are whole sections of his book which might easily be passed over as clever light verse by clever, light readers. And it is true, too, that in his most serious poems there is an element of mocking, or self-mocking. But the enveloping emotion that arises from his writing is helplessness: the helplessness we all feel in the face of the events of our time, and of life itself: the helplessness one feels as one's legitimate but chronically unfair portion in all the things that can't be assuaged or explained. And beneath even this feeling is a sort of hopelessly involved acceptance and resignation which has in it far more of the truly tragic than most poetry which deliberately sets out in quest of tragedy. I won't go on and on, and I won't name what I think are Mr. Nemerov's best poems, for I want each reader to find them for himself, and for all opinions to differ, and for each beholder to defend his own view, if necessary, with his life. But I do wish to end by saying that Nemerov has earned the best his particular Audenian censor can do for him, and that this censor, far from limiting him by putting up barbed wire at his boundaries, is busy showing him every day just how those boundaries may be pushed back, little by little, so that what stands inside them is *earned* ground, and will remain his. For what we all want, in the end, is just such a censor: a poetry-knowledgeable and poetry-divining being who could only be ours, and who is a good deal more alive and kicking than we are, is more vitally conscious and certainly more poetically intelligent than we, more able to tell the good from the bad, the essential from the inessential, the borrowed from the new. He is, really, all we have: the best of ourselves as writers. The value of the censor, the notion of the censor, lies not with Mr. Auden, who defined him and cleverly gave him a name which I have been using uncleverly: the value is not in the name but in the thing, the demonstration of its timeless importance and purpose: the poems of good poets.

[1961]

W. S. GRAHAM

W. S. GRAHAM's field of imagery is the sea, the seaside, shipbuilding, and fishing. It is a world of hard trades, and his poems* have an appropriate wrought, hand-finished, hewn or tempered

* *The Nightfishing* by W. S. Graham. New York, Grove Press.

quality. There are all kinds of violences to syntax, like "tonight in sadly need," but you feel you don't need to forgive these, since many of the poet's best effects depend directly upon such wrenchings. Reading them, I had the impression that the poems have been gentled down out of a syntactical and metaphorical wildness near (or even, perhaps, beyond) the ludicrous, into their present compact and ruggedly spare forms: that what the poet has gained, or earned, since *The Seven Journeys* is an increasingly personal *critical* sense, and that it has been this factor that has enabled the poems to break away from those of Dylan Thomas, which they followed very closely in Graham's earlier books. This is from *The Seven Journeys*.

> Answering the abstract annals of unhero'd floes
> The chimes of sweet Elizabethan turtled air
> Guide their soul cirrus monuments of azure
> Round the skull's thundery cathedral adored in ice.
> Let this head's unsearched gorge gird a fool's Philomel.
> Let this bird's moon bleach a swain's velvet bed.
> Let me from a Celtic sex with granite my costume
> Rise like a bangled Messiah in a saga's beak
> And break the Arctic girl with no seal's barrier
> And set her madrigals round my flint wrists.

The immense amount of stripping and paring necessary to bring out of writing of this kind the bare, forceful, and individualistic economy of the poems in *The Nightfishing* is an indication of both the nature and the successful completion of Graham's long apprenticeship:

> Burned in this element
> To the bare bone, I am
> Trusted on the language.
> I am to walk to you
> Through the night and through
> Each word you make between

Each word I burn bright in
On this wide reach. And you,
Within what arms you lie,
Hear my burning ways
Across these darknesses
That move and merge like foam.
Lie in the world's room,
My dear, and contribute
Here where all dialogues write.

Though he is not, despite everything, so impressive a poet as Thomas, he has a cleaner and harder grasp on some things, and the sea is one of them. It is hard to believe that the sea which Crane covered with flowers, prayers, hands, ice, and music, the sea which Thomas and Auden have mythologized almost out of existence, can be made, again, as capable of being experienced as Graham makes it. His sea strikes us immediately as being a much more brute-fact, lifting-us-letting-us-fall, worked-on, fished-in, sheltered-from sea than these others; for my money it is the livest sea since *The Seafarer's*. Graham has a vital, intense, and very personal stake in his sea, and now, after their trying-out or breaking-in in the earlier books, his words do it a kind of justice that makes you glad that human beings invented language, and that poets appropriate it and live in it.

The ocean, to Graham, is a field of experience where only essentials have their being, in a kind of inhuman mystery against which the human "I" is better defined than on land. Work itself, the work of fishing, say, becomes a communal and unknowing vigil where one is both alone and with the others, amongst the "continual other offer" of the sea. Graham develops this theme out of a quality of observation that must be a continuous, hard, and swelling joy to him, as it was to me when I read it; in their ability to *create* the subject, the poet's economy and force are in no sense short of marvelous.

At last it's all so still. We hull to the nets,
And rest back with our shoulders slacked pleasantly.
And I am illusioned out of this flood as
Separate and stopped to trace all grace arriving.
This grace, this movement bled into this place,
Locks the boat still in the grey of the seized sea.
The illuminations of innocence embrace.
What measures gently

Cross in the air to fix us so still
In this still brightness by knowledge of
The quick proportions of our intricacies?
What sudden perfection is this the measurement of?
And speaks us thoroughly to the bone and has
The iron sea engraved to our faintest breath,
The spray fretted and fixed at a high temper,
A script of light.

So I have been called by my name and
It was not sound. It is me named upon
The space which I continually move across
Bearing between my courage and my lack
The constant I bleed on. And, put to stillness,
Fixed in this metal and its cutting salts,
It is this instant to exact degree,
And for whose sake?

From the common ground of the sea, the dead speak, crying out on silence the name of the living person: his true and "defining" name, telling him who he is, in the light of the collective, inherited past and that of his own present. In Graham's tight, heavy, homemade-sounding, deliberately clumsy, jarringly moving lines, the sea takes on the quality of an impersonal and indispensable crossing-place of the dead and the living, the past and the present, the flesh and the spirit. Here, one's name is "spoken to the bone" by "all the dead brought to harmony," and identity is given a *basis* from which to claim its form, its essential definition: "My ghostly constant is articulated." Language, the poet's Word, is also given life through definition; it is alive or brought to life by individual "breath" out of the common experience, to speak from immersion in that experience, when, in the poet, "each event speaks through." Each moment is, for both man and the word he speaks, death and rebirth, and continuous and changing definition of the essential.

Graham's world is narrow, but it is deep and intense, intensely known and lived. Though there is a certain overreliance on a set of figures, breath burning, silence shouting, and so on, the vigor, the impacted, constantly-changing-about-a-center imagery, and the broken, rocky-mouthed, irresistible surge of his rhythms make him a poet in an entirely separate class. He has left himself, I think, little room for development, but who could advance that supposition in the face of what he has given us in *The Nightfishing*? Graham seems to me to be the most individual and important young poet now writing in English.

[1956]

SAMUEL FRENCH MORSE

LIKE any good book that one wishes were better, Samuel French Morse's *The Scattered Causes** sends the reviewer to verse he considers superior to that in question, in an attempt to find out

* *The Scattered Causes* by Samuel French Morse. Denver, Alan Swallow.

by comparison what the poet lacks, or what he does wrongly. Looked at one way, this is a safe and possibly fruitless enterprise, involving none of the risk and only a little of the trouble the poet underwent in writing the poem. After reading Frost, for example, it is quite easy to conclude that Morse's poems are far too discursive, that most of them lack immediacy, that often the too strict stanza forms stifle more than they release, so that frequently one feels a distinct sense of emancipation on turning away from a poem. These are all legitimate objections to Mr. Morse's work, and could be made to seem final judgments, not to say condemnations. But a definitive evaluation is rendered very difficult of attainment by the fact that Morse is a poet from the inside out, which is the only way to be one. Many of his single lines and several longer passages make a strong and even an exciting case for this assumption. It follows, then, that wherever his poems fail, the blame must be laid on the poet's approach to his material, on his technique in the larger sense, rather than on a defect of verbal sensibility or a want of personal insight.

Here is a fairly typical stanza:

> Leave well enough alone. You speculate
> On what is private and the public will,
> Like Aesop, who had seen, infatuate
> With paradox, the tortoise standing still,
> But understood the fable. What you fear
> Bewilders you with war: the bomber's speed
> Torn from your will to what end you must think
> Impossible and good. So you are here,
> Drawn to hope at the dead end of the year.

That is well said: logically worked out, clear, and, as proposition or argument, convincing. Yet it fails utterly to strike at least one reader with any sense of dramatic force. I am not led through the stanza upon an increasing sense of the necessity and importance of what is being said; certainly my own life seems quite remote from the experience of the shadowy protagonist, curiously called "you," though I suspect that the reverse of this effect was the intention. Like a great deal of contemporary poetry, the passage has the uninteresting patness of an exercise. Morse's practice here is that of picking up, as it were from a considerable distance, items from several disparate sources in his memory and placing them together in a relation calculated to bring from the aggregate a certain effect. To be explicit, by his juxtaposition of Aesop's meditation on the tortoise and a responsible twentieth-century American's bewilderment by "the bomber's speed," Morse wishes to show the eternal and even fabulous necessity of moral reflection, and the increasing difficulty of arriving at moral certainty in the contemporary world: Aesop arrived at hope, but we are driven (or "drawn") there. This in itself is an interesting assumption. Why then is it no more than moderately successful as poetry? It seems to me that the fault lies in Morse's having his eye consistently on the end, the Larger Sense, the Proposition, the General Truth, instead of on the concrete presentation of his subject in its living and particular identity. The details of his poems, always connected by rigid logic and presented in forthright language, are simply stages we pass through to reach "the really important thing," the oversoul of Meaning, the poet often going so far as to sum up in a neat final stanza what we should have gathered from the poem.

The master of this kind of discursive, inventory-like moral poem is of course Auden. And it is precisely the success of Auden's practice that has blurred the seeing and hearing and feeling of a whole generation of English-speaking poets. It is after all a good deal easier to *mention* a thing, perhaps according it a cleverly qualifying adjective, then another thing, and so on, the items of the poem being held together by their subsumption under an abstract quality ("Hope," "Fear," "Guilt"), than it is to set down each image in language by means of which it is realized as a valuable experience in itself. This discursiveness

works successfully for Auden because of the sharpness with
which he uses his immense fund of generalizing information; no
one who has read Howard Griffin's "Conversations" with
Auden can fail to remark that Auden's mind pulls naturally
toward abstractions, isolating principles which enable the initiate
to tell the difference between snobbery and opportunism, the
Saint and the Artist, the anti-Negro bigot and the anti-Semite,
and so on. From the evidence of his writings, I doubt very much
if Morse has the same fundamental affinity for generalization.
The best of his poems are written out of a specific situational
occasion, and have a simple assertiveness of diction that is very
impressive.

> Now grass with many flowers made
> A kind of sweetness, acrid, mild,
> Left loosely drying there, and piled
> As if for taking in, until
> One morning after rain, in chill
> Air shifting motionless and white,
> Somebody set the hay alight.
> And caught with fire, the field took form;
> Even the empty air grew warm,
> And the cloud held all afternoon.
> But nothing is consumed so soon:
> The drifting smoke mixed with the haze
> And air was fading blue for days.

Looking squarely at the object through his memory, Morse is
very much his own poet. Regardless of what he may do in the
future, he is at present a writer who never entirely fails us. If
this condition does not satisfy him, he may become very good
indeed.

[1956]

REED WHITTEMORE

As a poet with certain very obvious and amusing gifts, Reed Whittemore* is almost everyone's favorite. Certainly he is one of mine. Yet there are dangerous favorites and inconsequential favorites, and favorites like pleasant diseases. What of Whittemore? He is as wittily cultural as they come, he has read more than any young man anybody knows, has been all kinds of places, yet shuffles along in an old pair of tennis shoes and khaki pants, with his hands in his pockets, saying to every head-down, hustling graduate student he meets, "Shucks, fellow, don't take all this so seriously. Learn, as I was born to know, that all literature, all life, is secretly funny." How does this attitude get into the poems Whittemore writes? The mechanics of the transition, Whittemore tells us in "A Week of Doodle," are effected something like this:

> It [doodling] does, in my case, for my work, what others expect
> Of courses in writing—how to express and impress;
> And improves my condition no end in a different respect
> Since, in a pinch, I can sell it for (minor) verse.

That is modest enough, though fortunately Whittemore is a great deal better.

* *An American Takes a Walk* by Reed Whittemore. Minneapolis, University of Minnesota Press.

I prefer to sit very still on the couch, watching
All the inanimate things of my daytime life—
The furniture and the curtains, the pictures and books—
Come alive,
Not as in some childish fantasy, the chairs dancing
And Disney prancing backstage, but with dignity

There is a good soberness here, despite the whack at Disney. The passage is never very far from treating the whole mood as a joke, but it is never too near it, either. The felt and unspoken imminence of cutting humor gives the lines the characteristic tone, the good compression present in the best Whittemore poems, and from this balance of an almost fundamental distrust of appearances and a calculating good humor something else emerges: a sense that humor is used in these poems as the most adequate of defenses, or perhaps as the only defense, against things that no ordinary satirist would let in: serious commitment to the subjects he writes about (instead of commitment to their opposites), or total chaos, or poetry. You feel that you shouldn't insist on this too strenuously, however, for Whittemore is wickedly delightful, deft as Willie Hoppe, as good in spots as Auden himself, and a great deal more fun. Yet, as I have been suggesting, something else keeps grazing these poems, and the mind that reads them: something more valuable, more difficult than the poems themselves would have you believe anything is.

As he stands, Whittemore has plenty of whatever it takes to get you to "reassess the world around you," and is not much interested in the other thing, that makes you *like*, or hate in any significant way, anything you know, or think you know. The Subjects of the world stand around you, during your reading of Whittemore's poems, revealed in their inconsequentially ridiculous, very recognizable, and humorously contemptible attitudes, and never in their most deeply characteristic and unknown gestures, in unmanageable love. I suppose this is to say that Whittemore is essentially a satirist—yet even as I write I am not sure of that "essentially." But it *is* true that almost all the poems here are full of very telling satiric invention and observation, Americanized Auden, and "wonderful fun" (as in "Paul Revere's Ride," which is just that). For Whittemore is himself the perfect *Furioso* poet. Certainly I never saw anything published in that genuinely lamented magazine half so good of its kind as the best of these poems. Yet . . . what *is* it, exactly, in terms of the immovable values of real poetry, to be or to have been "the perfect *Furioso* poet"? To have been wittily uncommitted to anything save a few vague humanistic principles that have no issue except to mock, condescendingly and as from a great distance, inhumanly cool with the scintillant remove of knowledgeable superiority, a few of the things we are all against: War, the City, the Army, Science Divorced from Man? To have said to one's eager Cerberus, before the beginnings of dozens of poems, "Keep those three heads grinning. Not laughing. Not growling. Just keep the same expression that's always served us as the very Face and Image of Wit. Nothing living can get past that look." Strength of feeling, it is true, uncritical and breathless with unsanction, comes in a few times, but, save in one or two wonderful exceptions, the effect is that of a jar, and we tend to look up guiltily, saying, "What is *wrong* with Whittemore here, anyway?" Yet we are saying this of the poet who wrote, "And the laced-in hazards of the covert hills," and, for anybody's terror and helpless acquiescence, "Caught in an offshore breeze / A butterfly will turn / Too late to fight the air . . ." Truly hearing the way that "fight" works, no one could argue the effectiveness of this passage. Yet it is more than *effective.* If the theory of the "objective correlative" takes any value from examples, it ought to stand deep in the theorist's mind through this one, bearing with it all the latent terror of the natural world. The image realized here is part of that world, and finally that of man, gained, in an unforeseen and indispensable way, through Whittemore's words. Of the two (or more) poets in Whittemore, I should like most to see the one who wrote those lines emerge. Yet this is not really to posit a choice. May we not have cutting and transitory delight, and the unabashed lyric world, too?

[1956]

ALLEN GINSBERG

I FREELY admit that my own sensibility may exhibit terrible failures of eye, ear, mind, and nerve. Such an admission has grave consequences, and a good many of the terrors of responsibility. Because of my own defects of taste, I fear, for example, that I may diminish some perfectly respectable reader's pleasure in the work of Allen Ginsberg,* who has written the following lines.

What sphinx of cement and aluminum bashed open their skulls and ate up their brains and imagination?
Moloch! Solitude! Filth! Ugliness! Ashcans and unobtainable dollars! Children screaming under the stairways! Boys sobbing in armies! Old men weeping in the parks!

It is at least theoretically possible that I may do a certain amount of harm, also, to the celebrated "Bay Area Renaissance" if I say, with a tone of condescension I don't like but find myself using anyway, that Ginsberg's writings are of the familiar our-love-against-their-machines-and-money variety, strongly akin to those of Henry Miller, Kenneth Patchen, and Kenneth Rexroth, but lacking entirely the memorable and individual qualities of these: Miller's exacerbated sexual humor, Patchen's occasional

* *Howl* by Allen Ginsberg. San Francisco, City Lights Books.

beauties of imagery, and Rexroth's serious and moving contemplation of Time. There are some chances one must take, however; among modern poets, Ginsberg is the perfect inhabitant, if not the very founder of Babel, where conditions do not so much make tongues incomprehensible, but render their utterances, as poetry, meaningless. *Howl* is the skin of Rimbaud's *Une Saison en Enfer* thrown over the conventional maunderings of one type of American adolescent, who has discovered that machine civilization has no interest in his having read Blake. The pattern of introduction of works of this type is familiar: they are offered as. "confession," with the warning (here by William Carlos Williams) that their authors have indeed "descended into Hell" and come back with a marvelous and terrible Truth to tell us, all about ourselves and the world we have made. The principal state of mind is thus hallucination; everyone in Ginsberg's book is hopped-up on benzedrine, pot, or whiskey, and is doing something as violently and loudly as he can, in "protest" or "fulfillment." What emerges from all this is an Attitude, since most of the writing itself is in no sense distinctive. The Attitude, however, is really not worth examining either, since Ginsberg's idea of "revolt" seems essentially to consist in making of oneself "cocksman and Adonis of Denver."

If I pay Ginsberg more attention than he perhaps merits, I do so because I have long harbored what now seems to be a rather frightening assumption: that among the unschooled, self-educated, brash, and relatively mannerless poets whose books are issued by small publishers like City Lights Books, there might one day appear a writer to supply the in-touch-with-living authenticity which current American poetry so badly needs, grown as it has genteel and almost suffocatingly proper. *Howl* is certainly not the work I have been awaiting. And yet, and yet . . . Having established Ginsberg in (or as) Babel, is one, then, utterly sure that in this estimate some important things have not been left out? Isn't it true of his work, for instance, that somewhere amongst its exhibitionist welter of unrelated as-

sociations, wish-fulfillment fantasies, and self-righteous maudlin-
ness, a confused but believable passion for values is struggling?
Are there not a few indiscriminately scattered passages which
indeed do have upon them a good deal of the constricted,
screaming fury Ginsberg feels against his world? And is it quite
fair to say that he lacks *entirely* the better qualities of his literary kin: Patchen, Miller, and Rexroth? Is not, say, his description of the baggage racks in "In the Baggage Room at Greyhound" one of the funniest and most horrifying catalogues (and
typical baggage racks) in contemporary writing?

It was the racks, I realized, sitting myself on top of them now as
    is my wont at lunchtime to rest my tired foot,
it was the racks, great wooden shelves and stanchions posts and
    beams assembled floor to roof jumbled with baggage,
—the Japanese white metal postwar trunk gaudily flowered &
    headed for Fort Bragg,
one Mexican green paper package in purple rope adorned with
    names for Nogales,
hundreds of radiators all at once for Eureka,
crates of Hawaiian underwear,
rolls of posters scattered over the Peninsula, nuts to Sacramento,
one human eye for Napa,
an aluminum box of human blood for Stockton
and a little red package of teeth for Calistoga—

No; I must admit that the comic talent that noted and collected
these items seems to me considerable. And if a measure of craft
were to be exercised? What then? It is hardly fair to hope that
Ginsberg will ever come to agree with himself that this is necessary, but I for one will buy and read what he writes, should he
do so.

[1957]

. .

.

It is fun to imagine the exhilaration that must seize people who "always thought they might be poets" when they try the Allen Ginsberg method and find out that, after all, they *are* poets. In each case the needed equipment is very simple: a life, with its memories, frustrations, secret wishes (very important these!), an ability to write elementary prose and to supply it with rather more exclamation points than might normally be called for; these show transport, awe, horror, and other important emotions.

Later, refinements may be introduced, such as Zen Buddhism and the frequent use of words like "strange," "mad," "tragic," "visionary," "angelic," "apocalyptic"—and lo! the neophyte is revealed as a full-blown Ginsbergian or beatnik poet, qualified to read in coffeehouses, wear a beard, and serve as a "living symbol" of protest and freedom.

Mr. Ginsberg's new poems in *Kaddish*,* like his old poems, seem not so much themselves as a convenient prototype of all such writing: a strewn, mishmash prose consisting mainly of assertions that its author is possessed, is often if not always in "holy ecstasy," and so on. But the writing belies all such claims quite heartlessly; there is nothing holy about it in any sense that I can understand, and its obsession is evidenced only by its efforts to be so. Confession is not enough, and neither is the assumption that the truth of one's experience will emerge if only one can keep talking long enough in a whipped-up state of excitement. It takes more than this to make poetry. It just does.

[1961]

* *Kaddish* by Allen Ginsberg. San Francisco, City Lights Books.

DONALD F. DRUMMOND

DONALD F. DRUMMOND is a writer whom I have watched for several years with some admiration, but with more dismay and regret. That he is the best of a generation of the pupils of Yvor Winters I have no doubt at all. His poems, thoughtful, cleanly conceived and executed, and displaying almost a control-beyond-control of their material, have a great deal of compression, intelligence, and wit. Yet he seems to me a strangely unsatisfactory poet. In common with almost all other Winters-trained writers, Drummond appears to have assimilated entirely, and to have put to extremely effective use, the well-known principles and techniques upon which Winters insists with his characteristic air of finality. This enables Drummond to operate with a certain measure of success within disastrously narrow bounds, and cuts him off entirely from writing poems of permanent value. Worse; one often has the feeling that Mr. Drummond is not a poet at all, in the Platonic sense, but is by choice a kind of minor artisan in words, who has learned all he can from his guild-master, and is unwilling or unable to contribute anything of his own beyond. Many of the pieces in *The Battlement** are quite obviously (to use a phrase of F. R. Leavis) no more than "occasions for the exercise of the verse craft." Drummond writes:

> Excess of light, prohibited
> By the double-rayed diffusive terms

* *The Battlement* by Donald F. Drummond. Denver, Alan Swallow.

At source and sorcerer, becomes
The mystery which is scarletness
Seen in its whole, the violent red
Of quick, aerated blood, arterial
And central near the body's heart.

When one determines from the rest of the poem that this elaborate passage, involving human eyes seen as burning glasses, a
"mystery," and the color of the blood as it leaves the heart, is
simply an overingenious trope meant to define the color of a
woman's dress, it is hard to suppress an unbelieving smile at the
wasted seriousness and effort which concocted it; it is even more
difficult to avoid a certain amount of impatience regarding a
system of values that would reduce the rich, multiple excess of
the imagination to the bare, starved, and creatureless bones
strewn through this book and the several others like it which
Alan Swallow makes available to us.

In spite of their admirable concision, all of Drummond's
poems are denatured, dry, and in their lack of physical concreteness strike me as being no refutation at all to William James's
belief that "the deeper features of reality are found only in per-
ceptual experience." Rather than a refining and "understanding"
of experience, a kind of calculated bleaching process has taken
place, wherein life is reduced to a colorless abstraction of itself.
The body does not, for example, hurt, but "suffers indignity."
Something "portends" something else, so that a third thing may
"misinterpret where it apprehends." And so on. The result of
Drummond's practice: his carefully staged conceits, his logical-
as-a-timetable metaphors, his merciless regularity of accent, is
not the massive sense and depth of inevitability and rightness of
the great practitioners of the strict forms (Dryden, Yeats,
Valéry), but neatness merely: tidiness: the wrapping up of a
small ordinary parcel with habitual skill and dispatch.

I cannot, however, for the life of me get rid of the notion that
Drummond is a *larger* poet than he has yet appeared to be. The

release of this poet (if he exists) from the stone, will, of course, have to be effected by Drummond himself. I should like to see him lose himself for a year or so in the huge variety of Shakespeare, read modern continental verse, even wade shamelessly about in sentimentality. A glacial and sanctioned "purity" of the sort displayed in *The Battlement* has but little chance of contributing anything of value to either the language or the human beings who use it. In a few shocking, rebellious fragments in his book, Drummond appears to possess more individuality and insight than any of the other poets of his persuasion I have read; I would, if I could, enlist him on the side of humanity, rather than that of the Angels, whatever desperate remedies were required.
[1957]

JOHN ASHBERY

W. H. AUDEN's introduction to *Some Trees** is better than any of Mr. Ashbery's poems, but it doesn't help us much with Mr. Ashbery, a very difficult and perhaps impossible poet, since it notices him hardly more than any other writer who draws upon childhood or wishes he were somewhere other than where he is. To discover Mr. Ashbery we have to go beyond Mr. Auden, and struggle with going beyond the surface of Mr. Ashbery, too. *Some Trees* is made up of poems which display a great deal of irresponsible yet often engaging imagination. With one half of the mind feeling like a mystified but somehow willing accom-

---

* *Some Trees* by John Ashbery. New Haven, Yale University Press.

plice, and the other half becoming more and more skeptical, one follows the bright, faddish jargon Ashbery talks with considerable obscure brightness, trying patiently, with some engagement, to decide which of several possible meanings each poem intends. The poems have over them a kind of idling arbitrariness, offering their elements as a profound conjunction of secrecies one can't quite define or evaluate. One doesn't feel, however, that Mr. Ashbery has been at great pains to fabricate these puzzles; on the contrary, this manner of writing seems perfectly natural to him, which must, I suppose, qualify him as an original of some sort.

> A fine rain anoints the canal machinery.
> This is perhaps a day of general honesty
> Without example in the world's history
> Though the fumes are not of a singular authority
> And indeed are dry as poverty.
> Terrific units are on an old man
> In the blue shadow of some paint cans
> As laughing cadets say, "In the evening
> Everything has a schedule, if you can find out what it is."

This is a typical example of Mr. Ashbery's approach (or evasion), with its air of unspecified ceremony in the falsely religious "anoints," and its enigmatic close. Most of the poems are so much like this that I was surprised and even a little shocked to come upon a straightforward piece like "The Instruction Manual." It is not a really good poem, but amongst the sly quaintness, the wink-in-the-mirror attitude of the others, it assumes a certain stature, and even majesty. It may be that Mr. Ashbery realizes he is winking in self-congratulation not at his own clever image in the mirror, but at that of Wallace Stevens, who presides over *Some Trees* in many of his most tiresomely precious surface mannerisms, and little of his incomparable linguistic surety and tact. Though Mr. Ashbery enjoys a real facility with language, and is able to handle difficult forms, like the pantoum and the sestina, with remarkable ease, his poems amount to nothing more than rather cute and momentarily interesting games, like those of a gifted and very childish child who, during "creative play period," wrote a book of poems instead of making finger paintings. If one had no acquaintance with other poetry than Mr. Ashbery's, one would believe there were nothing more to the art than a vague, somewhat precious and connoisseurish liking for words and the puzzle interest of working them into difficult patterns. There is perhaps some value in the fact that the poems in this book were conceived and written, but it is part of the bargain that we not expect to share in their satisfactions to anything like the extent Mr. Ashbery would seem to have done.

[1957]

ROLFE HUMPHRIES

THERE is no need to say that Rolfe Humphries is a good poet. He is, and everyone who reads much poetry knows it. Most recent commentary, though, seems concerned with speculation as to why he isn't a better one. Surely, in the face of what he does, can do, this is one of the classic irrelevancies. In *Green Armor on Green Ground,** Humphries is working with material at the center of a very old affection: Welsh subjects and the traditional Welsh meters. These are, of course, original poems, not transla-

* *Green Armor on Green Ground* by Rolfe Humphries. New York, Charles Scribner's Sons.

tions, and with his tact, restraint, and a beautiful relishing confidence, Humphries sings into them in a way I can characterize only by the adverb "fully."

The first of the two sections, in which each poem is written in one of the classic Welsh meters, is perhaps the more successful. The latter, shorter section of poems in the "free" meters is charming, but (to me) a little thinner, less satisfying than the other. In all the poems, as in a kind of awe, or love, Humphries is never far from Wales itself, as subject. Part of the charm of the book derives from Humphries's extraordinary understanding of Welsh customs and beliefs, and his sensitive rendering of these against their traditionally pastoral background. The poems owe their value, however, to the subtly beautiful effects, in rhythm and music, which Humphries brings forth from these little-known meters. The book would be of immense value if only as *demonstration* (though it is far more than that), since it makes available to our poetic technique not only the mechanics, but the informing idea of systematic internal rhyme. This may, if taken seriously, result in a real love of, rather than an interest in, rhyme and the effects in sound of which it is capable, in sharp contrast to much contemporary verse, wherein rhyme appears to be used in slavish and grudging assent to what "the age demanded" of a classic, or classic-looking poetry. There is none of this empty formalism in Humphries, but a kind of deep executional delight in the complex and demanding uses of alliteration, assonance, and recurring sound. "Hard to do," he says in his introduction, "but how beautiful." Listen:

> Softly, let the measure break
> Till the dancers wake, and rise,
> Lace their golden shoes, and turn
> Toward the stars that burn their eyes.
>
> Softly, let the measure flow,
> Float in silver, and follow.

Softly, let the measure dwell
Slowly, as the spell is wound
Out and in, through space and time,
While the sandals rhyme the round.

Softly, let the measure stir,
Lift, subside, and go under.

Softly, let the measure prove
The bright cadence moving there
Changing, for unbroken dark,
The illumined arc of air.

Softly, let the measure be
Unheard, but never wholly.

Since the alternating stanzas are written in *Awdl gywydd* and
Cywydd deuair hirion, respectively, the second a couplet form
and the first a quatrain, Humphries is combining similar metrical
and rhyming structures (both these use the seven-syllable line);
he is also exemplifying, marvelously, the possibilities of experi-
mentation with these forms.

I have said little about the content of the poems, which is perhaps as remarkable as their structure. Humphries is constantly
seeking, through the music of his rich middle register, to fix
those real or imagined moments which obsess us without explanation: moments by which we have, rationally, least reason to be
obsessed. His ability is nearly without precedent, in these meters
or out of them, in conveying the nuances of these half-remem-
bered, half-seen, almost reachable scenes, memories, or states: he
is the only contemporary lyric poet I know who deserves (at
least by me) to be called *haunting*. His poems are glimpses of a
reality more profound than ourselves, that we yet, in some
powerful and undependable manner, contain. Humphries's success in transmitting these difficult, essential states through an ex-

tremely complex technique which seems as unstudied and inevitable as the flow of water, reminds us again, as Mark Schorer has pointed out, that authentic technical discoveries are spiritual ones, too, and are the means by which we reach those places in us which are least understood, and most typical, necessary, and profound.

[1957]

HERBERT READ

It may be that Herbert Read eschews the conventional sounds and structures of poetry in favor of another thing which seems to him more valuable: a thing which words and their combinations are capable of shadowing forth only in conjunction with ultimate sincerity and what Read calls "the sense of glory." Read has always committed himself to searching life at a very great depth. In so doing, he has deprived himself of almost all the traditional digging tools, taking it on faith that he must submit naked and without artifice to the presence of the Truth he is seeking. To some, he may appear to be mining coal with his bare hands. Others may see him in a nearly messianic light: a man getting at the lode of composite personal experience by the admittedly uncertain medium of words, which have served as well as they can if they show the reflected light of a Truth not so much sensory, but Absolute: opaque, heavy, and full of grandeur and mystery. It is a paradox it would be presumptuous to examine, to note that in his own poems,* Read's lifetime of deal-

* *Moon's Farm* by Herbert Read. New York, Horizon Press.

ing with the composition, structure, and psychological formation of works of art seems to have but little portion. His constant attempt to go beyond all devices of language establishes
Read as firmly as anything could among the Romantic poets he
has unselfishly upheld throughout his career. In doing this, he
takes the occasioning experience itself (and here I use an interesting phrase of Stephen Spender), "the poem behind the
poem," as of first importance, and the created work as successful
only as it embodies, through the necessary distortions of its
means, this experience. "But gently, lest the rhetoric steal / This
mood of quietness." Consequently he is occupied not nearly
enough with the words he must use, having his gaze fixed rather
upon the "far-off divine event" behind or beyond the poem: the
unfathomable mystery of a part of Being. The huge power of
Read's honesty is compelling, but I am bothered a good deal by
many of the poems in which it is set forth. To use words as
sparingly as Read does, shouldn't one see that each syllable pull a
great deal more weight than if it occurred in a somewhat denser
line? In many of these poems the employment of language is
fairly near being arid, and is substantially less successful than if
the poems were to be divested of their linear structure and written as Sir Herbert's excellent prose. Again, the inadequacy is not
entirely technical, but is inadequacy of insight also, the heart's
blood of poetry. In these cases, the moments in which Read believes with such passion and intelligence are given no true
chance to reach us. We have only Sir Herbert's word for it that
they exist, or have existed. There is too much of the will, here,
and not enough of the carrying flow of passion, which, in a great
poet, is inevitably and deeply connected with language. Read's
verse has over it, still, a strong cast of the would-be poet, the
straining inarticulateness of the amateur. In only a few places
does he display the exploratory and personal sense of language
that identifies the major poet.

It is amazing, therefore, after noting that it lacks the skill, the
insight, and the passion requisite to his subjects and approaches,

to find in Read's poetry a number of qualities which are nobly memorable, and (one hopes) of permanent value. The poems I think of most persuasively as Read's ("A World Within a War," "Moon's Farm") are about land, and its relationship to those who live on it. These poems have more of the feudal (and older) sense of *belonging* to the land than any I know since Wordsworth's. He writes, "When you live all the time in the same place / Then you become aware of time." At their most memorable, Read's lines in this vein have the profound authority of statement of words spoken by the dying, or by those who are in love: one has the same horror of asking the poet to change them for "effect" that one would have if they were, indeed, out of such actual situations. It is this naked and yet somehow imaginative and right simplicity, paired with the deep feeling for and of place, that gives Herbert Read's poetry its great spiritual and human resonance; it is fitting that after forty-five years of exemplary service to civilization, Herbert Read should make his ultimate contribution as a poet as "a man speaking to men."
[1957]

KATHERINE HOSKINS

THOUGH there are a great many difficulties in Katherine Hoskins's *Villa Narcisse*,* even the least of her poems are so full of invention and sharp, quirky aptness that there is not much point

* *Villa Narcisse* by Katherine Hoskins. New York, The Noonday Press, Farrar, Straus and Giroux.

in dwelling on her faults, which the virtues seem quite naturally to harbor and display in the bad poems and suppress or make inspired use of in the good ones. It will be very obvious to anyone who reads this book that Mrs. Hoskins is much influenced by Marianne Moore and by the seventeenth-century poets. This fact is by no means sufficient, however, to explain her most interesting pieces: poems in which Mrs. Hoskins is looking at bees, flowers, swimming pools, brooms, washtubs, and children with the fastidious and mathematic accuracy of a housewife lining up the eye of a needle with the light. Illustration will make the difference between good and bad in her work clearer than pages of talk could. This seems to me trivial and boring:

> Hero of poverty and time,
> Gordian hero of the senses' nets,
> Make frugal gala, gloss the Barmecide
> In entertaining world applauded guests,
> Your eyes', your heart's delight.

No matter what else may be said of the passage, it is trying truly hard to cram all kinds of disparate elements together. It makes you think sadly about skillful poets, and their ability to do this with a certain ease, and seem to bring it off. Skill makes all things possible, and one of the distressing characteristics of our verse is that it makes possible a great many poems whose parts, however cleverly arranged and persuaded that they belong together, are (in Bottrall's wonderful phrase) "Fused in no emotive furnace." This observation, which leaps angrily into the mind with the above and similar passages in *Villa Narcisse*, quite dies away as one reads the end of Mrs. Hoskins's "Far South."

> Grown up to exile, I remain
> This side the flowing green and watch,
>   Without touch or smell or smile,

The yellow grape-fruit fall while birds,
The red, the mocking and the long-legg'd
Gentle-handed black

Make of my childhood's plain and gay
Reality improbable,
Defenceless fairy tales.

When Mrs. Hoskins's odd verbal awareness and her memory
are two sides of the same spun coin, the resulting poems are
entirely though complexly direct, written closely around cool,
exact observation (the best of the things she has learned from
Marianne Moore to do and use for herself). Her intelligent employment of syllabic verse, with the air of quaint prosiness and
button-examining meticulousness it gives the lines, aids her in
exactly the way any formal usage should aid the poet, whose
principal aim is to discover the best means of communicating a
necessary state of being. Mrs. Hoskins infrequently allows her
writing to be *just* observation, *just* recording, but the boredom
occasioned by such passages is a very small price to pay for
poems like "After the Late Lynching," "The Sisters," "To
Clean Up," and "The Lost Re-found."

In sum, Mrs. Hoskins is almost totally authentic and profitable. Her poems, packed with domestic things, their descriptions
and meanings, are going to have a very good influence on later
writers, if I am not very badly mistaken.

[1957]

.   .

.

The main mission Katherine Hoskins has given herself is to
wind up the verbal spring as tight as it can be wound, to com-
press until the poem chokes and quivers with its own held-down
violence. One can feel the strain; one reads these poems* with

* *Excursions* by Katherine Hoskins. New York, Atheneum Publishers.

tight jaws and the beginnings of sweat on the forehead. It is often difficult, as well, to leap the logical gaps as blithely as Mrs. Hoskins seems able to do. And in many cases one suspects that these leaps are not entirely imaginative, but are the results of a very special and intelligent kind of literary contrivance.

Mrs. Hoskins, like John Berryman, is a "made" rather than a "natural" poet, and her high degree of skill and rigorous devotion to her art have brought her some outstanding rewards, such as the end of the poem called "After the Late Lynching." But reading through this large selection of her work, one comes to feel that Mrs. Hoskins depends entirely too much on what might be called the *wordiness* of words, or on giving the initiative to words, as Mallarmé advises. Her assumption appears to be that words themselves—in her case, these are usually peculiar, idiosyncratic ones, from the dictionary rather than from living speech—will do everything that needs to be done. She cares less for the perception that it should be the task of the words to embody. The result of her practice is a curiously bookish, heavy, pontificating diction.

> And sometimes drugged and visionary love
> projects beyond the boundaries of fact,
> as dearly waded brooks spring-drunk
> can brim their pastures' stoniest denials.

I have praised Mrs. Hoskins in the past, and I do as much here. At her best she is a very fine poet indeed, but I don't believe she can wring any more than she has already done from this particular idiom, and there are signs that she is falling back from her previous high accomplishment. Cocteau said to poets, I have heard, that they should find what they can do best and then not do it. A style, particularly as highly wrought and artificial a style as Mrs. Hoskins has so diligently—and no doubt painfully—developed, can pall more quickly than others that use forms of diction and rhythm closer to everyday language. Without taking anything away from her considerable achievement in this and her three earlier books, I would like—for the sake of human believability rather than predictable literary effectiveness—to see her try it another way.

[1967]

PHILIP BOOTH

I READ Philip Booth's *Letter from a Distant Land** trying as best I could to see the poems as coming from and illuminating a crucial center. There is none, however. Booth's is an American Georgian poetry, thinly descriptive, replete with easy answers, vacant, amiably bucolic. There are many attempts to feel, or at least to talk about feelings, but precision is lacking, and therefore consequence. Booth tries hard to particularize, but, though he lists many objects, none comes through with the immediate and fierce *haecceitas* that good poems demand and exact. Instead of being concrete, as some reviewers have claimed, Booth's verse is actually quite diffuse and vague.

> We floated on hope at flood,
> and over, over, the tide-
> sunk bar; there where the run
> of current, the waving sun,
> showed clear on the waterglass
> sand, on the seawind grass,
> how the islands were one.

* *Letter from a Distant Land* by Philip Booth. New York, The Viking Press.

Well, how *were* they one? Why is it "hope" on which the poet floats? Further, why "hope at flood," which implies some tremendous inner expectancy? True, Booth has previously stated that he and another had rowed ashore to swim "for love, a summer whim / when our limbs were all July," but that hardly seems adequate to justify the melting, grandiose assertion of the close. No; Booth's writing is undiscriminating in detail and thus mechanical, and so his feelings come to seem mechanical, too, and do not even seem possible without the full support of the Mode. Someone has remarked of this book that "there is not a really bad poem in it." This says exactly the reverse of what the statement intends. The fact that the poems are all no better than acceptably good, means, *sub specie aeternitatis*, that they are no better than unobtrusively or damnably bad; both good and bad, in these senses, will be equally lost. It reveals also, and devastatingly, one of the most pernicious results of the influence of the New Critics: the approval of poems on principle, as it were, if they sound like the thousands of others brought out by the same poetic weather. Booth sounds enough like the other poets his age and of his time to be all of them in one; in addition, he has a strain of complacent sentimentality which I find very much not to my liking. It may be that he will turn out well; I hope so. As far as I am concerned, however, his beginning does not indicate this as a strong possibility.

[1958]

KENNETH PATCHEN

Often at night, when I see that, indeed, the sky is a "deep throw of stars," I think of a poet named Kenneth Patchen, who once told me that it is. Because of this and a few other passages I remember years after first reading them, I have tried to keep track of Patchen, and have gone through most of his books (all, in fact, except *Sleepers Awake,* which I abandoned in despair). I have heard recently that he has joined the "San Francisco School," but in reality he was its only permanent member twenty years before the group was ever conceived in the impatient mind of Kenneth Rexroth, and is still, despite having produced a genuinely impassable mountain of tiresome, obvious, self-important, sprawling, sentimental, witless, preachy, tasteless, use-less poems and books, the best poet that American literary ex-pressionism can show. Occasionally, in fragments and odds and ends nobody wants to seek out any more, he is a writer of su-perb daring and invention, the author of a few passages which are, so far as I can tell, comparable to the most intuitively beau-tiful writing ever done. He is a poet not so much in form as in essence, a condition of which we should all be envious, and with which we should never be satisfied. To evoke the usual standards of formal art in Patchen's case is worse than meaningless. He cannot give anything through the traditional forms (those who suggest that he ought at least to try should take a look at some of the rhymed poems in *Before the Brave*). I do not like to read most of Patchen's work, for it seems to me a cruel waste, but he somehow manages to make continuing claims on my attention that other more consistent poets do not. If there is such a thing as pure or crude imagination, Patchen has it, or has had it. With it he has made twenty-five years of Notes, in the form of scrappy, unsatisfactory, fragmentarily brilliant poems, for a single, unwritten cosmic Work, which bears, at least in some of its parts, analogies to the prophetic books of Blake. Yet the words, the phrases, and the lines that are supposed to make up the individual pieces almost never coalesce, themselves, into wholes, because Patchen looks upon language as patently unworthy of the Vision, and treats it with corresponding indifference and contempt. This is the reason he is not a good writer, or a good prophet, either: this, and the fact that his alternately raging and super-sentimental view of things is too violent, centerless, convulsive, and one-dimensional to be entirely convincing. But he has made and peopled a place that would never have had existence without him: the realm of the "Dark Kingdom," where "all who have opposed in secret, are . . . provided with green crowns," and where the vague, powerful figures of fantasmagoric limbo, the dream people, and, above all, the mythic animals that only he sees, are sometimes as inconsolably troubling as the hallucinations of the madman or the alcoholic, and are occasionally, as if by accident, rendered in language that accords them the only kind of value possible to this kind of writing: makes them obsessive, unpardonable, and magnificent. It is wrong of us to wish that Patchen would "pull himself together." He has never been together. He cannot write poems, as the present book* heartlessly demonstrates. But his authentic and terrible hallucinations infrequently come to great good among the words which they must use. We should leave it at that, and take what we can from him.

[1958]

* *When We Were Here Together* by Kenneth Patchen. New York, New Directions.

MAY SARTON

MAY SARTON is not a profoundly original writer, but she is a beautiful one, with the casual balance, the womanly assurance and judiciousness that we look for in vain in many of our other women poets (I think at random of Edith Sitwell, and other names come flocking). Miss Sarton understands that we must mistrust the betrayals of technical facility fully as much as those of inarticulateness, and that we must employ whatever skills we may summon in the service of the things that move and shape us as human beings. In almost every poem* she attains a delicate simplicity as quickeningly direct as it is deeply given, and does so with the courteous serenity, the clear, caring, intelligent and human calm of the queen of a small, well-ordered country. The only regret Miss Sarton raises is that she is not likely to become much of an "influence." What good effects her practice may have on others will have to take place like the working of a charm or a secret spell: they must be felt in the loving skill with which her poems are built, rather than in the quiet, true, unspectacular sound of her voice.

[1958]

* *In Time Like Air* by May Sarton. New York, Holt, Rinehart and Winston.

WILLIAM JAY SMITH

UP to now, William Jay Smith has been noticed principally as one of our most gifted translators from the French. Though I agree with this entirely, I hope the present book* changes that estimate, for Smith is a fine poet, and as such deserves far more attention than he has been accorded. If sensuous delight and intellectual pleasure are among the important values conferred by poetry, we stand to gain more from Smith than from all but a handful of his contemporaries. He is a kind of dispossessed court poet among the ruins; in the leisured walk of his verse one feels a friendly, warm mind, a thorough and heart-quickening reliance on the things of this world, especially of the old, sumptuous South-European world. This is not to say that Smith is in any way superficial, though the extreme ease and fluency of the verse, and the great good humor and playful satire of some of it may occasionally suggest this as a possibility. Yet Smith never descends to the merely decorative. There is a strong sadness underlying these poems: the helpless acquiescence in decay and death, the falling-to-ruin of the old, man-made beauties, the dark hopelessness of departure. Through the deepening range of the later poems the voice richens, losing none of the clean, garnished grace that moves each line with intimate, musical authority. These poems show, again, how much of the dramatic the lyric attitude can hold, if managed by a very talented poet: one

* *Poems 1947–1957* by William Jay Smith. Boston, Atlantic-Little Brown.

who is privileged to bring instruction out of delight, a lasting
pleasure into the ear, and the things he knows and loves each
into its proper place, where it has always been, and where it
would never have been, had not the right eye seen, the right
voice said.

[1958]

ROBERT PENN WARREN

OPENING a book of poems by Robert Penn Warren* is like putting out the light of the sun, or like plunging into the labyrinth
and feeling the thread break after the first corner is passed. One
will never come out in the same Self as that in which one entered. When he is good, and often even when he is bad, you had
as soon read Warren as live. He gives you the sense of poetry as
a thing of final importance to life: as a way or *form* of life. In his
practice it is a tortured, painful, sometimes rhetorical means of
exploring man's fate, often nearer to tragic melodrama than to
tragedy, but never anything less than fully engaged in its problems, never inconsequential. Like any human poet, Warren has
his failings: his are a liking for the overinflated, or "bombast" as
Longinus defines it; he indulges frequently in examples of pathetic fallacy so outrageous that they should, certainly, become
classic instances of the misuse of this device. Phrases like "the
irrelevant anguish of air," and "the malfeasance of nature or the

* *Promises: Poems 1954-1956* by Robert Penn Warren. New York, Random House.

filth of fate" come only as embarrassments to the reader already entirely committed to Warren's dark and toiling spell. These two figures occur in possibly the best of all his poems: "To a Little Girl, One Year Old, in a Ruined Fortress." One regrets them, but in the end they do not greatly matter.

I cannot interpret for you this collocation
Of memories. You will live your own life, and contrive
The language of your own heart, but let that conversation,
In the last analysis, be always of whatever truth you would live.

For fire flames but in the heart of a colder fire.
All voice is but echo caught from a soundless voice.
Height is not deprivation of valley, nor defect of desire,
But defines, for the fortunate, that joy in which all joys should
    rejoice.

The massive, slow-moving, and leonine writing of this poem, in both its obvious imperfections and its near-sublimity, is the most succinct and moving presentation Warren has yet made of one of his principal themes: the impossible and obsessive desire of human beings for perfection, and the eternally corrupt and corrupting means of attaining it. His great arena for exploring this subject, in his poems as well as in his novels, is History. Somewhere within History, even as it is reduced to and manifested in the lifetime of the individual, abides the fearful and defining Revelation:

. . . and in that dark no thread,
Airy as breath by Ariadne's fingers forged.
No thread, and beyond some groped-at corner, hulked
In the blind dark, hock-deep in ordure, its beard
And shag foul-scabbed, and when the hoof heaves—
Listen!—the foulness sucks like mire.

Warren leads us through parts of History, through a starkly re-interpreted mythology, and through the static, terror-ridden world of his rural childhood as though at each turn of Time or corridor or path, in each change of light, behind each tree of the Kentucky woods, the Secret—terrible, unforeseen, inevitable— will appear, and either strike us dead, drive us into crime inexplicable to any but ourselves, or yield up in transfiguring and releasing pain our Definition. "Definition," in Warren's usage, is the result of the search for one's own *necessary* identity: for the place one has been ordained, by God or chance or self, to occupy in the tragic universe. When the individual discovers or makes "his own truth," the Truth he "would live," he has something to live for as well as by; he is then able to face "the awful responsibility of Time." With Warren we are seeking the identity, the definition, possible only to ourselves, and we are allowed no compromises either with the search or with the discoveries it entails. Warren's verse is so deeply and compellingly linked to man's ageless, age-old drive toward self-discovery, self-determination, that it makes all discussion of line endings, metrical variants, and the rest of poetry's paraphernalia appear hopelessly beside the point. Though it is good to notice in retrospect that Warren's best poems, like "Man in Moonlight," give us, too, the *formal* intensity of art, the sense of the thing done right, one is concerned finally less with this than with the knowledge that these poems invest us with the greatest and most exacting of all human powers: that of discovering and defining what we must be, within the thing that we are.

[1958]

RICHARD EBERHART

RICHARD EBERHART has long been an enigma for critics, and
doubtless will be so forever. To make things even harder for us,
he has all but perfected a number of devices that he employs,
cleverly and with increasing skill, to hide the fact that he is one
of the most authentically gifted and instinctively poetic minds
of our time. If we must choose, and in this case it begins to look
as if we must, between the *merely* formal and uninspired, and
the unformed and talented—if we cannot have inspiration *and*
executive form—we will choose the latter: we will choose Eberhart over Robert Bridges or Yvor Winters or Howard Baker.
That much is or should be plain. Yet Eberhart is often irritating
beyond belief; in this book* he has indulged himself increasingly
in a mannerism which first began to be obtrusive in *Undercliff:*
a gabby, jocularly pedantic dialect, largely of his own invention,
packed with awkward and ponderously frivolous word play like
"the election of erection" and "Enrapture my blessing / Immediacy of perception." One might imagine the heights to
which an untrammelled and enthusiastic use of this procedure
might take American poetry, but one does not have to imagine
them; they are all reached in *Great Praises:* surely it is hard to
believe any of us will ever see again, at least in the book of a
sometime superior poet, anything quite like "Superabundant /

* *Great Praises* by Richard Eberhart. New York, Oxford University
Press.

Faculty manifests sunburned rarity / As he eschews aridity and valley." It is an irony with aspects of the fabulous that Eberhart's main preoccupation as a poet—the achievement of true "immediacy of perception"—is made literally impossible by the heap of ill-digested bookish language he uses to try to persuade you that he is, too, writing from the center of the place "where everything is seen in its purity." Without this manner, on the other hand, Eberhart speaks with utter conviction and directness.

> I wanted to give him some gift,
> Small child dying slowly,
> With brave blue intelligent eyes,
> His form withered piteously.

> Only in the intelligence of those eyes
> Where life had retreated for a piercing look
> Was the enormous mystery justified,
> As he inhaled the betraying oxygen.

I don't know whether or not this kind of clairvoyant simplicity would be available to Eberhart if it were not for the unnatural and frequently ludicrous excesses of the other poems. I am willing to suppose that it would not, though surely his seems a strange route to take toward the first and only poetic Innocence. Yet there are wonderfully exciting times in which Eberhart *does* appear to be able to make of himself "flesh without a mind," and to speak with penetrating and involving spontaneity, and we must therefore grant him whatever means he adjudges favorable to such states, for at these times we recognize him for what he assuredly is: one of the writers who are opening up the world to our life, from the inside.

[1958]

EDWIN MUIR

EDWIN MUIR has come to occupy a distinguished position in contemporary letters. It is entirely deserved, and the reissuing of his 1953 *Collected Poems* in an attractive Grove Press edition* gives me a belated chance to indicate a few of the reasons why it is.

Before you have read more than five or ten pages of Muir, you recognize that he has in full measure the characteristic that more than any other separates the poet from the rest of mankind. He cannot believe in a thing, or even give it credit for existing, until he has mythologized it: made it part of a personal, self-consistent scheme of interpretation. Muir is probably the most determinedly symbol-making poet since Yeats, and quite likely the best. Within the bounds of his system he is capable of major intensity, though this quality makes itself felt slowly, with cumulative effect, since Muir is a reflective, philosophical poet, and not an instinctive one. He is occupied exclusively with Time, and the Mystery by which certain symbols develop a life of their own, and thus come to stand for the important disclosures of Time. According to J. C. Hall, Muir believes that "life is lived on two planes, the actual and the fabulous"; he chooses to deal with it, however, exclusively in terms of the latter, leaving the "actual" plane entirely out of account. Though this practice gives his work the temper of an inspired, distant revery,

* *Collected Poems* by Edwin Muir. New York, Grove Press.

it allows him to treat the symbols of Time much as Freud did those of dream: to make of them functional, interpretive con- centrations of meaning. His main icons are the Trojan War, the Greek myths, the Crucifixion, the Age of Innocence and the Fall, and certain legends of the Middle Ages. Past these Events runs the temporal Journey, which at times is motionless, im- mobilized at one of the "stages" where a symbolic Event occurs. At other times it runs backward, and at still others is able to trav- erse all History in a total, revealing flash. Most of the individual poems are engaged upon disclosing the eternal significance of these several Places, though some of them deal with the Journey between, through forests and fields of heraldic lions, deer, horses, and dragons, or with the entire Pattern, over which presides a kind of mystical determinism which is everywhere felt but no- where entirely understood.

As important and original as Muir's poetry is, one must admit that it is somewhat monotonous. It is easy to tire of his heraldic beasts and men, which are very much like the figures of a medi- eval tapestry: stiff, formal, richly woven, a little awkward and self-conscious in their stylized, symbolic postures. These poems, so deeply preoccupied with Eternal Recurrence, with the Maze, the Trojan War, and the Fall, seem oddly self-disqualified to deal with life as we must live it. Muir forgets that his readers must enter the Journey through the divine, meaningful, and ter- rible *surface* aspects of their existence; he does not really show these eternally significant Events as operative factors in our human condition. Even at their most successful, the poems are parts of an elaborate, serious shadow play ("The great non-stop heraldic show," as Muir calls it); reading them is like having a front-row seat in Plato's cave for command performances of the Iliad and the Crucifixion. Yet how heartening it is to have one's objections fade entirely away, in the light of pieces as good as "The Helmet," "The Animals," "Telemachos Remembers," and "The Transfiguration"! These assure Muir's place as an all-but-major poet, with all the qualities of greatness save a truly and recognizably human dimension.

[1958]

TED HUGHES

TED HUGHES has one or two very interesting poems, a good average in a first book.* Some of the rest of his work shows energy, also, though much of his violence appears studied and purely literary in origin. Ordinarily he uses the verbs which are employed by second-graders and lady novelists to denote strenuous action; there are many "cataclysms," "maelstroms," and the like, and lightning and storm clouds are everywhere. Yet there is something far better than this operatic décor in *The Hawk in the Rain:* a direct and powerful sense of the mystery resident within commonplace sights and occurrences, and a talent that really relishes the sound of words, not for themselves alone, but for the contribution they make to the audible part of poems. He is by no means limited to unintentionally amusing figures like "The abattoir of the tiger's artery," as passages of this caliber demonstrate:

> I listened in emptiness on the moor-ridge.
> The curlew's tear turned its edge on the silence.

> Slowly detail leafed from the darkness. Then the sun
> Orange, red, red erupted

* *The Hawk in the Rain* by Ted Hughes. New York, Harper & Row.

Silently, and splitting to its core tore and flung cloud,
Shook the gulf open, showed blue,

And the big planets hanging—.
I turned

Stumbling in the fever of a dream, down towards
The dark woods, from the kindling tops,

And came to the horses.
                              There, still they stood,
But now steaming and glistening under the flow of light,

Their draped stone manes, their tilted hind-hooves
Stirring under a thaw while all around them

The frost showed its fires. But still they made no sound.
Not one snorted or stamped,

Their hung heads patient as the horizons,
High over valleys, in the red levelling rays—

I can think of several ways in which this might be improved. I would do something about "the curlew's tear," in which no one could believe. "The fever of a dream" is a cliché, and the visual reference in the final simile is vague and inconclusive. But the overall effect is undeniably powerful. Because he has a strong, raw, and apparently natural sense of the way words and memory must interact, in his case, Hughes is able to transfer some of the *mana* of the scene to us. If he can succeed in doing this more often, he will fulfill a very considerable promise.

[1958]

LAWRENCE DURRELL

It is a real shame that Lawrence Durrell's poetry should have had to wait twenty years for American publication in book form. Again we have the Grove Press to thank for making a good poet available, though (despite the fact that Durrell himself made the selection) I don't believe that this book* does him quite the justice he deserves. I miss especially "Elegy on the Closing of the French Brothels," "At Epidaurus," and, most of all, the early, remarkable "Sonnet of Hamlet," perhaps too long to be included here. But the present book is withal a fairly good introduction to Durrell, and certainly displays his rich, slightly thievish sensibility in many of its most fascinating forms. Years after a first acquaintance with them, one still marvels at the freshness of Durrell's poems and at the poet's uncanny ability to bring the right things together in the right relation, to the right cadence, and to stop at the right time, on the cool, right note. With a masculine and beautiful concreteness, he writes of the agelessly lovely Near-East Island World, where every human action is given purpose and meaning by the life lived there forever, seemingly.

> Down there below the temple
> Where the penitents scattered
> Ashes of dead birds, Manoli goes
> In his leaky boat, a rose tied to the rudder.

* *Selected Poems* by Lawrence Durrell. New York, Grove Press.

Near the sad, intelligent, ignoble end of History, Durrell looks affectionately back on this world in some of the most expressive land-and-seascapes in contemporary verse: *paysage moralisé* at its most haunting, endowed with the marvelous and inexhaustible power of being learned from, under the sway of love. It is hard to leave off talking about Durrell, for he has long been a favorite of mine, but I must, and shall end with the injunction to the reader to buy these *Selected Poems*, and then to order his earlier collections (*A Private County*, *On Seeming to Presume*, *Sappho*, and *The Tree of Idleness*) from Faber and Faber, which wisely keeps them in print.

[1958]

CONRAD AIKEN

IN Conrad Aiken's remarkable "autobiographical narrative," *Ushant*, the "queer little top-hatted, frock-coated, Unitarian-minister-and-clairvoyant from California" says to "D." ("Demarest," or Aiken) ". . . at least two or three times you will have the most wonderful of experiences, the blessed experience of coming suddenly upon a veritable gold-mine of consciousness, seemingly inexhaustible, too, and with the words already hermetically stamped on the gold: perhaps out of some such experience you will even achieve one of those 'controlled' masterpieces that are both controlled and uncontrolled, and these are the best, the true artesian water of life: moments of abundance and joy, and the memory of power; but no, not the disciplined knowledge that will enable you to perfect, at will, and repeat-edly, true works of art." Aiken seems to have believed this prophecy *in toto*, and points out with some relish the emergence of the predicted pattern in the subsequent events of his life. Nevertheless, he has continued admirably to move in his own way in what he believes to be the direction of the "controlled masterpiece," "both controlled and uncontrolled," aforesaid. The later poems, beginning with those in *Skylight One* (1949) and continuing through *A Letter From Li Po* (1955) to the present volume,* are meditations (one almost says "musings") in which personal recollection and concepts drawn from reading combine to produce what might be called, in Aiken's handling, extended philosophical lyrics. The most interesting of these new pieces, "The Crystal," is apparently the last to be written, though it is certainly misleading to say, as the dust jacket of this book does, that "most of these poems have never been offered in book form before." Three of the longest—"Hallowe'en," "May-flower," and "Crepe Myrtle"—all appeared, ten years ago, in *Skylight One.* Though one may concede that Aiken is justified in reprinting these three poems as parts of a cycle, one can never-theless not help recording, also, that the last two mentioned are among his weaker, more "official" or external efforts. Not so "The Crystal." If I confine my remarks mainly to this poem, it is because "The Crystal" seems to me to deserve as extended a treatment as I can give it, and because one sees most fully here the resources which Aiken's later work uses, and most of the fruits of his unfashionable, characteristic way of approaching and dealing with his subjects.

In "The Crystal," as in "A Letter From Li Po," "Hallowe'en," and a number of other poems, Aiken is preoccupied with the search for a (or perhaps "the") realm of "timelessness," where all kinds of communication in depth are possible: communion with our own dead, with the great minds of the past, with each

* *Sheepfold Hill* by Conrad Aiken. Cranbury, N.J., Sagamore Press, A. S. Barnes and Company.

other, and, finally, with ourselves. To this end, Aiken has sought figures, "personae," whose various approaches to the Absolute might serve as dramatic projections of the quest for ultimate self-knowledge, which, when attained, makes possible the kind of communion with others that each human being seeks, often without knowing it, as the *raison d'être* of his life. Here the key figure is the philosopher Pythagoras, whose triple role of artist, mathematician, and mystic encompasses the most important functions of the mind. As one might expect in a poem by Aiken, the "timeless" world is found not only in the mind itself, but more importantly in the symbol, the fortuitously inspired and deliberately created work of art, represented in the poem by a figure of Venus carved on an emerald by Mnesarchos, Pythagoras' father:

> the emerald held in a vice, then the green
> ice of the clear stone gives up its goddess,
> the tiny wave bears up its Venus, green foam
> on the brow and the shoulder. The image?
> Of course! But beneath or behind it
> the knowledge, the craft: and the art, above all.
> Would it not be for this, for ruler and compass,
> brother Pythagoras, that we would return?

The spiritual voyage, at the beginning and end of the poem presented as a real sea voyage "to the west" taken by Pythagoras, thus becomes a Proustian "return" into the past in search of the definitive moment of "abundance and joy" which has come by its own mysterious alchemy to be the principal focal point of personal meaning. The crystallization of this moment is, ideally, the work of art in which it may be embodied: the final form it takes as a result of the uniquely human act by which man possesses his deepest experience. The poem is full of marvelous pulses of insight into the nature and significance of the creative mind. One would have to go back to Valéry's notebooks to find so good a description of organic form as, "Design shines implicit

in the blind moment / of self-forgetful perception." Such pronouncements are obviously the high points of the poem; the in-
tervening passages are actually no more than pleasant transitional
devices, opportunities for description: a pagan religious ceremony (somewhat after Pound), the voyage, and the inevitable
quick-change of past into present, where the poem ends with
what must surely be the most astonishing apotheosis of a cocktail party (save perhaps Eliot's) in all literature:

> The cocktails sparkle, are an oblation.
> We pour for the gods, and will always,
> you there, we here, and the others who follow,
> pour thus in communion. Separate in time,
> and yet not separate. Making oblation
> in a single moment of consciousness
> to the endless forever-together.

Despite the ending, however, and over and above some routine
passages, "The Crystal" is an extremely rewarding, closely
worked poem. As always in Aiken's verse, the lines move beautifully, and with such ease and assurance that one often has the
impression of hearing the poem sing itself into existence fully
formed, spontaneously, with no intervention of "craft," no deliberate calculation of effect, as if the poet had indeed found the
"gold-mine of consciousness" of which he speaks in *Ushant,*
' with the words already hermetically stamped on the gold."
That this quality, amounting in Aiken almost to genius, is capable of producing a masterpiece "both controlled and uncontrolled," or several of them, I have no doubt at all. But in spite of
its great merits, "The Crystal" is not one of these. Just as the
mind, effortlessly musical or not, is not always interesting, neither is Aiken's poetry. Perhaps this is because his eye is a much
less subtle and valuable poetic instrument than his ear. Though
in *Sheepfold Hill* his ability to record memorably things seen
and known is markedly better than it has ever been, the flow and
glitter of the verse still cannot help reducing the details of the

poems to a kind of rapt, unindividualized equality. Aiken's symbols, much as they are insisted upon *as* symbols, seldom have the quality of bringing the single life-experience to the reader not merely as a piece of expert writing, but as a moment of heightened consciousness shared.

As he stands, Aiken is in many ways a richly compensating poet. He gives back an immense amount, as from unsuspected resources of the reader's own mind, which has not (it should be said) forgotten a good many banalities and standard beauties. "The Crystal," the end of "Portrait," and the earlier "Hallowe'en" give rise to some very exciting expectations. The next few years should tell us whether Aiken is merely very valuable to us, or whether he is indispensable. Meanwhile, with the poet, his Fates, and these poems, we can

   . . . only wait in the Absolute, and see.

[1959]

.   .

.

The course of poetry appears to have turned away from Conrad Aiken, leaving him an industrious and unfashionable Historic Personage with space in all the textbooks and anthologies and very few readers. Beside the work of those poets who sweat for the ultimate concentration—Thomas, Robert Lowell, John Berryman—Aiken seems terribly low-keyed and diffuse. His long later poems, in fact, seem very like words murmuring endlessly to themselves in poetic terms without in the least resembling poetry as we have come to believe it should be. Part of this neglect—surely unfortunate—results from the fact that Aiken is consistently evaluated by standards which are inimical to his temperament and the characteristics of his verse: concentration, ambiguity, verbal eccentricity, irony, paradox, concreteness (*à la* Williams), and the ability to produce powerfully suggestive phrases suitable for quotation in reviews. Aiken has none of these attributes to any marked degree; he is obviously after other things.

*The Morning Song of Lord Zero** contains twenty-three new poems of some length, including a sequence about vaudeville performers written in 1916 and revised and published—mistakenly, to my view—in 1961. The other three sections are drawn from earlier books, *A Letter to Li Po, Skylight One,* and *Sheepfold Hill,* a fact which calls further attention to Aiken's enormous output, for these books have all been published since his monolithic *Collected Poems.* The huge bulk of his work is closely related, I think, to his basic orientation toward writing, which allows not so much for individually distinct poems to be made, but for poetry as a continuous act to go on uninterruptedly. For Aiken, language is quite simply a self-sufficient interior universe. In this respect his poems are radically different from those of almost all other poets now writing. In Williams, for example—or in newer writers like Theodore Roethke or William Stafford—the poem has a curious power to return you to the actual world with a deeper sense of the meanings that lie hidden in it. There is a profound and mysterious connection between the moment of illumination in the poem and the thing that the poem is about; one feels an interchange between language and reality, each gaining from the other, and in this sense the poems of Roethke, Stafford, James Wright, and others have a life-enhancing quality that is, I suspect, ultimately unanalyzable, but is nevertheless unmistakable. When we turn to Aiken's verse, though, we are not likely to feel that this is the case. We come to suspect, instead, that words are being used not to point back to things that exist independently of words, but as a kind of substitute for them, leading us farther and farther from the realm of hard edges and experienceable relationships into the bodiless

* *The Morning Song of Lord Zero* by Conrad Aiken. New York, Oxford University Press.

toils of syntax, verbal legerdemain, and symbol-making in which the primary virtue of any evoked rose, stone, or tree is that it *is* a symbol.

> We'll summon in one dream all motives forth
> and you shall be the south and I the north
> and we will speak that language of the brain
> that's half of Portugal or all of Spain
> or of those yet unsounded seas
> that westward spawn beneath the menstrual moon:
> what are we but divided souls that live
> or strive to in the sundered self of love?

Nothing quickens here. It is a poetry of thoughtful but perhaps not necessary musing, a kind of verbal daydreaming according to long habit. There are no hard and fast rules as to what is admissible; literally anything may come in, from an occasional genuinely imaginative observation like "sudden as a tree of lightning" to the most random and trivial associations that have never quite managed to find the oblivion they deserve. Consequently, Aiken's poems *are* terribly diffuse, and seem much of the time to be portions lifted from an endless reverie, the reverie that one begins at birth and continues uninterruptedly until death. The sense of necessity that art alone makes possible is almost totally absent, and one surrenders to the serious, musical murmur as to a long after-dinner nap in which one dreams of poetry dreaming that it is poetry.

In regard to Aiken's writing as it has come to exist on the page, I have two complaints. The first is against the frequent juxtaposition of words that have similar sounds but different meanings: the uninteresting and coyly mannered verbal jugglery that all but runs off with Aiken's autobiographical *Ushant* and figures here more obtrusively than in his earlier books of verse.

The Man
  Perfection, it may be—or imperfection it may be—

The Woman

> Or confection perhaps. What a delicious garden. The leaves
> are not of the fig, nor figment, one believes
> in neither.

The other difficulty is more pervasive and more damaging to
the poetry: it is what might be called the "metaphor-or-bust"
syndrome.

> the hawk hangs over his beloved hill
> as love hangs over the destined heart:
> and once more joyfully we begin
> the ancient dance of meet and part,
>   wherein
> each is in turn the hawk and each the heart.

One is struck immediately by both the obvious strain and the
total irrelevance of the figure to any conceivable real passion;
the hawk—to say nothing of the hill and the dance—is only an
arbitrary poetic device distantly and somewhat predictably
standing for what may or may not have been an actual emotional
experience. The danger here is that such poetic bombinating in
the void can take place more easily without genuine experience
than with it, requiring nothing but itself, a pleasant and conventional "sensible emptiness" of words. Despite his compulsion to
follow an analogy until it drops dead of exhaustion, Aiken does
not appear to recognize that such a practice, as he uses it, is
essentially anti-poetic: that this particular trope, for example,
was not a good idea to begin with, being mechanical and unsug-
gestive. Over the whole book there is this effect of straining
to *make mean:* to assign to the fortuitously drifting and re-
combining materials of one man's eternal reverie—the innumerable and intolerable details of memory—significance, order,
value. None of these significances come out of the matter of the
poems with anything like a feeling of inevitability; the details,
some of them very good in their own right, are simply saddled

with them and told to rise and walk, resulting in an air of contrivance and falsity more and more difficult to dispel as one reads on. If nothing else, however, *The Morning Song of Lord Zero* should help to establish one thing definitively: that the lyric impulse extended beyond its proper limits is at best a questionable vehicle for philosophic musings.

And yet, through the clouds of poetic vapor that Aiken exudes, through the long-winded and unworkable analogies, the unprofitable word play, the vagueness of reference and the on-and-on-*and*-on of his grave, muffled words, a kind of kingdom exists. One is troubled on going into it, and remains troubled on coming out of it, as though haunted by a sensibility so astonishingly rich, various, and self-obsessed that language is inadequate to express it. Perhaps the aim of Aiken's lifelong reverie is not to send one back into one's external world, where the thorn draws blood and the sun shines differently from moment to moment, but into the endlessly ramifying labyrinth of one's own memory. And it is no small compliment to Aiken to say that, once one enters there with the total commitment Aiken's example encourages, one is struck by its likeness to Aiken's: to that vast, ectoplasmic, ultimately inexplicable—though one tries to explain—and often dimly beautiful universe whose only voice he is.

[1963]

MARGARET TONGUE

MARGARET TONGUE has evidently read Cummings and Marianne Moore to advantage, but the deepest impression on her writing has been made by the Oriental poets, particularly the Japanese. Her method also has something in common with that of Francis Ponge, the poet of *Le Parti Pris des Choses*, wherein the poem tries to discover the essence of a given object or animal not so much as it exists in the mind of the beholder (though of course this is what it comes to), but as it seems to want to exist in itself. In most of these poems,* Miss Tongue is able to enter the life of the thing she is writing about (in her world, frost and rivers live as individually as camels and unicorns do), and so comprehend it by an entirely original act of understanding. Her approach is oblique, touching at several sides of an object (a shell, a rose), hinting at characteristics, and then retiring when the reader has been given all the information needed to make an imaginative summation of the qualities, which then, almost magically, assemble in the mind into the thing described. This method has its dangers: it demands the most extreme delicacy, and the poem cannot afford anything resembling a false note. The poet can never *say* exactly, but must always *hint* exactly. Miss Tongue does not invariably find ways to avoid the hermeticism and arbitrariness that she risks; one would be hard pressed to say just

* *A Book of Kinds* by Margaret Tongue. Iowa City, The Stone Wall Press.

what is going on in some of these little poems, did not the titles furnish the necessary identification. Yet look at "Fawn":

> On is it up
> Yes upon
> It is and now
> Endure.

To make an authentic poem—an entire drama of awakening and weakness and trying to stand on new legs in a difficult, strange, and unsteady world—all this in eleven words: surely this is a remarkable achievement, deserving to rank with the best of Cummings's short pieces. Like Cummings, Miss Moore, and Bashō, Miss Tongue has the gift of being able to reveal the things of her poems in their own fastidious and irrevocable immediacy, and of involving the beholder, beyond judgment, with each subject, his fate bound intimately to the unfolding of the words. I hope that people buy *A Book of Kinds* not to read once, or to give to friends because of its attractive illustrations and typography, but to live with. The poems here will repay everything of himself that the reader can bring to them.

[1959]

ELLEN KAY

ELLEN KAY is a tractable student of the Wintersian virtues, and seems to take as axiomatic that learning to concoct acceptable little quasi-philosophical proposition-making verses that scan constitutes all that one can hope to achieve in the way of human expression. One sees immediately that nature is never itself in Miss Kay's poems;* nor does it belong to Miss Kay in any intimate and revealing connection. It belongs to the Proposition which it may be made to yield, if the poet rigs a satisfactory set of syllogisms. For this kind of writing, the myths do as well as (or perhaps better than) things seen and known; consequently there are poems on Pluto and Ceres, Eve, the unicorn, Tiresias, "The Living Narcissus," and, no less wonderful in the pantheon of West-coast neoclassicism, "One Intent upon the Doctorate." Perhaps this is all just as well, for Miss Kay's powers of observation are decidedly slight. But when one sees, also, that her ability to make decisive generalizations is not much above that of the average graduate student, one becomes restive. She says that a stone found in the sea is "licked small and smooth by rough / Tongues of wave, in beauty / Its own cosmography . . ." Isn't this a kind of predictable dressing-up of a poetic commonplace? What more haggard cliché could the poet have come upon than *waves* seen as *tongues*, albeit rough? I find this going-a-platitude-one-better occurring so frequently throughout Miss Kay's book that it has all the appearance of being systematized, and I can't, despite my best efforts, escape the conclusion that Miss Kay is an almost frightening example of all the worst faults, quickly acquired, and middling virtues, come by somewhat more slowly (but I should think not much) of the average Winters-trained poet, primly preaching a set of academic homilies ("the mind is . . ." "lust is . . ." "love is not . . ." etc.), wherein painfully contrived arguments in rhyme substitute for genuine insight, and the whole is delivered in diction like nothing ever spoken in truth or understandable error: "Comfort cannot insure / Life is no sinecure . . ." or (my personal favorite) "April holds their last breath; / Catabolic law, guiled / By the mind's strategy, / Moves to finality / Without return." In the end one reads this kind of writing only as another more serious-minded and semi-

* *A Local Habitation* by Ellen Kay. Denver, Alan Swallow.

codified form of jargon verse; in any meaningful sense it is sub-
jectless, all "strategy" and no passion, all will power and no luck.
[1959]

JAMES MERRILL

JAMES MERRILL is the most graceful, attractive, and accomplished
of the "elegants": the highly skilled, charming, agreeable crafts-
men of the forties and fifties who promised most and delivered
least. These are the leisurely European travelers: the rootless,
well-mannered, multilingual young men: the sophisticated, talented, slightly world-weary occasional poets of the last twenty
years, who have done everything perfectly according to quite
acceptable standards, and have just as surely stopped short of
real significance, real engagement, of the daring and self-
forgetfulness that might have made the Word come alive, preferring as they did to settle for décor, decorum, and the approval of a body of like-minded critics who affirmed the
assumptions of this approach, and pointed out little tricks of
rhyme and phrasing as if these were permanently valuable addi-
tions to the spirit. The goals which Merrill has set himself have
served as ideals for dozens of books of verse during the last two
decades, among which Merrill's two volumes* are both entirely
typical and distinctly superior. Reading them, one is content and
even glad to set the stronger passions aside, and most of actual

* *First Poems* and *The Country of a Thousand Years of Peace and Other
Poems* by James Merrill. New York, Alfred A. Knopf.

life aside, and to enter a realm of connoisseurish aesthetic contemplation, where there are no things more serious than gardens (usually formal), dolls, swans, statues, works of art, operas, delightful places in Europe, the ancient gods in tasteful and thought-provoking array, more statues, many birds and public parks, and, always, "the lovers," wandering through it all as if they surely lived. It is a strangely Jamesian poetry, though lacking James's strongly moral point of view; it has enough of James's insistence upon manners and decorum to evoke a limited admiration for the taste, wit, and eloquence that such an attitude makes possible, and also enough to drive you mad over the needless artificiality, prim finickiness, and determined inconsequence of it all. One tires very quickly of the exquisite, nonvital kind of sensibility, and is inclined to yearn with increasing restiveness for precisely those qualities which Merrill, Anthony Hecht, and Richard Wilbur do not give, rather than being permanently content to assimilate the merits of the calm, perfectly assured poems they do. This is not to say that their poems are not beautiful, in many cases. They are, but it is not a beauty that grows and lives and changes with one. It is, instead, a thin, orderly, lifeless, and somewhat self-consciously beautiful beauty, not coming as an unlooked-for and miraculous visitation, as it seems to do in the best poetry, but quite openly a quality sought, by intricate and yet still very obvious means, as an end in itself.

> There are many monsters that a glassen surface
> Restrains. And none more sinister
> Than vision asleep in the eye's tight translucence.
> Rarely it seeks now to unloose
> Its diamonds. Having divined how drab a prison
> The purest mortal tissue is,
> Rarely it wakes. Unless, coaxed out by lusters
> Extraordinary, like the octopus
> From the gloom of its tank half-swimming half-drifting
> Toward anything fair, a handkerchief

Or child's face dreaming near the glass, the writher
Advances in a godlike wreath
Of its own wrath.

The complex technique of rhyming, in which the last syllable of
every other line rhymes, or half rhymes, with the penultimate
syllable of the line before, shows with what fastidious, almost
disdainful ease Merrill can move in whatever verse form he
wishes. Yet within a very large variety of forms, all the poems
are pretty much the same. Each of them entails the weaving of
an elaborate figure of speech in a shimmering mesh of its own
correspondences and identifications, its connotations and its
teased-out reciprocal agreements. Like Wallace Stevens, whose
manner has provided a haven for shoals of young American
poets who have nothing much to write about, Merrill operates
exclusively in that area where objects are engaged in becoming
assemblages of approximate comparisons of other things to
themselves. Unlike Stevens's poems, whose meanings are usually
implicit and frequently open to a number of interpretations,
Merrill's nearly always make neat summations, prefigure, insist
on, furnish explicit judgments, instruct, edify, so that experience
itself comes to resemble a kind of dandyish, Gidean private-
school teacher. This is, I suppose, a way of making the world
safe for poetry, but somehow one hates to think of its being
made *this* safe. One feels a moment of very real delight, therefore, on hearing Merrill say, "My eyes fill with a seeing not their
own," or, in the best of all his poems, "Dream (Escape from the
Sculpture Museum) and Waking": "Exhaustingly the wayfar-
ers / Breathe out white and pass by blind." One's heart leaps;
one wishes that Merrill might do something *else:* that, with or
without his permission, his "lovers" might cease to wander
through parks and art galleries and public gardens as part of the
scenery, but simply come into each other's presence and stare.
With that kind of help, the sheer linguistic ability of a singularly
gifted poet might begin to matter, we be shaken by the power of

insight which until that time had lain dormant in our lives waiting for the right words, and James Merrill escape from the
sculpture museum, at last.

[1959]

E. E. CUMMINGS

WHEN you review one of E. E. Cummings's books,* you have to
review them all; you have to review Cummings. Perhaps this is
true to some degree of reviewing all poets, but it is entirely true
in Cummings's case. His books are all exactly alike, and one is
faced with evaluating Cummings as a poet, using the current text
simply as a hitherto unavailable source of quotations. Let me
make my own position clear right away. I think that Cummings
is a daringly original poet, with more virility and more sheer,
uncompromising talent than any other living American writer. I
cannot and would not want to deny, either, that he dilutes even
the finest of his work with writing that is hardly more than the
defiant playing of a child, though the fact that he does this with
the superb arrogance of genius has always seemed to me among
the most attractive of his qualities. I love Cummings's verse,
even a great deal of it that is not lovable or even respectable, but
it is also true that I am frequently and thoroughly bored by its
continuous attitudinizing and its dogmatic preaching. I have
often felt that there must be something hiddenly wrong with his
cult of spontaneity and individuality, that these attributes have

* *95 Poems* by E. E. Cummings. New York, Harcourt, Brace and World.

to be insisted upon to the extent to which Cummings insists on them. I feel, also, that "love" and the other well-known emotions that Cummings tirelessly espouses are being imposed on me categorically, and that I stand in some danger of being shot if I do not, just at that moment, wish to love someone or pick a rose or lean against a tree watching the snowflakes come down. The famous mannerisms, too: aren't they, by now, beginning to pall pretty heavily? Were some of them, even when they were new, worth very much? I can, for example, think of no two literary devices which interest me less than the countless "un"-words Cummings is fond of using, and his wearisome, cute, and mechanical substitution of other parts of speech for nouns ("a which of slim of blue / of here will who / straight up into the where . . ."). Yet when you come on a passage like this, what can you feel but silence, gratitude, and rejoicing?

> now air is air and thing is thing: no bliss
>
> of heavenly earth beguiles our spirits, whose
> miraculously disenchanted eyes
>
> live the magnificent honesty of space.

Here is something entirely beautiful, with the odd, arresting, directness-from-another-angle that characterizes the best poetry, and can change your life. One thinks of Blake's observation about the crooked roads without improvement, and is glad of the quotation, and even more glad that Cummings has lived along those roads with vitality and constancy, and has defended them against the cheapjacks of life and of the word with the belligerency and the withering scorn he has. A few years ago, reviewing Cummings's *Poems 1923–1954* in *The New York Times Book Review*, Randall Jarrell deplored Cummings's insistence on his difference from other men. Whether or not Cummings does this to the extent Mr. Jarrell suggests, and I think he does, I am more delighted than dismayed by it. Just this

jealous treasuring of his individuality, his uniqueness, has enabled Cummings's personality to flower in a number of perfectly
inimitable poems, and in countless passages in other poems beside which the efforts of all but a few other contemporary poets
pale into competent indifference. It has encouraged also, I suppose, the various devices and mannerisms for which Cummings
is celebrated. The important thing, however, is that Cummings
has felt the need, and followed it, of developing absolutely in his
own way, of keeping himself and his writing whole, preferring
to harbor his most grievous and obvious faults quite as if they
were part and parcel of his most original and valuable impulses,
which perhaps they are. The poems in *95 Poems* are no better
and no worse than Cummings's best and worst poems in his
other books, though the percentage of good poems over bad is
considerably higher here than is customary. As always, Cummings is his own most distinguished and devastating parodist,
able with penetrating wit to hold his own work up to the ridi-
cule some of it deserves, and then, in the next poem, or even in
the next line, to restore it to an eminence which seals the critic's
mouth and changes him into a more perceptive being than he has
been since his fifth year. But how is this done? I attempted to
answer this question by doing my best to determine which of
the two or three writers present in Cummings I admire most. It
is certainly not the one who depends on a number of elementary
and quite predictable tricks of typography to make points which
could be made more easily, and probably more effectively, by
other means. In Cummings's experiments in breaking up words
and using syllables in various permutations and combinations on
the page, I have only the faintest interest.

```
l(a

le
af
fa
ll

s)
one
l

iness
```

There is not much doubt as to what the vertical arrangement of
the letters, here, is meant to do. Within the enveloping context
of "loneliness," the motion of the leaf, set parenthetically, the
initially unexplained "l" which completes the key word when
one goes back to it, all show pretty well how this device in Cummings's poems usually operates. Although this treatment (one
can hardly call it a technique) has, in addition to a simple kind of
puzzle interest, the slight advantage of approximating kinaesthet-
ically the falling of the leaf, and of literally surrounding it with
the human emotion which it connotes or causes, I cannot for the
life of me think of this piece as particularly good poetry, or
particularly good anything; certainly I do not think of it in the
same way I do of some of Cummings's poems. No; I am most
drawn to the Cummings whose quirky, indignant sharpness of
observation produced the unforgettable pages dealing with Jean
le Nègre in *The Enormous Room*, over which no typesetter
asked for a raise or cut his throat: to the writer whose fantastic
and uncompromising devotion to a spontaneous, outward-going
(and typically American, if we would just *be* Americans) view
of the world permeates his prose and most of his poems with
gorgeous, unpremeditated energy: to the Cummings whose entirely personal daring with diction and image brings us into a
Chaplinesque, half-comic, half-holy reconciliation with the

events through which we live. His excesses are, most certainly, enormous, as one feels they should be in a genuine poet. Cummings is without question one of the most insistent and occasionally one of the most successful users of pathetic fallacy in the history of the written word. He is one of the most blatant sentimentalists, one of the most absurdly and grandly overemotional of poets, one of the flimsiest thinkers, and one of the truly irreplaceable sensibilities that we have known, with the blind, irresistible devotion to his exact perceptions, to *his* way of knowing and doing, and to his personal and incorruptible relation to the English language that an authentic poet must have. Immediacy and intensity are Cummings's twin gods, and he has served them with a zeal and single-mindedness which we should learn to appreciate even more fully as these traits tend to disappear from our verse, giving way, as they seem to be doing, to a more withdrawn, philosophical, "considered," and altogether safer point of view. I can think of no other qualities so much needed in contemporary poetry as those which Cummings has spent his life discovering ways to make viable.

Whether or not successful in every instance, all of Cummings's skill, so special to himself that we cannot imagine anyone else making use of it, has gone to establish and consecrate the *moment:* the event which is taking place *now:* the thing which will never be repeated in quite this same way, and which, quite likely, would ordinarily not even be noticed as it happens. Cummings's several devices are all ways to get at this, and to show "what happens" in its pure, inexplicable, purposeless instancy and intensity: in its meaning-beyond-meaning. He has never felt the need to broaden his subject matter, or to systematize its implications, or even to *notice* anything beyond the experiences and scenes which attain the highest degree of intuitive meaning *for him:* love, love with sex, sex without love, spring, flowers, snow, death, sunlight, moonlight, leaves, birds, his family, hatred of money and money-makers and public figures. No one would insist that Cummings be a more systematic thinker than he is, because of his spectacular success in *feeling* responsively and deeply and verbally, but I for one often wish, when reading his poems, that they had *somewhat* more intellectual structure or firmness under them. I had as well withdraw that statement, though, for poems 48 and 49 in this book are wonderful poems, and are so quite without taking any notice whatever of my objections. Aside from his big *Poems 1923–1954, 95 Poems* is Cummings's best book; there are so many good things in it that to begin to quote whole poems would necessitate my going on for pages. I note this with relief, for to point out all the brilliant passages would entail having to indicate ludicrous failures also, and with having to reckon again with the fact that Cummings has long since passed (perhaps with his first poem, perhaps when he was born) the point where writing correctly, well or badly according to other lights than his own, made the slightest difference to him. He is so strongly of a piece that the commentator feels ashamed and even a little guilty in picking out flaws, as though he were asked to call attention to the aesthetic defects in a rose. It is better to say what must finally be said about Cummings: that he has helped to give life to the language, for language is renewed by the best perceptions of its most valuably intuitive and devoted users, and by no other means. Cummings belongs in the class of poets who have done this, not by virtue of his tinkering with typography, but because of his superior insight into the fleeting and eternal moments of existence: not because of words broken up into syllables and strewn carefully about the page, but because of right words with other right words, which say what they do whether they are upside down, right-side up, inside out, backward, or any other way.

to stand (alone) in some

autumnal afternoon:
breathing a fatal
stillness

Cummings is an important poet because he has insisted, by virtue of his fine, irascible talent, on the primacy of the perpetually happening, never-repeated "natural miracle," and on our feeling with what we see, and seeing with what we feel, spontaneously, thoughtlessly, and totally. I do not in the least mean to slight his typographical innovations, which may well be of greater import than I have been willing to concede; I only wish to reiterate that what I consider Cummings's finest moments are dependent not on these innovations, such as they are, but on combinations of words that deliver the necessary insights regardless of what splintering process may or may not take place among them. These poems, such as "Paris: this April sunset completely utters," and "Always before your voice my soul," show that part or perhaps most of the miracle is in our observing and responding: that it is we who must do the seeing and feeling, unashamedly and faithful to nothing but our actual responses. In poems as strongly charged with as unforeseeable and as unique a personality as Cummings's, that is a very great deal.

[1959]

EMMA SWAN

EMMA SWAN's poems* suffer from a certain tightness and nervelessness, but the best of them are unassuming, unpretentious, and very likable. Miss Swan strikes me as being sincere, grave, and a little naïve in the ordinary, unpoetical way. In her case, naïveté emerges as quite a good quality, for her verse has a refreshing,

* *Poems* by Emma Swan. New York, New Directions.

wide-eyed acceptingness about it: not exactly the innocent gaze of Blake or of a real child, it is true, but still an eye that sees instinctively, quickly, and with finality, without hesitation or blurring of focus.

> As if the snow were not enough,
> The air, the sidewalk slicked with ice,
> Extend the sunlight at each step,
> And freeze the dazzled passer twice.

No one not perceptive to the degree that poets must be, both to life in its particulars and to language in its efforts to embody and outdo what we have known, could have believed in this observation enough to record it, or have come up with the word "extend" in this context, to make it worthwhile. Miss Swan's poems are like this; they have the clearness of conviction, unfurnished with anything but the essential words, and the straightforwardness of intuition accepted unquestioningly as fact. She has no wish or need to expand her poems beyond the feelings she has actually undergone, on such-and-such occasions. "I would breathe differently if you moved / The finger of one hand," she says, and casts a spell into which we enter deeply as human beings, bringing our own personal relations with us and judging them to be true, and unbearably intimate, on the strength of Miss Swan's words. These poems have nothing in them remotely resembling greatness; they are perhaps not even outstandingly good, but they are real poems, and all real poems are as necessary to us as they are to their creators.

[1959]

HAROLD WITT

HAROLD WITT says that "close observation of what is most familiar—the regional and known—is the way to universals." This is
probably true or at least it ought to be, but it is hard for me to
believe that things like "the in absentia bees" constitute much of
value in the way of "close observation." *The Death of Venus**
displays a good deal of verbal busyness, an air of brilliant slap-
dash improvisation, and very little real feeling or consequence.
The poems only infrequently *engage* their subjects: instead,
they take off from them, circle them, skirt them, and, in essence,
play with them. Despite Witt's avowal of "close observation,"
his clever figures are maddeningly vague; to say of a "strayed
opossum" that it is "disturbing as *stars*" (italics mine) is to say
little more or less than that it is disturbing as diamonds, raspber-
ries, head colds, birds, airplanes, atomic bombs, or almost anything else you might want to pick, for all things, seen in some
perspectives, are "disturbing" in some sense; in point of fact,
stars are usually counted (unless you are Pascal) as relatively
reassuring.

Most of his work shows Witt to be a decorative poet: the
decorative being defined as the writer who, because he cannot
say exactly the right thing, hopes to say the interesting thing. If,
as Malcolm de Chazal maintains, poetry is the art of transmitting

* *The Death of Venus* by Harold Witt. Francestown, N.H., The Golden
Quill Press.

life, or the sense of life, at its most meaningful, then the presence of a living human being must somehow make itself felt behind the language. This does not happen in *The Death of Venus* any more than it does in the sardonic and contrived poems of Weldon Kees, which Witt's somewhat resemble. As must be apparent, I don't much like Witt's kind of writing. Nevertheless, he has an enviable store of energy, and obviously he loves the language. He may yet go through a thousand changes, and one of them may be the right one.

[1959]

WINFIELD TOWNLEY SCOTT

I HAVE been wondering for several weeks what combination of circumstances might have led an American poet, Winfield Scott, to undertake the writing of a long narrative poem about a voyage to America supposedly taken four hundred years before Columbus by Leif Ericson's half-sister, Freydis.* Beyond the possibility that Scott was drawn to the subject by whatever impulse or compulsion leads writers (or some writers) to want to say something about America from the standpoint of beginnings and symbolic figures, I have not made much headway in my speculations, and must be content to say that *The Dark Sister* is a very good narrative poem indeed, no matter how it may have been conceived. When I first began to read it, I was afraid I had simply opened another American history high-school pageant play,

* *The Dark Sister* by Winfield Townley Scott. New York, New York University Press.

this time in verse: one of those determined, ready-made epics where all the characters speak in voices excruciatingly appropriate to their roles, and the author's careful scholarship is everywhere painfully evident, as though it were the logical substitute for vision. This feeling did not last long, for the following passage occurs seven pages from the beginning:

> Gudrid cried: "I tell you
> there is evil in that place.
> That land was not meant for us—there is something against us,
> Something beneath the soft grass and the bright leaves,
> More than threat of savages native there. Some
> trick of the sun
> Gentles its uttermost kingdom and lures us into it
> as if it were
> A shining paradise beyond the black cold sea. Those
> who go in
> Are netted with a silken skein of light, move as
> dreamers in dream,
> Fancy themselves gods of a sort come miraculously to
> an earth-garden of Valhalla
> —And are welcomed with poisonous arrows, and yet dream still:
> those spared,
> Lulled to birdsong and the great shards of the sun
> on the coast rock,
> The way of the wind in the tall trees, the forested hills
> Sighing of peace and wealth and a kind earth
> flowering under their feet
> —They are sucked weak. I tell you trouble and
> danger weave in the air.
> Almost I believe again the spinning Norns brood
> Watching that foreign thread. It shines bright on the fields,
> Yet I think it drags darkly into the ocean and whirls
> coldly somewhere out to the sky.
> It spins, and they wait."

I doubt very much whether the abiding menace America must have been for these people—a land having as yet no gods, or anything but the tremendous, veiled entrancement of the un-known—has been given a more convincing statement than it has here. Furthermore, the accent of imaginative rightness struck in this passage is sustained throughout the rest of the poem. Frey-dis, upon whose personality the poem depends, is entirely be-lievable not only as a ruthless, acquisitive woman, but as the first embodiment of the self-destructive greed that was to character-ize America, as she, her crew of Greenland Vikings, and another ship commanded and manned by mercenary Norwegians sail to "Vinland" to cut and bring back timber to be sold in "treeless Greenland"; the voyage turns out to be, of course, though none of the participants realizes it more than dimly, a first try at claiming the land: it is a spiritual or symbolic exploration to de-termine the *meaning* of the new continent first visited by Leif Ericson, whose only marks upon it had been graves and a few huts along the shore of "Hop," or Narragansett Bay. Once the ships beach in Vinland, however, strange and terrible things be-gin to happen. Greed impels Freydis and the Norwegian captain apart, and they fall to haggling over the division of the timber even before it is cut; but over and above the passion for personal gain, the dreaming enchantment of the land exerts an influence on Freydis which she can neither understand nor control. She has all the Norwegians murdered, and sets sail with the timber, pursued by the guilt that drives her husband Thorvard eventu-ally to suicide and herself into near-madness, so that in the end the wood bought in Vinland with unnecessary bloodshed is stacked unsold in the fields of Greenland, and left to rot.

A large measure of the success of *The Dark Sister* comes from the fact that Scott has gone beyond treating eleventh-century America merely as a backdrop for the actions of his characters, but has envisioned it as spiritual ground, as a place that stands for something equivalent in the developing psyche of man: a new inner continent more important than the geographical one. My main and only large objection to the poem is that it does not explore this possibility, set forth with such magnificent promise in the passage quoted above, with sufficient stubbornness or insight, abandoning it for the commonplace that "we carry with us / That which we journey toward." Scott's ability as a poet is gratifyingly robust, and I for one hate to see him settle things the easy way. Perhaps because he handles the extra-long line with great dexterity and variation, and because of the dark and bloody events of the poem, much of *The Dark Sister* is reminiscent of Robinson Jeffers. Yet Scott is a great deal more inventive than Jeffers is, and far more sensitive to language. His poem is not so fanatically one-sided as Jeffers's long poems are, and is altogether a more successful creation than anything Jeffers has written, with the possible exception of *Hungerfield*. *The Dark Sister* has, however, in addition to what I must take as a slighting of its most interesting stated theme, one or two structural weaknesses that are damaging to it. Since the narrative movement is direct and forceful, I should have thought that the poet would be content to let his meanings come through the action itself. On the contrary, he has seen fit to include a great many asides, soliloquies, and explanatory dialogues. Some of these are extremely good, but many are not, and even if they were all as good as the passage above, there would still be too many of them, all encouraging the reader to get from the poem exactly what the poet believes he has put into it. There is far too much editorializing, by Freydis, by Leif Ericson, whose function toward the end of the poem comes to resemble that of a Greek chorus, and by almost everyone else present. I was particularly disappointed to find Vinland coming to nothing more than is indicated in the MacLeish-like

"Did we find more than we were meant to find? Come
     by long westward sailing
Where we were never meant to go, since we could not
     stay? Once having walked that land

We knew all others harsher. And though it could not
    be ours we set names on its shores
And marked it with some of our dearest bones; but we knew
    all the same it was not evil.
Only that it was not ours, only that it waited."

And yet, had this poem come down to us from the time it treats, it would have been reckoned a masterpiece, and dutifully enregistered as such in many a textbook and anthology. At first I regretted, a little foolishly, that it *doesn't* come from that time, for I found myself wishing that the author might be able to give it the final authenticity of saying, "I am the man, I suffered, I was there." But the only authenticities that matter in poetry are those of the imagination and the emotions, working together to pass from fact to vision. Knowing this, I am doubly glad, now, that we may credit *The Dark Sister*, not to an eleventh-century Norse scop, but to a contemporary American poet.

[1959]

ELDER OLSON

To my untutored mind, which probably shouldn't be allowed an opinion of this sort, Elder Olson has always appeared the most gifted of the influential University of Chicago "neo-Aristotelian" school of literary aesthetics. From time to time he publishes a few poems, too. I have come to watch eagerly for these, and have noted with especial delight their difference from the complicated and rarefied trafficking with universals that he and

his colleagues do in the pages of the learned journals. All of Olson's poems that I have seen are in his new book,* together with
five short plays which are witty, ingenious, and amusing, but
which are not up to even the lesser of the poems in originality
and lasting effectiveness. The plays are marred by excessive reliance on literary gimmicks and surprises, and do not impress me
as being anything more than mildly successful, even within their
modest intentions. *Faust,* for example, is a humanist parable on
the old story, but with the twist that Faust, in quest of youth
instead of knowledge, is taken at his word in an entirely different sense from that which he intended, becomes the victim of a
purely scientific retribution, and is made to suffer "regressive
evolution" back to the state of the primates, and beyond. *The
Illusionists* makes use of Huxleyan "illusion machines" which
the populace of the earth, habituated for years to illusions by
other means such as television, the cinema, and advertising, eagerly adopts, because "real individual happiness is incompatible
with the good of the State; besides, it isn't possible." Men no
longer see any reason to distinguish reality from illusion, and
embrace the illusion machines even though they must pay the
machine masters with their flesh. As may be inferred, these five
small plays are exclusively dramas of ideas, with the characters
simply serving as a number of stand-ins for various points of
view. Once the surprise packages of their *dénouements* have
been opened, they come to seem contrived and a little thin.

The poems are in another class altogether. Obvious influences
there are, to be sure, and not all of them good; to note one, the
well-known "Ballad of the Scarecrow Christ" is disastrously in
the shadow of Dylan Thomas's "Ballad of the Long-legged
Bait":

> Look, look! amid what pomp of waters
> He lordly rides like the light of day;

* *Plays and Poems 1948–58* by Elder Olson. Chicago, University of Chicago Press.

All the sea-robed waves throng round,
Sea-foam garlands all his way

This is not Olson's best manner. But "Crucifix," "Jack-in-the-box," and, above all, "A Nocturnal for His Children" are models of difficult thinking made profoundly clear, and of a power of organization which brings the Great Questions into perfectly convincing *rapport* with the actual circumstances of everyday life. I am delighted and even awestruck by Olson's capacity to assemble the materials of his poems around the ideas they dramatize, and by the ease with which he wields his verse forms upon basic and eternal considerations, steadily and evenly.

Not in God's image was man
First created, but in
Likeness of a beast;
Until that beast became man,
All travailled in death and pain
And shall travail still
Till man be the image of God
And nothing shall transform
Man to that image, but love;
And this I believe is God's will.

And all shall work that Will:
Planet and planet shall spin,
Atom and atom, until
The scriptures of heaven and earth,
Mountain and ocean, spell
The one unnameable Name
Of One we know nothing of,
Save what we learn from love

Reading this, and many other poems and parts of poems in Olson's book, I keep asking myself why his work is not better known. I can think of no adequate answer, and must leave Olson's relative neglect a mystery, trusting I have done what I could to rectify what seems to me a really unfortunate situation, and hoping to enlist the aid of Time.

[1959]

NIKOS KAZANTZAKIS

NIKOS KAZANTZAKIS's *The Odyssey: A Modern Sequel** appears among all other contemporary poetry more as an elemental force of nature than as a "work of art," or as a thing that can be bound between the covers of a book. In sheer force of invention, in its primitive, unleashed, fleshly splendor and a kind of gluttonous ravening over the world of the senses, it is unmatched by anything I have ever read, long and involved as it is.

I suppose that by now most people know Kazantzakis's story, which begins in the twenty-second book of Homer's *Odyssey,* and takes a still-questing Odysseus to sea again and to Sparta to abduct Helen, then to Crete to destroy the decadent civilization at Knossos, then to Egypt to attempt the same thing at Thebes, then south to the source of the Nile, where he founds a short-lived ideal city, then into the South African wilderness to become an ascetic, then into the Antarctic ice floes to die, or to become pure spirit (one cannot quite determine which). The philosophical meanings of these events are painstakingly indicated by Kimon Friar, who has done a beautiful job of transla-

---

* *The Odyssey: A Modern Sequel* by Nikos Kazantzakis. Translated by Kimon Friar. New York, Simon and Schuster.

tion and commentary here, but who, to my mind, is inclined to make a little too much of Kazantzakis's "ideas." One of the difficulties about the poem, though, is that Kazantzakis apparently took them just this seriously himself, with the result that he has made of his Odysseus one of the most unflaggingly doctrinal heroes of all time. No bird flies past, no one eats or sharpens a sword or makes love without sending Odysseus into a long disquisition on the destiny of man, on man's duty to himself to surpass even his God, to make the earth fecund, to strive and to search, and many another *idée fixe* about spirit, mind, fate, soul, and body, all of which become—can't help becoming—somewhat tedious, as they recur time after time, leaping at us out of the sun, the moon, the wind, from the sails of ships, from the lyres of minstrels, from the dead, from wine cups and flagons and worms and bulls. There are so many dreams and visions, all equipped with symbolic purposes, that one soon begins to have forebodings each time night comes on, or one of the characters falls to musing. The essential difference, of course, between Homer's *Odyssey* and this one is that Kazantzakis is consciously and deliberately writing an allegory, or symbolic poem, giving embodiment to aspects of his Nietzschian-Dionysian-Bergsonian philosophy, his ideas on the growth and decay of cultures, the transmutation of matter into spirit, and so on, the inevitable outcome of which is that his Odysseus, as impressive a creation as he is, constantly runs the risk of losing his vital identity and becoming nothing more than a Voice. I am bothered, too, by a few of the literary devices of the poem, which, repeated countless times over the tremendous span of twenty-four long sections, tend to lose most of their effectiveness. Chief among these is personification. It does not help much to note that personification is one of Homer's principal devices also; I imagine that even he would be dismayed if confronted by the excessive, even monstrous use to which Kazantzakis puts it; the figures of speech for the sun alone, most of which compare the sun to a human being, fill a page and a half of Friar's introduction, and are very nearly as obtrusive in the poem itself. Surely this is too much of a moderately good thing.

But I get all these objections down only to dispense with them and enter into praise. Though they are frequently over-long and there are a great many of them, the countless soliloquies, asides, dreams, and digressions do, in actuality, but little to impede the wild, barbaric onrushing of the narrative from scene to scene, from place to place, from event to event, as Odysseus and his followers plunge through a gorgeously sensuous world which matches the hero's own tremendous animal vitality as well as his moments of reflection and the turns of his "many-sided mind." The feeling of life extravagantly, deeply, and meaningfully lived is in every line of the poem; not only are the personages unforgettably vivid, down to the least slave serving wine in a harbor tavern, but the very objects of the poem seem to have an independent life of their own, too: swords, shields, the robes of women, the stones on the road, and the stars above the ship all pulsate with uniqueness, mystery, beauty, and immediacy, so that the reader realizes, time after time, how very little he himself has been willing to settle for, in living: how much there *is* upon earth: how wild, inexplicable, marvelous, and endless creation is. The real effect of Kazantzakis's immense poem is to bring forward (and with what unbelievable fullness!) the incalculable value of a total response to experience. The greatest tribute I can pay to the poet is to say that his grafting of various symbols onto the actions of his hero soon falls into a kind of secondary or parallel interest, and that the prime fascination of the poem comes out of Kazantzakis's tumultuously vital evocation of the physical world itself, apprehended in a joyously primitive splendor that dazzles, dazes, and finally overwhelms the reader with his own admiration and gratitude.

When one looks back over Kazantzakis's *Odyssey* and recalls it in its thousands of vivid details as well as in its irresistibly forceful major passages: when one remembers it, in all its seven hundred and seventy-six pages, twenty-four books, and thirty-three thousand, three hundred and thirty-three lines, one sees that one has had part in what is very likely the most remarkable sustained accomplishment in verse that the modern imagination has been privileged to record. When one notes, too, that this huge, questing hymn to daring and fecundity has been written, not at all in a Miltonic striving for "greatness," but in the most intense and personal creative joy, one is but the more impressed, and the more indebted to both poet and translator, to say nothing of one's feeling of gratitude toward the publisher who had the courage to take a chance on a book of this kind, and make it available, at ten dollars, to a public habituated to thirty-five cent paperback editions of Mickey Spillane and Norman Vincent Peale.

The final good of the new *Odyssey*, I suspect, will not be to glorify the Nietzschian hero, or to make aesthetically viable the ideas of Bergson, Nietzsche, or Spengler, or even "man's dauntless mind," but to restore the sense of the heedless delight in living to a jaded populace. To poets, it is and will be a living demonstration of the profound vitality that words may be made to carry by a poet who is himself profoundly vital, and of the human power that makes the best poetry nearly as valuable as life. It shows, also, that this power at its most significant issues, not tentatively and fraught with contingencies, but directly and unalterably from the deepest, unanalyzed springs of personality. It is this power which appropriates the forms of writing and uses them to create and explore new realms of the imagination, and ultimately to establish them, so that they become the most enduring ground of the spirit. In this connection, Odysseus is likely to prove a hero to us in more ways than even his chronicler has envisioned, and Kazantzakis himself in all ways.

[1959]

THOM GUNN

THOM GUNN* has already taken quite a beating from some very good American reviewers, notably John Thompson in the November 1959 issue of *Poetry*. On the other hand, he is very highly regarded in England, wins all sorts of prizes there, and has things like this said about him by critics as acute, learned, and perceptive as A. Alvarez: "Gunn's *Fighting Terms* is the most impressive first book of poems since Robert Lowell's." I see him somewhat differently: as a fashionable, rote versifier of some skill and intelligence, the very perfect model of the young Americanized British poet, writing solemnly about the sect of eagle-jacketed motorcycle riders and about Elvis Presley, who turns out (naturally!) to be a Symbol of impending war. All his work is smoothly executed. It can exercise your logical powers by putting before you a number of problems and resolving them neatly, but it has not the slightest power to touch you (or to touch *me*, perhaps I should say), or to make you feel that the situation with which it is dealing has any importance whatever, except as material for the kind of poems Gunn writes. Here are the motorcyclists:

> A minute holds them, who have come to go:
> The self-defined, astride the created will

* *The Sense of Movement* by Thom Gunn. Chicago, University of Chicago Press.

They burst away; the towns they travel through
Are home for neither bird nor holiness,
For birds and saints complete their purposes.
At worst, one is in motion; and at best,
Reaching no absolute, in which to rest,
One is always nearer by not keeping still.

This sort of writing invites you to go on and on, line after line, stanza after stanza, murmuring, "Yes, I think I see . . . Yes . . . Yes . . . Yes . . ." without actually assenting, or doing so only because the poet seems to have such utter confidence that what he is saying is true, and because some of the problems involved look pretty knotty, and would probably take some work to unravel. Eventually, though, you get a little tired of this diet of half-ideas, and begin to read the book all over again. And you ask questions like these, about the above quotation: Isn't it a little silly to characterize a group of sideburned toughs on Harley-Davidsons as "the self-defined, astride the created will"? How about the reference to "the towns they travel through"? Doesn't dragging in the supposed fact that birds and saints are *not* in the towns introduce a whole train of possibilities that, when examined, turns out to be completely irrelevant? For example, what if birds and saints *were* in the towns? Even though they "complete their purposes" (whatever that may mean), would this make any appreciable difference to the cyclists? Is it even true that there are no birds in the towns? I had thought previously that some birds can make a home anywhere. Perhaps I am being overliteral, but overliteralness comes to seem the only defense against Gunn's pedantic, pontifical manner, and his irritating pose as a universal Wise Man. From these poems you go back to the things and beings Gunn has written about, to the cities, the women, the magicians, the airedales of Yvor Winters, even to the motorcyclists, with relief, realizing that, after all, they're not, they can't be like these poems at all. And you feel, too, what a very sad thing it is that the poet in our time is an intellectual, and that his thinking sets him increasingly far from his subjects. If the poet's search is for "truth" and "reality," and for means by which to communicate these, one must drearily conclude that he is now farther from being able to do it than he has ever been. He has taken on a knowing, wise-seeming no-voice, a limbo voice like Gunn's, completely unconvincing, mannered, unmattering. He performs endless labors to make simple ideas complex and important-sounding. I have seldom read a duller book than *The Sense of Movement*, and I have nightmares thinking of the energy and the good intentions that went into it. Before the concrete of his approach and his "style" hardens around him, Gunn would do well to remember that his two favorite words, "will" and "define," are, in poetry, uneasy bedfellows. It is not the will but the imagination that defines, or better still, holds, embodies, presents, and finally gives.

Gunn's book brings up the whole question of the recent influ-ence of American on British poetry. In my opinion, it has not been good. The chief culprit, I am afraid, is Wallace Stevens, whose mannered artificiality and poetry-about-writing-poetry-about-poetry have driven large numbers of writers delightedly back into their shimmering, wordy sensibilities and buried them there. Gunn resembles Stevens no more than he does, say, Yvor Winters, but he has picked up the attitude that Stevens's work has fostered in the now influential next-to-youngest generation of American poets. According to this view, writing a poem is simply inventing a complex proposition about life or one of its manifestations, and illustrating it with whatever material appears to fit in. It seems to me that this leads to a particularly debili-tated kind of puzzle-making sterility, where to overcomplicate and then resolve is considered the criterion of artistic excel-lence. The great simplicities, the illuminations that should come like the sun from behind the cloud of ordinary perceptions and everyday judgments are not given a chance to come through, even if they could. These moments are hard to have, hard to discover and embody. Why bother, when it is so easy to be a "career poet" and to make one's way in a society of opinion which gives good marks to poems like Gunn's? Reading book after book of these poets, one is reminded of nothing so much as of Edmund Wilson's wonderful remark about the poems of Stephen Vincent Benét, which are "just about the same kind of poetry that the ordinary man would produce if he'd gone in for writing poetry instead of for investment banking or selling real estate." No; we must look to writing in other languages than English for the creative *joie de vivre* that poetry must above all embody: to the poems of a thousand young Frenchmen full of sentimentalities at which Brooks and Warren might laugh, but which come out of an unselfconsciousness that enables these writers to use their imagination at full stretch, resulting in poems that are as far as anything could possibly be from the constipated verses we are accustomed to reading, with their carefully market-tested and approved kind of significance. Or we would profit by going to the South Americans, especially to Neruda, whose magnificent abandon includes whole schools of wonderfully good and atrociously bad poets with the strength and delight of a demiurge. We have had enough of calculated effects in poetry, or at least of effects calculated as we have calculated them. Even the beatniks, though none has much imagination, can teach us things about opening up, for what we need most is the simple belief that a human being has said something because it matters.

[1960]

BROTHER ANTONINUS

REVIEWING religious poets, determinedly religous ones, always makes me a little nervous. I feel somewhat as if I were reviewing God, and am intimidated at flying in the face of all that goodwill with the mere instruments of my own taste and judgment. This is especially true when I come to Brother Antoninus. I remember him from several years back as William Everson, who wrote some of the first poetry I ever truthfully liked. Along with his new book,* I went back and read his old one, *The Residual Years*,† and found it full of the hatred and necessity of sex, and of a very convincing and powerful, from-inside-the-thing feeling about California farmers and farming:

> Deep sun, deep sky;
> No wind now for the dance of the leaves;
> But the light clean on the shape of the neck;
> And the deep sound of the heart.

Everson is (or was) best in simple, tactile description. His poems in *The Residual Years* are unforced and open, and I renewed my acquaintance with many of them gladly, noting their imperfections and setting them aside in favor of the living quality that these pieces give off. And yet I was also struck, as I had been

* *The Crooked Lines of God* by Brother Antoninus. Detroit, University of Detroit Press.
† *The Residual Years* by William Everson. New York, New Directions.

before, by the author's humorless, even owlish striving after self-knowledge and certainty, his intense and bitter inadequacy and frustration. I suppose I should have known, when I first read him fourteen years ago, that these problems would be resolved in religious orthodoxy, though I could not have guessed that Everson himself would become Brother Antoninus in the Catholic Church. In *The Crooked Lines of God* I encountered a good deal less of what I am pleased to call poetry than in *The Residual Years*, though if there were any justice there would be more. The verse here is of the kind I had hoped not to find: page after page of not-very-good, learned, dry sermonizing which in several places leans toward an attitude which I cannot help believing is somewhat self-righteous and even self-congratulatory. Before the poems proper ever begin, it is disconcerting to hear a writer say that what follows is "tortured between grace and the depraved human heart," as though he were presenting his poems, not as the tentative, hopeful ventures that all poems must be, but as a confident course from the mere estate of being human to the extreme Beatification. He talks of "my new poetic vision" as though it were an irrefutable fact. But alas, it is not so. What Brother Antoninus offers, instead of the "vision" he speaks of, is a sober, unimaginative forthrightness and a nagging insistence that he is right and you are, no matter what *else* you may believe, wrong. What I find peculiarly disagreeable in Brother Antoninus's work is his basic dislike of people and of sex, and this seems to me to be based at least as much on secular reasons as on religious, especially considering the fact that he shows the same distastes in *The Residual Years*, though there they are offered simply as personal feelings instead of Enlightenment. It may be that I am being unfair to Brother Antoninus, and if so I hope he will forgive me. Nevertheless, I still must say that the material offered here is much nearer to being apologetics than poetry. Worse; the author's determination to make his subjects as important and impressive as he believes they should be only succeeds in puffing them up into unbelievability.

Good Peter, upside down,
Straddles the Roman sun,
His legs like aqueducts
Bloody the down-hung head.
Already here the packed arena fills;
Its martyrs mount their yardarms.
The starveling lion
Snuffs the blood-stung air,
And the maiden's coif
Mats the tiger's jaw.
All, all are here. Their pain
Reaches already to this swollen Heart
That lugs and labors like a giant sea
Clasping its wounded islands,
Toning its solemn note upon that shore,
To weep out its geologic woe alone.

Unfortunately, as I have said before, the means, risks, and results of poetry are the same for religious verse as they are for
any other kind. Hopkins knew this, and he labored mightily to
see what the world had to show him. If inspiration is religious,
and is also inspiration, the result will be good religious poetry,
provided the words are adequate to express it. If the writing is
religious in theme, but without the spark that only imagination
can supply, the result will be much like the verse of Brother
Antoninus and Thomas Merton: all argument, good intentions,
and no light. It is too bad that, in verse coming to us from intensely devout, serious, and dedicated men, we get enough solemn, dead metaphors to fill the stuffed owl's mouth for generations to come, enough laborious theology to make us wish
Thomas Merton were still an undergraduate Bohemian, and
Brother Antoninus still a farmer in the San Joaquin Valley,
ploughing God's land with his horses.
[1960]

HAYDEN CARRUTH

HAYDEN CARRUTH has been around a long time, as "younger poets" go. Up to now, I have never been favorably impressed with anything of his I have seen, and have passed him off as one among many of the same. But that is not the way to begin a review of his first book,* for as it turns out I *am* very much impressed. As I think of *The Crow and the Heart*, I find myself believing not in its sustained power or concentration of language, but in a carefulness which bursts, once or twice or three times, into a kind of frenzied eloquence, a near-hysteria, and in these frightening places sloughing off a set of mannerisms which in the rest of the book seems determined to reduce Carruth to the level of a thousand other poets who can do, just as easily as he, most of the things he does in about three-fourths of these poems. Often, Carruth appears not to have learned the Gresham's Law of poetry, which states that the more sounds and images you crowd into a line, the less effect they have. He seldom lets you forget that you are reading something which has been written, and written again, and then written some more. These poems strike me as being completely mechanical and lifeless, with more than a hint of academic dilettantism about them. They are Suspect, and I for one cannot take them seri-

* *The Crow and the Heart* by Hayden Carruth. New York, The Macmillan Company.

ously. The subjects of the poems are completely obscured in a
blur of likely sounding words.

> This is the white king's palace: snowflakes flounce
> On every draught, dally in secret aisles,
>
> Bow and depart, an instant clap of fury,
> And winds, O sparrow, shake your chandelier
>
> That leaps and branches toward the reeling walls.

This is supposed to be a description of a snowfall, but it is a
decorator's description, with a great deal more emphasis on the
describing than on the snow, and so we get a little shimmer of
words and no sense of winter at all. And the same thing happens
over and over again.

> What kind of thing, here where my mother's flowers
> Bark colors only, like a tranced bazaar,
> Is my late lingering love for you, which flows
> Beyond all those events, past the Azores?

I guess (and I am only guessing) that "bark colors" is intended
to indicate that the colors are raucous and irritating, and call
attention to themselves mindlessly and unnecessarily. Actually,
though, this is not what happens in the beholder's mind. He
thinks momentarily only of a preposterous image of flowers like
dogs, or like sideshow barkers, and then dismisses it, his attention
having been retained by neither flowers nor dogs. Because the
objects which are called to our attention are vertiginously dis-
embodied in language, considerable doubt is cast on the veracity
and imagination of the mind that brought them up and presented
them in this way. As Auden says, the poet's job is to find out the
images "that hurt and connect," and a great many of Carruth's
don't, at least not for me. They are like musical exercises that one
wants to hear dissolve into the real playing.

The point where this happens is page nineteen, for those who

wish to consult the text. "On a Certain Engagement South of Seoul" is as fine a poem as an American has ever written about the ex-soldier's feelings, and that takes in a lot of territory. It is only after the Inevitable has clamped us by the back of the neck that we go back and look carefully at the poem, and see that it is written in *terza rima*. And so, hushed and awed, we learn something about the power of poetic form, and the way in which it can both concentrate and release meaning, when meaning is present. This poem suggests, too, that Carruth is one of the poets (perhaps all poets are some of these poets) who write their best, pushing past limit after limit, only in the grip of recalling some overpowering experience. When he does not have such a subject at hand, Carruth amuses himself by being playfully skillful with internal rhyme, inventing bizarre Sitwellian images, being witty and professionally sharp. And there is much of this. But through Carruth's verses-by-anybody we are led slowly and a little restively, like the true mad, into "The Asylum," surely one of the most remarkable sequences of recent years. It is a low-keyed, extremely intelligent, tremblingly helpless poem about insanity and its terrible cure. It draws conclusions that no one but Carruth could have drawn, and which, by the miraculous process that takes place in poetry as good as this, manages also to speak for the rest of us, too, and for our society. I hope I am not making Carruth's powerful writing appear ordinary by talking about it as I do, but you must let him, and not me, convince you that it is neither. I should like very much to quote long stretches of "The Asylum," but I restrain myself in order to give the poem the chance it deserves of building up in the reader's mind as it was meant to. I suggest, then, that you buy Carruth's book and read "On a Certain Engagement South of Seoul," "The Fat Lady," and "The Asylum." They have done us proud.
[1960]

. .
.

Hayden Carruth is a writer with strange and terrifying shifts in quality. His last year's *The Crow and the Heart* contained the finest sonnet sequence that I have read by a contemporary poet, "The Asylum," and a great deal of ordinary, jargoning stuff which Mr. Carruth should have been ashamed to print in the same volume. "The Asylum" showed, however, that Mr. Carruth might be one of the few modern poets capable of writing a good long poem. *Journey to a Known Place** is it. I can only give an inadequate, betraying sketch of this beautifully conceived and imagined poem, into which Carruth blends his tremendous and sensitive vocabulary (surely the largest and most precise since Hart Crane's) with a mixture of cold, steady fury and nightmarish passion in the presence of which I can do little more than record my amazement and gratitude. Mr. Carruth's Known Place is the world itself, seen and experienced in and through its classic elements, earth, water, air, and fire. Each of its four sections begins with the protagonist's apprehension of one of the elements and follows him as he goes into it, comes to know it, *lives* it through a process of primal metamorphosis, and then emerges in preparation for his entry into the next element, until all is resolved in fire. Since part of the immense force of the poem depends upon its closely packed, slow-rolling diction over long stretches, quotation in brief can hardly do more than suggest its quality. But when Mr. Carruth's man-fish goes

> Down, down to the stiller mid-regions
>   Where giant sea-snails hung torpid in copulation,
>   Half out of their shells, white flesh rolling, exposed
>
> Obscenely in the slow coiling and cramping of a cruel
>   And monstrously deliberate ecstasy

we have had a vision of the blind and necessary horror of nature which is, for my money, very nearly absolute.

* *Journey to a Known Place* by Hayden Carruth. New York, New Directions.

Like his man-bird, Mr. Carruth is "skilled now in the / profound and lovely / necessities," and his wonderful new poem, very possibly a great poem, which begins with a huddle of refugees and ends in the City of the Sun, is bound to be discussed and reread for many years. *Journey to a Known Place* is a painful and magnificent poem; it really hurts and it really sings, and I can only urge readers to buy it and live with it.

[1961]

JAMES KIRKUP

DEPENDABLY and often remarkably brilliant, James Kirkup* is a professional poet in every sense the term has ever had. He is the only poet I know of who can interest you in the difficulties of sitting down at the writing table each morning to dream up a new poem. With Kirkup's work, however, I don't feel that facility is the problem, as it is with many writers. He is, instead, one of those poets to whom writing is a continuous process, natural, simply a part of living. He cannot summon the tragic, but is unfailingly direct and graceful. He can find an acceptable meaning for each of his subjects, and can write about anything, apparently at a moment's notice. He is really a *beautiful* poet, by which I mean that he keeps everything harmonious and in proportion; but of the strangeness that Bacon said is or should be a part of all "excellent" beauty, there is none at all. His poems are what you

* *The Prodigal Son* by James Kirkup. New York, Oxford University Press.

habitually find in the better medium-circulation magazines; everything said is just a little better than what you would expect to be said, and is what *you* would have said, if you were as talented as James Kirkup. One is bothered as much as delighted by the cleverness of the poems, and by seeing many promising themes dissolve into conventionally pretty descriptions. You feel, not really the painful search to know and to grasp something, but that, for the bright and the witty, everything is already known. These poems don't *develop* well, either; they stand still and elaborate, somewhat like those of Laurie Lee, a less intelligent but far more sensuously gifted poet than Kirkup. But there is immense delight to be had from Kirkup's writing: tremendous variety, lovely cadences, a seemingly inexhaustible ability to make telling comments on anything and everything. And what might prove to be an interesting new direction for Kirkup begins to show itself, too. The influence of Oriental poetry seems to be having a good effect on him.

> You said that if only you could find
> One man who would let himself be touched
> By your poems, then you would die happy.

> I have come too late to tell you
> How your brief poem moved me
> With its modesty and longing.

The important thing about Kirkup is that a poet who can do so many things superbly may yet do the one Thing, that he is exceptionally talented, and that he wrote, a few years ago, the magnificent *Descent into the Cave*. Perhaps he will descend again, possibly this time into a cave in Japan.
[1960]

ANNE SEXTON

ANNE SEXTON's poems* so obviously come out of deep, painful sections of the author's life that one's literary opinions scarcely seem to matter; one feels tempted to drop them furtively into the nearest ashcan, rather than be caught with them in the presence of so much naked suffering. The experiences she recounts are among the most harrowing that human beings can undergo: those of madness and near-madness, of the pathetic, well-meaning, necessarily tentative and perilous attempts at cure, and of the patient's slow coming back into the human associations and responsibilities which the old, previous self still demands. In addition to being an extremely painful subject, this is perhaps a major one for poetry, with a sickeningly frightening appropriateness to our time. But I am afraid that in my opinion the poems fail to do their subject the kind of justice which I should like to see done. Perhaps no poems could. Yet I am sure that Mrs. Sexton herself could come closer than she does here, did she not make entirely unnecessary concessions to the conventions of her literary generation and the one just before it. One can gather much of her tone and procedure from quotations like "You, Doctor Martin, walk / from breakfast to madness," and "All day we watched the gulls / striking the top of the sky / and riding the blown roller coaster." "Riding the blown roller

* *To Bedlam and Part Way Back* by Anne Sexton. Boston, Houghton Mifflin Company.

coaster" is a kind of writing I dislike to such an extent that I feel, perhaps irrationally, that everyone else including Mrs. Sexton ought to dislike it, too, for its easy, A-student, superficially exact "differentness" and its straining to make contrivance and artificiality appear natural. One would hope that a writer of Mrs. Sexton's seriousness, and with her terrible story to tell, would avoid this kind of thing at any price. Yet a large part of her book is composed of such figures. In the end, one comes to the conclusion that if there were some way to relieve these poems of the obvious effort of trying to be poems, something very good would emerge. I think they would make far better short stories, and probably in Mrs. Sexton's hands, too, than they do poems. As they are, they lack concentration, and above all the profound, individual linguistic suggestibility and accuracy that poems must have to be good. As D. H. Lawrence once remarked in another connection, they don't "say the real say." But Mrs. Sexton's candor, her courage, and her story are worth anyone's three dollars. [1961]

GALWAY KINNELL

I LIKED Galway Kinnell's poems* mainly for their wholehearted commitment to themselves, and for what I can only call their innocence. Mr. Kinnell cares quite openly and honestly about almost everything he has ever seen, heard of, or read about, and

* *What a Kingdom It Was* by Galway Kinnell. Boston, Houghton Mifflin Company.

finds it rather easy to say so. There is nothing very tragic or tearing about him, or nothing very intense, either. He seems to me a natural poet: humanly likeable, gentle, ruminative. But he is dishearteningly prolix. Prolixity is, of course, the foremost and perhaps only natural enemy of the natural poet, and Mr. Kinnell is going to have to do battle with it if he is to realize himself. Some of these pieces are almost too trivial to be believed, and even the best of them keep blurring into each other, since there is no real division, nothing to *individualize* them, make them separately experienceable. They are just part of the amiable weather of the book. Poetry can do better than this, and so can Kinnell. The last long poem, "The Avenue Bearing the Initial of Christ into the New World," has some beautiful lines about such unbeautiful objects as carp in grocer's tanks and vegetable pushcarts. Here, you feel quite strongly a genuine presence, an integrated personal reality, powerful and *projected*. Kinnell realizes the difference between knowing something because you have been told it is so and knowing it because you have lived it. And this latter kind of knowing is what good poetry can give, and what Kinnell in some of his work gives, too. His first book is not as deep and abiding as we might like; I find myself remembering his themes and a few scattered details, but not the way in which they are told, or, as happens with the very best poems, the *words* in which they are told. But Mr. Kinnell has made an authentic beginning, and many poets die without getting even this far. Perhaps to a degree more than is true of other poets, Kinnell's development will depend on the actual events of his life. And it is a life that I think we should watch. It is warm, generous, reflective, and friendly. And as poetry it holds out some promise, largely because of this necessary involvement with the author's life, of being in the end magnificent. It is not entirely impossible that the Wave of the Future may turn out to have begun at Avenue C, or some place within walking distance of it.

[1961]

CHARLES OLSON

CHARLES OLSON is one of the elder statesmen of the Beats, and his "Maximus" poems* have been appearing in the very small and very rebellious magazines over the past several years. They have apparently gained a fairly enthusiastic reputation among the readers of these periodicals, and their collection has been anticipated with a good deal of excitement in some quarters, for at such a time the master plan was to be revealed, the relation of the parts to the whole shown. There was even speculation that the completed work would bring about a radically new kind of American poetry. Olson helped this supposition along by generously furnishing his followers with his theory of "projective" verse or "open" verse, which notion I should imagine he picked up from the French critic René Nelli, author of *Poésie Ouverte, Poésie Fermée*. The kind of poetry which he describes is written, evidently, by means of a method entitled "composition by field." The poem, according to this, is "energy transferred from where the poet got it . . . to the reader." It must therefore be "a high energy-construct, and . . . an energy-discharge." Stripped of the language of physics, which in his use turns quickly to jargon, Olson's theory comes down to the simple and ancient one of organic form: "right form, in any given poem, is the only and exclusively possible extension of content under

* *The Maximus Poems* by Charles Olson. New York, Jargon/Corinth Books.

hand." As to the process by which this laudable goal may be reached, Olson tells us that "ONE PERCEPTION MUST IMMEDIATELY AND DIRECTLY LEAD TO A FURTHER PERCEPTION." These *dicta*, when taken in conjunction with a less easily understood set of ideas concerned with the relation of breathing to "the line," make up most of what Olson has to say about poetry. For the reference of those who might wish to put it into action, I reproduce Mr. Olson's key formula. "Put baldly," he says, "the two halves are:

> the HEAD, by way of the EAR, to the SYLLABLE
> the HEART, by way of the BREATH, to the LINE."

If rightly applied to syllable and line, this process is supposed to give "the play of the mind" which shows "whether a mind is there at all." In the poem—or the "field," as Olson calls it—the syllables, lines, images, sounds, and meanings "must be taken up as participants in the kinetic of the poem just as solidly as we are accustomed to take what we call the objects of reality." These elements "are to be seen as creating the tensions of the poem just as totally as do those other objects create what we know as the world." Well, fine. But this is all nothing very new. And when you come, finally, to see that Olson's trump card, very nearly, is "the advantage of the typewriter," which ostensibly gives the poet "for the first time" the "stave and the bar a musician has had," it is pretty evident that Olson's contribution to the aesthetics of poetry is likely to be something less than epoch-making. All the things he says are in various ways true enough, but "projective verse" has no claim on them; most of them are true of any poetry, or at least of any that is worth reading. Certainly, organic form—the poem growing naturally from its own materials and creating its own best internal relations and overall shape —is the form that all good poems must have: do have. What Olson's notion of "open" verse does is simply to provide creative irresponsibility with the semblance of a rationale which may be

defended in heated and cloudy terms by its supposed practitioners. All "schools" theorize endlessly, it may be noted.

The Maximus Poems themselves, issued in a handsome format
by Jonathan Williams's small and splendid Jargon / Corinth
Books, are reasonably interesting, though by no means as original as one might have been led to expect. I kept looking in them
for the HEAD by way of the EAR to the SYLLABLE, but found only
a great number of syllables which go back to Ezra Pound's head
via the kind of jigsaw organizational techniques of William Carlos Williams's *Paterson*. Instead of "Mr. Paterson" we have Maximus, and instead of Paterson itself we have Gloucester, Mass.
There is much of the history of Gloucester; there are lists of the
crews of ships, what they carried, descriptions of their figure-
heads, and so on, evidently selected around one of Mr. Olson's
principles, though I'm not sure which one. There are also a great
many small, terse, prosy snapshots of Gloucester life both past
and present, with Maximus now participating, now reading, now
remembering, now dreaming. Some of these episodes are effective, especially a short prose section on cod fishing, but I have
difficulty in taking the whole seriously as a poem, as I do with
Paterson also. Yet I have a weakness for long poems of this kind,
for the *Cantos*, for *Paterson*, for *Maximus*, and particularly for
the most obscure and ambitious of them all, David Jones's *The
Anathemata*, which perhaps provides in its brilliant, thorny introduction the best justification for this kind of writing, for this
kind of organization (or anti-organization), that could be made.
Jones says, quoting Nennius (or whoever composed the intro-
ductory matter to the *Historia Brittonum*): *coacervavi omne
quod inveni:* "I have made a heap of all that I could find." Jones
then goes on to explain that he has allowed himself "to be di-
rected by motifs gathered together from such sources as have by
accident been available to me and to make a work of this mixed
data." This, essentially, is what Olson has done also, and there is
always some amount of fascination in seeing what things have
been made available to another's mind "by accident" and have

emerged in print as the details of a poem. In presenting his material, Olson is both observant of the way his world, including its history, looks and feels, and determinedly bookish, with the cantankerous and pedantic bluster of his self-educated colleagues Rexroth and Edward Dahlberg. But with or without the help of his theories, he has managed to write a few moderately interesting sections of a long, unsuccessful poem which must have been the labor of years, and these are worth reading. The structure of the poem is only the structure of fortuitous association plus the more obvious devices and literary mannerisms of Pound and Williams, but his mind seems to me quite a capable one, and at all points is working hard to say what has been given it. That is enough, because it has to be.

[1961]

WILLIAM STAFFORD

THERE are poets who pour out rivers of ink, all on good poems. William Stafford* is one of these. He has been called America's most prolific poet, and I have no doubt that he is. He turns out so much verse not because he is glib and empty, but because he is a real poet, a born poet, and communicating in lines and images is not only the best way for him to get things said; it is the easiest. His natural mode of speech is a gentle, mystical, half-mocking and highly personal daydreaming about the landscape

---

* *West of Your City* by William Stafford. Georgetown, California, The Talisman Press.

of the western United States. Everything in this world is available to Mr. Stafford's way of writing, and I for one am very glad it is. The things he chooses to write about—I almost said "talk" —seem in the beginning more or less arbitrary, but in the end never so. They are caught up so genuinely and intimately in his characteristic way of looking, feeling, and expressing that they emerge as fresh, glowing creations; they *all* do, and that is the surprising and lovely fact about them:

> The well rising without sound,
> the spring on a hillside,
> the ploughshare brimming through deep ground
> everywhere in the field—
>
> the sharp swallows in their swerve
> flaring and hesitating
> hunting for the final curve
> coming closer and closer—
>
> the swallow heart from wing beat to wing beat
> counselling decision, decision:
> thunderous examples. I place my feet
> with care in such a world.

Let Mr. Stafford keep pouring it out. It is all good, all to his purpose.

[1961]

LEWIS TURCO

In his introduction, Donald Justice speaks of Lewis Turco's playfulness and his penchant for difficult exercise poems, like "a gifted musician practicing scales, arpeggios, and the sonatas of Clementi." I must say that I don't feel this is a promising sign in Mr. Turco's work.* As a game it is all right, I suppose, but why play games with Mr. Turco when one can be reading real poetry? Skillful Mr. Turco may be, but his is the most ordinary of all kinds of skill, and shuts off more of the potentialities of poetry than it opens. As far as I am concerned, Mr. Turco has not yet learned the cardinal point about one's relation to what one writes: that, of a given subject, one can say many things, with much aplomb and all the versifying skills in the world, and yet not have (or make) them worth saying. The important thing is not to say something, anything, with wit and skill, but to say the right, the unheard of, the necessary thing: necessary because the subject is what it is, and because the writing man, including his relationship to the subject, is what *he* is. Without this kind of live conjunction nothing else really matters, and we are left with the sonatas of Clementi and apologetic introductions rather than with something that we must, because its urgency and its means leave us no choice, live with until we die.

[1961]

* *First Poems* by Lewis Turco. Francestown, N.H., The Golden Quill Press.

W. S. MERWIN

W. S. MERWIN is probably the most widely published poet of his generation. That he is a fine writer I have no doubt at all, and that in his new book* he displays signs of a power I had not hitherto noticed is equally true, though one has certainly re-marked the low-keyed monotony of some of his descriptive poems and the endless fascination that the mechanical problems of writing verse have always had for him. What he has lacked up to now, and still lacks, is intensity, some vital ingress into the *event* of the poem which would cause him to lose his way among the intricacies of what is so easy for him to say concern-ing almost anything on earth and suffer a little at the hands of his subjects: in a word, *earn* them emotionally. Control of one's ma-terial is one thing, and dictatorship over it is another. It is this, I suppose, that led "Crunk," the lively amateur critic of the inter-esting little magazine *The Sixties*, to speak of Merwin as being "like a great general born into the world again as a member of the animal kingdom." It seems to me, also, that Merwin has never given enough of himself to his subjects: of the self that somehow lies beyond the writing self. He has always seemed so sure, so utterly sure of what he knew and could tell about them that the strokes out of Heaven, or out of the subjects themselves, have never quite managed to hit him between the eyes. One of

* *The Drunk in the Furnace* by W. S. Merwin. New York, The Mac-millan Company.

the difficulties about Mr. Merwin's writing generation has always been just this, as I have noted before: the dominations and powers of poetry itself—of the surface effects and the learnable manipulations as opposed to the profound marriages of technique and personality that make up the poems we remember—are constantly in danger of becoming a kind of mask which takes, automatically, a more or less pleasing, predictable shape, but which also with tremendous effectiveness obscures and kills what the poet should want to get at: those areas which only he is capable of discovering. In a land where all poems are masks, good ones or bad ones, it behooves the poet to construct the best faces for himself that he can. And yet when the right kind of simplicity reveals itself, how artificial all such construction and its products come to seem!

I think a new, strange kind of simplicity is now becoming available to Merwin, and the fact that it is slowly emerging from the techniques of one of the master prosodists of our time makes its advent doubly worth watching. There is still far too much gilded stuffing rounding out the contours of Mr. Merwin's poems, and I can't yet see his features clearly through his various masks, but I hope that one day in the not too distant future I shall be able to do so. After a prodigal beginning Merwin may now seem to be stalled. But it is my impression that he is gathering force. The title poem here and "One-Eye" avail themselves of an odd kind of roughed-up, clunking diction and meter that I found quite attractive, and which involved me in their poems more than in any of Mr. Merwin's others that I have read. With tools like these and with the discoveries about himself that this book shows him intent on making, Merwin should soar like a phoenix out of the neat ashes of his early work.

[1961]

THEODORE WEISS

THEODORE WEISS's new book,* for which we have waited far too long, is well worth waiting for. Weiss is a writer who works his language hard, and he knows exactly how to cultivate it for what it can give him. The opposite of poets like Lee Anderson and Charles Olson, who build for years a kind of complicated and contrived deadness into their poems, Weiss arrives at a clear, intense, vivid verbal life through the most laborious analytical processes, and it is apparent that he could not have achieved the extraordinary intensity of these poems by any other means than this approach. One has the feeling that Mr. Weiss has lived with each phrase for a long time, testing it in all sorts of ways, like a man edging cautiously out over thin ice, trying each footstep carefully before putting his full weight on it, until, in the center of the lake (for this simile must pertain to poetry rather than to fact), he can not only dance on the ice but on the water itself when the ice melts. Many of his passages seem to me to be nothing more or less than visionary, with the vision-seeing that only the poet's truest and most personal language can attain, with "the world / lit up as by a golden school." And yet you never lose the sense of Weiss's presence, either: the poems never seem to be the products of anything but a knowable and very human mind. The mind is an exceedingly complex one which operates by building small, deeply observed details ("the wood / in its

* *Outlanders* by Theodore Weiss. New York, The Macmillan Company.

own dark / middle lost") into difficult and rewarding structures: poems which never give all they have to give on any one reading but withhold, withhold, always retaining something essential of themselves, something to bring the reader back and reward him again. The poems have both the immediacy one wishes for and the power of engaging the remoter, more abstract regions of thought; they have both the concreteness of things, objects, and whole ranges of meaning which the things inform, until the world does, indeed, turn into a "golden school." It is in the vicinity of such a school, after hours, that I like to think of Weiss and his intelligent daemon sitting down together to have a beer, and of the daemon idly throwing onto the tabletop the great keys to Mr. Weiss's splendid imagination which together they have designed and made over the last twenty years. Weiss has worked for a long time, and in a way right for him, to understand his means and to employ them as they were intended to be employed. This labor has paid off fully, and with interest, in the present book, and what must certainly be Mr. Weiss's very great pride in looking back and seeing how the thing was done is my pleasure to try to imagine. Readers who want to connect first with the poems *I* like best should begin with "The Fire at Alexandria," "A Canticle," and "To Forget Me." From there they should go in any direction, knowing that it is the right one. After all, Mr. Weiss is on every page; *Outlanders* is in all senses his book.

[1961]

JOSEPHINE MILES

IN the case of Miss Josephine Miles, I find myself confronted with thirty years of poems of a kind that I have never much liked.* Yet after reading Miss Miles, I find also that all my standards, never very strictly defined, have been upset, so that I am not exactly sure what I like and what I don't. Though, like most people who read poetry at all, I was aware of Miss Miles's name and of her rather muffled but nonetheless quite apparent reputation, I have never until now taken a good look at the totality of her output. The first quality of her work that struck me was a uniform sort of unrelieved and often drab intellectuality. There are plenty of intelligent comments, plenty of shrewd, narrow-eyed observations, but I kept wishing for a little more feeling and a little less knowledge. The poems are so self-contained that they come to seem automatic, including as they do all the things that poems need in our time in order to exist respectably: they have beginnings, middles, and ends, and one is never in any doubt about which is which. There is none of the opening out into a Beyond greater than anything the poems have to tell: nothing to assure the reader that what *he* brings to the poems of his own life is at all important—Miss Miles has neatly packed everything for him. And yet I did not continue to feel this way for long. I came to believe what Miss Miles says, and believe it in

* *Poems 1930–1960* by Josephine Miles. Bloomington, Indiana University Press.

a way that also includes a large measure of admiration for the gentle assurance with which she deals with her material. If there is such a thing as making a cardinal virtue out of deliberately letting alone larger subjects in favor of smaller ones, Miss Miles has made a modest and authentic triumph of it, and any reader who is at all alive will be enriched by her quick, penetrating looks from the odd angles of hidden corners.

[1961]

THEODORE ROETHKE

I SHALL have very little to say about the Indiana University Press's new paperback edition of Theodore Roethke's collected poems, which he calls *Words for the Wind*, and his charming but much slighter book for children, *I Am! Says the Lamb*.* Roethke seems to me the finest poet now writing in English. I reiterate this with a certain fierceness, knowing that I have to put him up against Eliot, Pound, Graves, and a good many others of high rank. I do it also cheerfully, however, for stating his own idiosyncratic and perhaps indefensible views is part of a reviewer's business. I think Roethke is the finest, not so much because of his beautifully personal sense of form (approved even by Yvor Winters, our most insistent watchdog in these matters), but because of the way he sees and feels the aspects of life which

* *Words for the Wind* by Theodore Roethke. Bloomington, Indiana University Press. *I Am! Says the Lamb* by Theodore Roethke. New York, Doubleday and Company.

are compelling to him. The powerful, almost somnambulistic statements of his observations and accountings come to us as from the bottom of the "deep well of unconscious cerebration" itself, from a Delphic trance where everything one says is the right, undreamed-of, and known-by-the-gods-all-the-time thing that should be and never is said. The best of Roethke's poems are very nearly as frightening and necessary as "darkness was upon the face of the deep," and as simple and awesome as "let there be light." It is this world of perpetual genesis, his own genesis, re-curring, continually available if only the perceiver is up to it in mind and body, that Roethke has somehow got down in words. The few objects that define his personality—stones, flowers, sunlight, wind, woman, darkness, animals, fish, insects, birds—tell his entire story, and the changes and similarities he finds among them are his poems. They are simple, tragic, profound, and un-utterably joyful. They are, and will be, permanent parts of our perception of reality, and one feels guilty of an unjust act, of a dislocation of nature, in referring to them as "literature" at all. [1961]

．　　．
．

The remainder counter of any bookstore is a depressing con-frontation for all writers, but worst for poets. There are always large numbers of poetry books there, and among them the writer may find—frequently does find—his own work, marked down to seventeen cents. The books of only a very few poets of each generation survive, and it is good to imagine these, inevita-bly thrown on the sale counter of a department store in the general indifference to poetry in which Wallace Stevens is remaindered along with Jesse Stuart, as giving off a special glow perceivable only by those with the power to receive their vision.

I first picked up Theodore Roethke's *The Lost Son* on such a counter, and paid twenty-nine cents for it. With its first few words I knew that I had something far beyond the capacity of money to command, reward, or comment upon, but I was not quite sure what it was. I had the illusion (perhaps not an illusion) that I had been looking for the book all my life without knowing it. I had long been disturbed by a strange and doubtless indefensible distinction in my mind between poets who *merely* tell you of their experiences ("My grandmother's walking-stick had a brass knob") and those who are able to relate *you*, the unknown but potentially human Other, to the world that all of us exist in. If you have heard wind, you have heard Roethke's wind; the wind of your experience comes doubly to life. If you have touched the bark of a tree, you have touched one of Roethke's trees, and understand through the words of the poem what you felt years before, standing there in the pine grove speechless. Roethke is of the company of the great Empathizers, like Rilke and D. H. Lawrence, and in this association none of those present need feel embarrassment. They are the Awakeners, and can change your life not by telling but by showing, not from the outside but from within, by the lively and persistently mysterious means of inducing you to believe that you were *meant* to perceive and know things as Rilke, as Lawrence, as Roethke present them. Roethke's poems make you remember and rejoice in Lawrence's magnificent little jotting: "We don't exist unless we are deeply and sensually in touch / with that which can be touched but not known." Roethke's marvelous sensuous apprehension of the natural world—finer in its way than Rilke's because more immediate, less withdrawn and contemplative—and his total commitment to both his vision and to the backbreaking craft of verse, are what should have put a peculiar shine on that book on Davison-Paxon's remainder table. I must admit, though, that blind luck is almost as good. From that first encounter I went on to buy his other books as they came out, and was struck by the increasing mastery of form as well as by the reckless willingness to throw everything out the window and start over again, get back to first things, to primal sources, to

risk sounding ridiculous and awkward in the quest of things that
cannot be made to appear smooth and easy. I was moved also by
the deepening of perception and the steady increase in joyous-
ness as the man himself became older. These qualities are all
present in blazing fullness in the present book,* and now that
he is gone one cannot help being haunted by the unwritten, unlived poems which might have existed for Ted—which undoubtedly *would* have existed for him, for he was that kind of
man and writer.

He wrote two kinds of poems: song poems (as all the pieces of
this sequence are) and long free-verse meditations. These are
successful poems in different ways, but I shall not be moved to
comment on them as *performances*, as dazzling as this kind of
consideration could easily show them to be. What matters to me
is not so much the form the poems took as the sensibility that
lived in them, the superior quality of observation that made
them possible: the presence of insight, of vision.

There was something of a cry in each of Roethke's lines: a cry
of astonishment at finding the thing—tree, stone, shell, woman—
really there, and himself also there at the same time: a cry of
affirmation at knowing somehow that he and it *would* be there.
This may account for the fact that there is some mindless, elemental quality in the sound of his voice, something primitive
and animistic, something with the wariness and inhuman grace
of the wild beast, and with it another thing that could not be and
never has been animal-like. His poems are human poems in the
full weight of that adjective: poems of a creature animal enough
to enter *half* into unthinking nature and unanimal enough to be
uneasy there, taking thought at what the animal half discerns
and feels. This position, which at times seems triumphantly an
extraordinary kind of wholeness impossible to animals and possible to men only on rare occasions, is the quality that Roethke has
caught in his best poems. They are the cries of a creature in a

---

* *Sequence, Sometimes Metaphysical* by Theodore Roethke. Iowa City,
The Stone Wall Press.

landscape which is beautiful and filled with mystery and does not know that it is: the utterances of a perceiving mind which cannot enter wholly into nature and yet yearns to, set off from the mindless flow it would become by a mind that reflects and assesses. The balance, the tranquil awareness that comes occasionally and wonderfully from this state is in his case the product of a terrible tension not far from madness at times, not far from total despair, but also not far from total joy.

In these twelve poems in this handsome book, sadness and joy, the unthinking eye and the reflecting mind are balanced, sometimes swaying one way, sometimes the other.

> What's madness but nobility of soul
> At odds with circumstance? The day's on fire!
> I know the purity of pure despair,
> My shadow pinned against a sweating wall.
> That place among the rocks—is it a cave,
> Or winding path? The edge is what I have.

It is no accident that Roethke' favorite word is "spirit." Spirit to him was meaningless without body. Yet body without the capacity to understand, be terrorized by, and finally to be reconciled with the eternal unknowable Self is only a kind of walking death. The body's response to the movement of waterweed, for example, is, for a super-selfed, selfless instant, the spirit's movement also. The hand moves unconsciously with the weed, the body sways, and something within moves also.

There is great joy in Roethke's poems, great sorrow, and great fear as well; one feels that unspeakable dread is never very far from any line, any perception. But everything he says has the authority of the earned vision, paid for with part of an extraordinary human life. Roethke is one of the few great poets (and I am prepared to retract no adjective in sight) who have been able to make effective *statements:* ones you believe, and believe in, at first sight, like a look into the one right pair of eyes in the world.

And who can shake off his magnificent Questions? If they were answered, so would everything be.

In the second of these poems, Roethke says

> Make me, O Lord, a last, a simple thing
> Time cannot overwhelm.

I would like to reply now, beyond the reach of his huge clumsy affectionate modesty, "Rest easy, Ted. The thing is done."
[1964]

LOUIS MACNEICE

In several important ways Louis MacNeice is my favorite poet of the Auden era, though even to state it in this manner indicates how inferior he is to Auden both as a poet and as an influence. I must admit, too, that I have been and am greatly attracted by MacNeice's modest and sensible statements about poets and poetry, and about his own stake in the game, so that I have always *wanted* to like him, and to find in his writing the qualities that he consciously tries to embody in it. In the introduction to his 1940 collected *Poems,* he says "I write poetry not because it is smart to be a poet but because I enjoy it, as one enjoys swimming or swearing, and also because it is my road to freedom and knowledge." This strikes me as a healthy and valuable approach to poetry, and MacNeice's Drydenian, superbly rational style embodies it as well as any style could. No one else of his generation has raised common sense to such eminence, has turned it on so many areas of contemporary experience, has drawn such lucid and thoughtful conclusions by means of it. He has not Auden's large implications and penetration, but within his limits he is masterful. His loose, conversational idiom is in fact severely classical in structure, deliberately slangy as much of it is; it never means more than what it says, and never less. On the other hand, there is a certain breeziness that I find more and more irritating as I reread MacNeice, for it comes to seem the breeziness not only of the disillusioned intellectual, but of a rather patronizing superiority; it often seems that MacNeice could not have the attitudes that make his poems unless the world furnished him objects to contemplate at an uninvolved, somewhat disdainful distance from which he always, somehow, still manages to talk as though he were in the thick of things. Again, he inclines too much toward fashionable jargonizing which dates quickly, though it always seems timely and even prophetic at the time it is written. In the new poems in *Solstices* as well as in the old ones of *Eighty-Five Poems*,* there is too much listing and cataloguing, too much lumping things together and not paying sufficient attention to any of them, too much easy sliding from one detail to another, passing over and through without touching. There are too many things used as "instances" of something or other, illustrations, counters to be moved around in a poem. Poetic discipline, at least as he conceives it, sits easily on MacNeice and he adopts one form or another simply as it amuses him to do so, all being equally available to a skill which never seems skill at all, but merely the pleasure of speaking, at that moment, in that particular way. That is why there is so *much* of MacNeice, and why so little of it is really memorable. The medium of verse is *too* ready to serve him. Common sense is, after all, not inspiration, not intuition. It is only common sense, and (paraphrasing a remark from the old Keith circuit), the trouble with common sense is that it's so damned common. MacNeice has been and is

* *Solstices* and *Eighty-Five Poems* by Louis MacNeice. New York, Oxford University Press.

always well informed and readable, and he is an authentic master of the committed, noncommitted, ironic tone which has been passing with us for the true voice of twentieth-century man. This is much, for who would want the future to remember us from the "prophetic" poems of George Barker? But in the end, reason pulling energetically at its own bootstraps, half smiling and intelligent, is not enough. Not really.

[1961]

CHARLES TOMLINSON'S VERSIONS OF FYODOR TYUTCHEV

I DON'T know Russian, and if I did I would try to forget it, so as not to interfere with my pleasure in reading Charles Tomlinson's "versions" (he doesn't call them translations) of Fyodor Tyutchev,* the nineteenth-century Russian poet much admired by Tolstoy and Dostoevski, then forgotten, then resurrected by Blok, Pasternak, and others when symbolism made its belated appearance in Russian verse. With a major assist from Henry Gifford, Tomlinson has selected and rendered thirty-seven of these strange, still poems, and the results are rewarding in a way translations rarely are. Tomlinson's withdrawn, meticulous, and scholarly-accurate diction makes of Tyutchev an English as well as a Russian poet; it is hard to believe that these pieces are translations, though they don't sound like Tomlinson's own poems,

* *Versions from Fyodor Tyutchev* by Charles Tomlinson. New York, Oxford University Press.

either. The reader must conclude that Tomlinson and Tyutchev (and Gifford) have met in the Great Good Place where all translators and makers of versions should go: where the individual characteristics of the translator's own style and personality give him a profound rapport with his subject without devouring it, as, say, Roy Campbell's Baudelaire is devoured by Campbell's style. It would be too much to say that Tomlinson and Tyutchev are alike; I'm sure they aren't. But their tendency toward quietness, their curious and highly effective use of scholarly and at times pedantic diction, of the unusual but precise word as well as the ordinary and precise, are similar. Note, for example, the beautiful use of "incursion" played off against the equally beautiful "lets":

> Steady incursion of the blade
> Lets space into the crop:
> Emptiness over all, save where
> Cobweb on idle furrow
> Stretches its gleam of subtle hair.

It is not often that we get translations (or even "versions") as good in their own right as poems as these are. Tyutchev and Tomlinson have struck it lucky, and so have we.

[1961]

MARIANNE MOORE

THOUGH her new *Reader** contains a generous sampling of all
the forms her writing has taken, her poems are, of course, Marianne Moore's main work. They depend largely upon her volu-
minous memory of things she has read in an unimaginable variety of places, from highly technical reference books on animal
species to the daily columns of sports writers, on her ability to
draw judgments from these and to make points which the culled
items themselves would never have thought of, and on her own
power of description, which is dazzling:

> The barnacles which encrust the side
> of the wave, cannot hide
>   there for the submerged shafts of the
>
> sun
> split like spun
>   glass, move themselves with spotlight swiftness
>   into the crevices—

Surely few poets have had so keen and so *right* an eye for the
ways in which one thing resembles another, or one aspect of a
thing suggests an aspect of another. Her capacity for finding,
fastening onto, and transmuting the wayward, the peculiarly
apt, the odd and the interesting fact, the little known and the

---

* *A Marianne Moore Reader*. New York, The Viking Press.

universally known is constantly astonishing, and so is her faculty
for making these dovetail into a careful, reticently revealing assessment of what, together, they illustrate or seem to prove. Few
poets, either, have shown how endlessly various, how ingenious
and idiosyncratic and inexplicably fascinating, how sheerly *interesting* the world is in its multifarous aspects, many if not all
of which are constantly modifying the beings and meanings of
others in secret and half-glimpsable ways: have shown how the
world is always becoming more and more absorbing, divulging
to the imagination behind the practiced, practical eye a continual
metamorphosis of illuminating correspondences and potentialities, some of which were always there, only waiting to be discovered, and others which have just come into being, from the
outcome of a baseball game played yesterday, a new statement
by a physicist, a new treatise on rare animals or on the fur trade
in the Hudson Bay area in the 1880's. Though there are notes to
some of these poems, the poems are readily graspable without
them, and are in no sense like the sterile paste-ups of William
Empson and Charles Madge. Though Miss Moore is learned and
sometimes devious, her poems have a way of coming wonderfully clear in the end, for their details are first lived before they
are written into their forms of language, and she cares about
communicating.

The dangers that Miss Moore's method runs are two. First,
there is the risk of her disappearing behind her quotations, and
of the essential secondhandedness of this part of her approach
becoming obtrusive and therefore self-defeating. The second
danger is that, in a universe of correspondences such as she posits, the resemblances and cross-fertilizations of her selected items
will, if inspiration fails, seem simply fortuitous or "yoked by
violence," a danger somewhat alleviated by Miss Moore's use of
syllabic meters, whose slow, sober matter-of-factness can be
made to *seem* to carry anything and makes even the ridiculously
diverse appear not only to belong together, but to *want* to belong together. Miss Moore's task as she has set it is to bring forth

only the best and most humanly useful, the most telling, the *essential* parallels: out of the infinitude of possibilities of comparison and illustration, only those we most need. In firm tones, over the half-prose substructure of syllabic verse, Miss Moore has only to say "Like the . . ." and anything could be admissible. It is perhaps not the least tribute one could pay to her work to say that anything is definitely *not* admissible, and that her exquisite tact and insight into her materials enable her to surmount both these dangers—though she is never very far from them—with a quiet and responsible assurance that amounts to triumph. Surely there has not been such imaginative and evocative precision since the Hopkins of the *Note-books*, and one can only regret, here, the exclusion of so many of the other poems Miss Moore has written, for nothing that she has touched is unprofitable, and we should welcome all the contact we can get with her watchful, spoken songs, with her way of putting the world together.

Her essays are as particularizing, judicious, modest, and incisive as her poems, and one realizes in reading them that in a sense the poems are inspired verse essays which make use of the daring leaps in logic and sequence which poetry permits more readily than prose. Except for the obvious omission of Miss Moore's metrical patterns and her cunning rhyme schemes, the essays are not greatly different from the poems; the packing of the text with quotations is still very much in evidence, as is her method of weaving together the thing being said from a number of other sources. Miss Moore's piece on Ezra Pound, for example, is the best on Pound that I can remember, and this is largely because it is Pound writing on himself as he should have written; it is hardly more than an extremely discriminating choice of citations from Pound's verse and prose, but these are arranged in a manner which reveals strikingly what his principles and his practice offer in their essences; even though Miss Moore seems hardly to permit herself to get a word in edgewise, we see Pound a great deal more clearly than before. That, I take it, is what is meant by interpretive criticism at its best.

Miss Moore also includes a number of translations from La Fontaine's *Fables*, published and much discussed several years ago. Howard Nemerov and others have shown that her French is not quite certain, and that she positively misreads more than a few passages, all of which adds up to demonstrating, I suppose, that her *Fables* are more Moore than they are La Fontaine. That is all right with me. Though I don't know La Fontaine except through Miss Moore, I suspect her of being the same kind of translator that Pound is, in, say, his renderings from the Chinese: being, even at his wrongest, somehow righter than right. If La Fontaine sounds like Miss Moore, he's lucky. Few writers are, this many years after death.

The one thing I most strongly regret about *A Marianne Moore Reader* is the inclusion of the so-called Ford Letters: the correspondence in which, at the instigation of Robert B. Young, of Ford's Marketing Research Department, Miss Moore undertook to find a salesworthy name for a new automobile. What I dislike most intensely in the whole affair is the assumption on the part of Mr. Young and his associates that there must be, might be, *some* practical good to be got from poets, who after all use words, just as copywriters do, but conceivably a little better; I keep imagining one executive at Dearborn saying to another, "Why, if poets can sell cars, let's use 'em." I have had considerable experience with this viewpoint myself, and I admire the perspicacity with which Miss Moore handles Mr. Young and his ghost-writer and/or stooge Mr. David Wallace, and the characteristic tenacity with which, without knowing anything whatever of advertising methods, she attempts to discover a usable trade name. But it is distressing, too, to see her struggling, with all her good faith and the same painstakingness that produced her poems, to come up with either the first thing that a junior copywriter would know enough to discard ("The Ford Silver Sword") or names so recherché and esoteric that they must have made the members of Ford's marketing team smile in amazed disbelief, as they did me, as I tried to imagine the company's money being paid out to publicize something called the "Triskelion," the "Turcotingo," or the "Utopian Turtletop." But I have also a vicious and continuing delight in recalling that the car, eventually named the "Edsel," was on all counts the biggest failure in recent automotive history, and must have been a financial disaster as well. Miss Moore's part in the whole thing was honorable and mistaken, and I hate to have such evidence of her exploited naïveté included in the only comprehensive selection that has been made of her work. It is a small price to have to pay, though, for the amassed riches of her *Reader*. To use her words, which are better than mine, her writing is a prime example of the "intensified particularity" of which we must be capable in order to get all the way *into* life, into the world both as it is and as it can be when we have achieved the "simplicity that is not the product of a simple mind but of a single eye." One relishes saying of Miss Moore, as one passes her book along, what she says of Paul Rosenfeld: "When everything has its price, and more than price, and anyone is venal, what a thing is the interested mind with the disinterested motive. Here it is."

[1962]

·   ·

·

Heaven is a vision, and so is earth; or at least it can be. Of one of these we know something; about the other we have to speculate. A question: What poet would we most like to have construct a Heaven for us, out of the things we already have? Construct it from his way of being, his particular method of putting the world together and endowing it with consequence? And what would we end up with, picking one rather than another? Would we prefer to inherit the cowled, ecclesiastical, distantly murmuring twilight of Eliot? Should the angels sing in a mixture of Provençal, Greek and frontier American, presided over by the perfect Confucian governor, as Ezra Pound might have it? Or would Paradise be the Artificial one of Baudelaire, a place like nocturnal Paris: a Heaven which—the maker might argue—contains those elements of Hell without which our joy could not exist?

If the question were put to me, I would choose Marianne Moore. And I suspect that this is so because of her persuasiveness in getting the things of this world to live together as if they truly belonged that way, and because the communal vividness of her poems suggests to me order of an ideal kind. In a way, she has spent her life in remaking—or making—our world from patticulars that we have never adequately understood on our own.

Well, what kind of Heaven would Miss Moore's be? Much, most probably, like the earth as it is, but refined by responsiveness and intellect into a state very far from the present one; a state of utter consequentiality. For what is Heaven, anyway, but the power of dwelling eternally among objects and actions of consequence? Miss Moore's Heaven would have a means of recording such objects and actions; it would have a history, and a way of preserving its discoveries and happenings: it would have books. But it would be, first of all, a realm of Facts: it would include an enormous amount of matter for there to be opinions about, and so it would make possible vivid and creative and personal parallels between things, and conclusions unforeseeable until they were made. It would take forever from Fact the deadness of being *only* fact, for it would endow what Is with the joyous conjunctions that only a personality itself profoundly creative, profoundly accessible to experience—a personality called a soul—can find among them. Truly, would we have it otherwise in the Eternal City?

This is how Miss Moore might do it. Or, more truthfully, how she has done it, by taking—literally—everything as her province, as the province of her poems. Her Heaven would be not only an artist's Heaven—though it would be that with a magnificent authority—but a Heaven to show the angels what they have missed. Missed, for example, by not knowing, or caring *enough*, about the story in Meyer Berger's "Brooklyn Bridge: Fact and Symbol" of the young reporter of the 1870's who, drawn by some unknown imperative, climbed one of the cables of the bridge, became spellbound to the extent that he couldn't come down, and simply hung there all night. Who ever knew this but Mr. Berger, the reporter, and Miss Moore? Miss Moore knew it not only because she encountered it, but because she *cared* to encounter it, and then came to possess it, first by knowing it and then by using it.

Each of her poems employs items that Miss Moore similarly encountered and to which she gave a new, Mooreian existence in a new cosmos of consequential relationships. What seems to me to be the most valuable point about Miss Moore is that such receptivity as hers—though it reaches perhaps its highest degree in her example—is not Miss Moore's exclusive property. Every poem of hers lifts us toward our own discovery-prone lives. It does not state, in effect, that I am more intelligent than you, more creative because I found this item and used it and you didn't. It seems to say, rather, I found this, and what did you find? Or, better, what *can* you find?

Miss Moore's critical intelligence is not destructive, as criticism is almost always taken to be, but positive in the richest and best sense. As a result of its use, who knows better than she how sheerly *experienceable* the world is, and in how many ways and on how many levels? She has asked, and the world has answered, for it understands, in all its billions of parts, how to answer when questions are rightly put.

This is Miss Moore's first book of poems since 1959,* and it is probably the finest of them all. It is, of course, much like her others, for she is not the kind of writer who goes through phases, but rather one who deepens down into what she already was: a poet of surprising particulars that also happen to be true. Here, some of her particulars are large, like the Brooklyn

* *Tell Me, Tell Me* by Marianne Moore. New York, The Viking Press.

Bridge, and some are small, like the bear in the old Frank Buck animal-trapping film she saw. (And, come to think of it, "Bring 'Em Back Alive" is not an unrevealing way to characterize Miss Moore's poetic method, either.) What you find out from these new poems is what Miss Moore has learned from in the last seven years: what she has read, what ball-players she has watched, what museums and zoos she has gone to, what people she has talked to.

In one poem, for example, she juxtaposes a quotation from Sir Kenneth Clark's "Leonardo da Vinci," another from da Vinci's own notebooks, and a statement by da Vinci that Henry Noss, a history professor at New York University, cited in a television lecture. These become entities which strike whole showers of fresh sparks from each other, and one feels that their conjunction is possible only because Miss Moore so thoroughly understands, by an act of the acutest intelligence, these quotations in all their expressive possibilities, and not simply in the contexts in which they originally occurred: she knows what they are *all* about, instead of merely what they think they are all about.

Informing Miss Moore's work is a lovely, discriminating, and enthusiastic involvement with the way things are: *are*. In her poem to the Brooklyn Bridge, it is part of her involvement to know as much as she can learn about the engineer who built the bridge, and also something of the purely technical problems of its construction: to know what a "catenary curve" is. As it turns out, this "curve formed by a rope or cable hanging freely between two fixed points of support" is not only interesting in itself, but it becomes a poetic as well as an engineering term: the next time you ride by it or on it or see a picture of it, feel how the bridge deepens not only its structural Thereness for you, but its range of suggestiveness as well, being now a construction as much like a poem as a bridge, and requiring on both levels its own laws, its own initiates.

In her "burning desire to be explicit," Miss Moore tells us that facts make her feel "profoundly grateful." This is because knowledge, for her, is not power but love, and in loving it is important to know *what* you love, as widely and as deeply and as well as possible. In paying so very much attention to the things of this earth that she encounters, or that encounter her, Miss Moore urges us to do the same, and thus gives us back, in strict syllables, the selves that we had contrived to lose. She persuades us that the human mind is nothing more or less than an organ for loving things in both complicated and blindingly simple ways, and is organized so as to be able to love in an unlimited number of fashions and for an unlimited number of reasons. This seems to me to constitute the correct poetic attitude, which is essentially a life-attitude, for it stands forever against the notion that the earth is an apathetic limbo lost in space.

Who knows of Heaven? It may be only the convenient fiction of a reviewer, after all. But whatever her labors in the realm of the celestial—and I personally would never discount the possibility of their existence—one thing is certain: Miss Moore is making our earth.

[1966]

JOHN LOGAN

IN the only lines of his I have ever found memorable, Kenneth Rexroth says that the poet is "one who creates / Sacramental relationships / That last always." I have often been struck by the profundity and necessity of this statement, and I have also wondered why it is that the creation of sacramental relationships takes place so rarely in the work of most of our religious-oriented poets, men of good intent and lifelong devotion to God and to writing, like Thomas Merton, Daniel Berrigan, and Brother Antoninus. A sense of the sacred, which these men labor to make available, is probably the most important quality that poetry can possess, and it is not, I think, excessive to say that all poets, regardless of their orthodoxies, beliefs, or unbeliefs, are trying to embody and project such a sense according to their various lights and abilities.

John Logan's approach to the problem of sacramentalism in poetry is an interesting one. To begin with, he is on the surface a very literary poet, drawing constantly on quotations from church fathers, ecclesiastical writers, and also others, like Lorca and Rimbaud (you would think, from the number of poets who attach Rimbaud's words to their poems as though they were *mana,* that he made his living writing epigraphs), and in his present book* not only precedes his poems with multiple quotations but also furnishes them with explanatory afterthoughts ("After Antonina Valentin and after a memorial to Heine in Kilmer Park"), a practice that I simply loathe, and which I fervently wish that Logan would forget about. From a description of the subject matter of most of Logan's poems—a description citing their preoccupation with saints, with the sacred writings, with holy days, and with ecclesiastical rituals—one would be tempted to think that his approach to the creation of sacramental relationships is based exclusively upon an eminently orthodox symbology, and that it would thus run some chance of failing to convey this sense to those not of like faith and persuasion. One might conclude, also, that an habitual use of such time-worn symbols and images from an age of greater and more universally acknowledged faith would result, even at best, in a kind of museum or textbook poetry based upon matter which no amount of sincerity or ingenuity could ever restore to its former urgency.

* *Ghosts of the Heart* by John Logan. Chicago, University of Chicago Press.

Though it is true (at least in my opinion) that his poems about saints and martyrs are not his best, the surprising thing about this part of Logan's work is that the churchly bookishness is not dry and dead; it is oddly alive and *felt,* for in addition to being a Catholic, Logan is a man for whom intellectual excitement exists. Even so, to a religious outsider like myself, his formidable and detailed knowledge of church history and ritual is rather forbidding, and there are a good many times when I get lost in it. If one is patient, however, one comes to see that Mr. Logan's sense of what is sacred in his own experience is by no means limited to what is officially supposed to be sacred; it does not in the least depend on his having read Saint Augustine or on any of the rest of his orthodox or unorthodox learning. His poems at their best—and Mr. Logan's work is remarkably "level," with few peaks and declines—convey to a remarkable degree that degreeless and immeasurable and unanalyzable quality which Albert Schweitzer has called, in our century's greatest phrase, "reverence for life." In the face of this feeling, which is constant throughout Mr. Logan's writing, one does not really care much about talking of his literary means. His technical abilities are relatively slight, and really begin and end with an uncommon capacity for coming up with a strangely necessary and urgent observation and setting it among others by means of ordinary, unemphatic but rather breathless language which makes his lines read something like a nervous, onrushing prose. The heavy machinery of his religious symbology looks at times a little incongruous in this setting, but Logan himself never does. The day will come, I am sure, when he will lay less stress upon the symbols provided by his church, and rely more upon what he has so abundantly and joyously: the spirit of love without which all the dogma of Christianity would be valueless. I know of no other writer of my generation who so consistently is able to project this quality, and Logan does so entirely without recourse to that awful and professionally useful kind of "love" that is no more than a word on a page, and is often mistaken for the spirit that infrequently underlies it. Logan mentions love very few times in his two books, but it informs, illuminates, and transfigures everything he writes about. One closes Logan's books—particularly the present one, markedly superior to the first—thinking, "Yes, this is what poetry can sometimes do; this is what it can sometimes be." One understands what the religious faculty in man really is, and the human miracles it can perform even in its impure modern environment.

Mr. Logan's poems have not, perhaps fortunately, been widely or well reviewed; perhaps they could not have been. His strange kind of innocence, walking in and out of his ecclesiastical and literary knowledgeableness, is not an easy thing to talk about, though anyone who reads Mr. Logan cannot fail to be excited and uplifted by it. He is very much out of place, too, in the pathetic and vicious jostling and literary back-scratching for prizes and favorable notices that shows his generation of American poets at its ineffectual worst. He is far beyond the Idols of the Marketplace, and works where the work itself is done out of regard for the world he lives in and the people he lives among because he is helplessly and joyously what he is. As (and if), in Logan's work, the letter of religion fades away in favor of its spirit, he stands, in my opinion, an exciting chance of being one of the finest poets we have ever had in this country. (It might help, also, if he could find a less prosaic way of writing, and if he would explore a little among the dynamics of language, always retreating when they became too interesting for their own sake). It might be given to Logan to show in exultant urgency and truth what so many have labored and failed to show, but only said: that the spirit that makes Christianity Western Man's greatest triumph and hope is always and perpetually available in everything the human creature is privileged to do, from bringing children to birth to caressing the head of a dog.

[1962]

JOHN FREDERICK NIMS

JOHN FREDERICK NIMS has skill enough to dazzle Franz Liszt himself. Some critics—Randall Jarrell, for one—dismiss him because of his glitter. To my mind that is taking the short view. Mr. Nims has worked for a good many years to achieve his style of unremitting brilliance, and it behooves us to look closely at what he is doing. The question his verse always raises—at least with me—is what is the brilliance *for?* Reading Nim's first book, *The Iron Pastoral,** one wants to say quite loudly that if there is no originality or individuality of vision in the poet's apprehension of his subject, the mode of expression does not actually matter very much: that the determined effort to raise banalities, through verbal manipulation alone, to what passes for consequence is the worst danger our poetry runs, and has contrived to give much of it the appearance of smooth-tongued and systematic lying. And with some of Nim's cleverer poems you do feel this: that the poet is not trying to come at something which could be truth, but is only looking for a way to make commonplaces linguistically lively, substituting the result, decked out in current poetic fashionableness to which he adds his own fillip, for the profound experience of revelation which a good poem is. Even in the poems where Mr. Nims is at his most prodigiously empty, however, one can always marvel at the extremely difficult bra-

* *The Iron Pastoral* by John Frederick Nims. New York, William Morrow and Company.

vura-cadenza effects he brings off with zest and aplomb. Even if he offered nothing but the rapid-fire fingering, Nims would still be worth reading. But there is a lot more to Mr. Nims than artfulness. Whenever I think of him it is as the author of "The Masque of Blackness," for my money one of the most memorable, moving, and *believable* elegies in English, and as the translator of San Juan de la Cruz, a rendering so good that you tend to forget that the poems were ever written in Spanish. In his new book* there are a good many poems which have all the sparkle one associates with his work, and a few, like "The Young Ionia," which only have some.

> If you could come on the late train for
>   The same walk
> Or a hushed talk by the fireplace
>   When the ash flares
> As a heart could (if a heart would) to
>   Recall you,
> To recall all in a long
>   Look, to enwrap you
> As it once had when the rain streamed on the
>   Fall air

After taking part in the lovely fall-and-hover of this, one wants to catch a train and simply go and shake Nims's hand without saying a word. I sincerely hope that in future his writing will be more like this and less like that in many of his other poems, all concocted in the extremely self-conscious literary lingo of the forties that makes you say to yourself, after reading a poem composed in it, "I'm glad to get back to the naked truth, which mercifully has no words for itself." The best poetry—and Nims's best poetry—somehow partakes of this kind of nakedness, and one is shaken and exalted on coming back to it and seeing that it *is* in words. Nims's difficulties, if they are such,

* *Knowledge of the Evening* by John Frederick Nims. New Brunswick, N.J., Rutgers University Press.

stem mainly from his enterprising and energetic nature, which has tended to make him a "busy" poet, always prodding language to get up and work for its keep, and to work *hard*, for work's sake, as the nature of the Dutch prompts them to their compulsive cleanliness. The practice absolves Nims from the harder thing, which is only hindered and traduced by his verbal whizz-bangs. But I hope that people buy and read this book for "The Young Ionia," "The Evergreen," for its marvelous title (the best of the year, if Robert Duncan's *Opening of the Field* isn't), for a fine though niftied-up translation of Machado, for a great many incidental beauties of phrasing and cadence which Nims's resourceful technique and sensitive ear make possible only to him. Mr. Nims is quite a considerable poet, and gives occasional promise, without even trying, of becoming more. [1962]

RICHARD WILBUR

I HAVE never liked Richard Wilbur for the reasons his reviewers have generally given: his lightness, grace, wit, the assuredness of his technique, and his delight in making complexities sound natural, amusing, and easy. If this were all I would long ago have tired of him, for there are plenty of other poets who have these qualities, if not to the extent that Wilbur does, at least sufficiently to be comparable. It is true, though, that these *are* the first qualities that strike you about his verse. When you open a book—a new book or an old book—by Wilbur, you relax as into a lively yet orderly conversation in which your greatest pleasure is in listening to your host talk disarmingly about his house, his grounds, and his reading. Such conversation proceeds with friendly modesty; there is a happy, tranquil marriage between words and things, there are charming surprises and satisfying disclosures, and every anecdote has its point; when you leave you hope to be invited again. Up to now, though, there has been no *development*, or even change, in Wilbur's work, and there is something vaguely disturbing in this, even though you hear people on all sides saying that if someone is already the most charming and amiable man in the world there's no need for him to try to be something or somebody else. And yet it's hard to shake off, too, the feeling that the cleverness of phrase and the delicious aptness of Wilbur's poems sometimes mask an unwillingness or inability to think or feel deeply: that the poems tend to lapse toward highly sophisticated play. Yet even in this book,* which is not Wilbur's best, there is, underlying the grace and negligent mastery, the thing that should eventually make him the truly important poet that he deserves to be: the thing which his superlative manipulation of verse forms, his continuous and unobtrusive skills never fully state but never lose sight of. This is the quietly joyful sense of celebration and praise out of which Wilbur writes: the kind of celebration that is done, usually, without anyone's being told, and of the things that cause joy to rise unexpectedly, excessively, and almost always voicelessly in the human breast. This sense underlies Wilbur's work as the sea underlies a ship, or rather a garlanded Shelleyan boat which we admire so much that we forget that the sea makes its movement possible. Wilbur's celebration is sweet-natured, grave, gentle, and as personal to him as his own breath, a praise of small moments in which there is profound and intense life, and in his best poems (such as the one a few years back about burying the pet dog) it rises as it deserves to rise. This undercurrent, this

* *Advice to a Prophet* by Richard Wilbur. New York, Harcourt, Brace and World.

feeling of the steady joy of life as it exists, waiting for us, in "the things of this world," is the most valuable quality in Wilbur's work, and it may be that he has already found his own best and final way of getting it to us. But I'm not sure of that; the translations of Guillén, Quasimodo, and Nerval included here are a good deal more forthright than Wilbur's own poems, and may presage a widening of his concerns, though perhaps the difference I note is only in the poets whom Wilbur is translating.

Though there are grave shades in it, Wilbur's is not essentially a tragic mind, and the lack of this one quality will probably keep him, in the estimates of literary historians and other fossils, from being called a "major poet": one having made large Miltonic or Poundian flights. And yet his poems as they stand are as true and heartening a picture as we are ever likely to have of the best that the twentieth-century American can say of himself or have said about him. They are intelligent, good-humored, tolerant, imaginative, witty, resourceful, affectionate, candid, openhearted, and eminently responsible to and involved in their own business. These are the qualities that make Wilbur's kind of celebration possible, and if there is no other way for him to get this sense across to us, that is all right. I am only suggesting that there might conceivably be other ways, too, and that it is at least a *little* worth while to try to find them, considering the importance of what he has to give. Yet a new book by Richard Wilbur is surely an occasion for celebrating on our own in our own ways, which, as it turns out, are Wilbur's ways all the same.
[1962]

ROBERT DUNCAN

ROBERT DUNCAN is certainly one of the most unpityingly pretentious poets I have ever come across, even down to his past par-
ticiples, which for no particular reason that I can see he spells
without e's. As he keeps telling us, he is a mystic, which of
course allows him to say anything in any order. Sometimes I am
glad that he has given himself this freedom, but more often I feel
suicidal about it. When it doesn't fail him and ravel out into
quotations, Duncan's wide-eyed dreaminess is often wonderful
in individual lines and phrases, but the poems themselves are
drifting conglomerations which could be shuffled and dealt again
as different poems with results equally good and bad. Most of
them are crammed with the deadweight "filler" that inspired
poets fall back on when inspiration has failed and pride, or something equally vitiating, bids them pretend that it hasn't. What
we get, usually, is a poem of about a hundred lines purportedly
about the making of poems—I don't believe that even Duncan
does or could make poems according to these formulae—shot
through with a good many startling lines and ideas, tag ends of
quotations with and without inverted commas, and a general air
of inconclusiveness and waste. Though at best he is quite an
original writer, Duncan has some obvious and heavy literary
debts, notably to the Pound of the Italian and Provençal translations and to Pound's own poems: "There / disorder is not, order
is not, not no / Even simpleton need demands my ear." But the

part of Duncan's writing that is really his, that seems natural to him—or would seem natural to anyone—makes buying his book* worth one's money, though perhaps only so much of it as the paperback edition costs. His symbolistically ecstatic universe is vague, but it is real enough in its way, in the fashion in which dreams would be real if they occurred in words instead of images. The best thing in it is Duncan's ingenuousness, which shows through the sloppy rhetoric and the undigested quotations and the false mystery-mongering like the sun through clouds. It is no accident that the cover design is of children dancing in a ring; one imagines Duncan as one of the few modern grown-ups who could join such a dance without self-consciousness. Duncan also interests me because he demonstrates pretty well that at least one kind of original mind—the revery-prone, introspective, willful kind—withers under the conventional disciplines; there are some haunting images and at least two marvelous poems in his book which I don't think would have been possible under the teachings of any school but the self.

There are memories everywhere then. Rememberd, we go out, as in the first poem, upon the sea at night—to the drifting.

Of my first lover there is a boat drifting. The oars have been cast down into the shell. As if this were no water but a wall, there is a repeated knock as of hollow against hollow, wood against wood. Stooping to knock on wood against the traps of the nightfishers, I hear before my knocking the sound of a knock drifting.

It goes without will thru the perilous sound, a white sad wanderer where I no longer am. It taps at the posts of the deserted wharf.

Now from the last years of my life I hear forerunners of a branch creaking.

* *The Opening of the Field* by Robert Duncan. New York, Grove Press.

All night a boat swings as if to sink. Weight returning to weight in the cold water. A hotel room returns from Wilmington into morning. A boat sets out without boatmen into twenty years of snow returning.

Except for the "white sad wanderer" and the inclusion of the last sentence—which I was sorely tempted to leave out so that the poem, even if only once and in somebody else's quotation of it, could end where it should—this seems to me not so much a "successful poem" as a visionary statement of obsessing beauty, not a model of current writing proprieties but something dictated by an angel or one's wild, necessary, and incontrovertibly personal daemon. Duncan has the old or pagan sense of the poem as a divine form of speech which works intimately with the animism of nature, of the renewals that believed-in ceremonials can be, and of the sacramental in experience; for these reasons and others that neither he nor I could give, there is at least part of a very good poet in him, somewhere and somehow; there would have to be to get anything memorable said through the heavy traffic of his influences. This poet's supreme indifference to what we mean nowadays about form gives Duncan a chance, though perhaps only a slight one, to achieve the kind of form that his vision requires, and to avoid having his insights strait-jacketed by preconceptions as to what poetry has to be like in order to be poetry. This approach necessarily requires a tremendous amount of lost motion and dead wood; anyone who says "faith's fiefs" is not thinking about either small or large considerations of the ear, or of what is even sayable in English; anyone who advances propositions like "when the sky is in the sky it is uncertain it is an elephant" is just drifting and hoping. Some poets drift forever and nothing happens, but Duncan doesn't. If his drifting is tedious and often ridiculous, it is also sometimes productive, and that is all we can ask.

[1962]

.   .

.

Robert Duncan's way, his orientation, is largely that of Ezra
Pound.

> where the Day slept
> after noon, in the light's blur and shade
> the Queen of the Tree's Talking
> hears only the leaf sound,
> whirrr of wings in the boughs,
>
> the voices in the wind verging into leaf sound.

As may be seen, Duncan has managed to reproduce a little of the
older poet's sound, although at a very great remove. Duncan has
a good many of Pound's mannerisms and almost none of his superb talent, his *instinct* for significant or interesting juxtaposition, his marvelous sense of timing, his ability to make of many
fragments a whole greater than any one of them. Consequently
one feels in Duncan's work mainly arbitrariness. Some poets
drift well, but Duncan only periodically does so. He is intelligent in a special sort of narrow way, he is learned in the
curious matters that one can become learned in if one has the
time and the inclination, but none of this ever seems to come to
much on the page.

> If I think of my element, it is not of fire,
> of ember and ash, but of earth,
> nor of man's travail and burden
> to work in the dirt, but of the abundance,
> the verdant rhetorical.

The failure of such dandified writing is, I think, apparent
without further comment, but the kind of failure it is might be
instructive in certain ways. The tone is high and bookish, a self-
conscious mixture of Victorian pomposity and humbleness-from-

a-high-remove. It is easy to write like this—again, if you have the time. One brings away from Duncan's book* only a sense of complicated inconsequence, of dilettantism and serene self-deception, of pretentiousness, of a writer perhaps natively gifted who has sold himself the wrong bill of goods (or, one wants to say, trappings), and so has come out gorgeously arrayed in other men's garments, predictably beautiful, "artistic," elaborately dead. Duncan is not fulfilling his early promise.

[1965]

HORACE GREGORY

HORACE GREGORY is unfailingly urbane and informed and precise, though I wish he weren't quite so insistent upon devices of contrast, particularly the past-present, myth-reality, urban-pastoral contrasts which he has always relied upon. But once he is well into his subjects, these or any others, he goes to town. Not spectacularly to town, but to town just the same. Gravely witty and slow-building, his verse playlets and poems are conceived at a deliberately low intensity, without self-conscious brilliance, to give them a better chance to come through as wholes without asking the reader to dwell in fascination on single passages. About half these pieces† are monologues and capsule verse plays

---

* *Roots and Branches* by Robert Duncan. New York, Charles Scribner's Sons.

† *Medusa in Gramercy Park* by Horace Gregory. New York, The Macmillan Company.

concerned with characters like Boris MacCrearey and Effron Siminsky, personages similar to those whom Gregory began writing about in the late twenties in *Chelsea Rooming House*. Neither the plays nor the characters would have been possible without the Eliot of the Sweeney poems and the dramatic fragments, but I am very glad that they are. They are good vehicles for projecting Gregory's main preoccupation or obsession: the undefinable dread that obtrudes into even the most ordinary happenings of everyday existence: the dread—compounded about equally of the fear of death, guilt over the unlived or the useless life, the frustrations of modern society, and the threat of universal extinction—that seems to concentrate itself in large American cities and among the leisured rich. Gregory's dealing with this *angst* is suave and worldly, and the subject emerges and is felt as somehow all the more terrible for the wit and reasonableness that set it forth. We realize that wit and urbanity—indeed all the devices of speech and social intercourse, comfort and "enjoyment" and instruction, including Gregory's poems—are only distractions from the terrifying realities that can't in the end be avoided, but only purged beforehand for a little while from consciousness. Gregory is, I think, our best chronicler of the universal *devices* of distraction, of the ruses—especially alcohol and opulence— modern man employs against the unthinkable and the inevitable. (If I were ever to meet Gregory, I would expect him to say, before I had the first one, "Have another drink.") The variations he plays on this nameless hysteria, the settings he gives it, the characters who act it out, are amazing in their aptness. There is a kind of civilized gallows humor in their telling which Gregory uses with what would seem very nearly like sadism if it were not for the underlying pity that one feels also in his rendering of people at bars, official dinners, open-air concerts, or sitting at night in rich apartments in New York with "The city washed away like time beneath us, / And nothing there except the perfect view." Yet one wonders, sometimes, if his work doesn't depend a little too much on décor, on descriptions of settings, and such. I won't dwell on this, though, for it really doesn't disturb me more than faintly. I am too much in favor of Gregory's kind of subtlety in depicting the condemned playground that the diseased unconscious makes of our world, the extraordinary ways in which he shows the eruption of the timeless myths into modern life, and the inability of moderns to rise to the myths and their meanings, though they live them, unrecognizing.

Of the lyric pieces, all in Gregory's finely tuned, middle-distance manner, the best are "Gifts of the Age" and "On a Celtic Mask by Henry Moore." The rhetoric of the latter is surprisingly forthright and powerful for Gregory, and is a good last poem for his book, pointing, as is the right function of a tailpiece, toward the future.

[1962]

I. A. RICHARDS

SCREENS, according to the dictionary definition that I. A. Richards quotes, are both partitions and things on which other things or their appearances can be projected and so shown. The central metaphor for the book* and all its poems is Plato's famous one of the cave and its shadows, for which Richards sometimes substitutes the motion picture or the slide projector. Using devices of this kind in a variety of ways, Richards deals with different kinds of shadowings-forth of individual identity and with the

* *The Screens and Other Poems* by I. A. Richards. New York, Harcourt, Brace and World.

question of whether each or all of these—the individual as he sees himself (at what time?), as others see him, as eternity sees him, and so on—is the self, or none. The poems are, then, actually about the soul. Sometimes it is merely the mind or consciousness, sometimes an abstraction like what is usually meant by the word "identity," sometimes it is like the Hindu Atman, passing unchanged through innumerable births. The poems are about how the soul acts without appearing to, how it influences without seeming to, how it changes and doesn't change, how it makes us who we are without our ever knowing who we are. These are delicate themes, vastly complicated and perhaps impossible of solution, but Richards does very well by them, according his vast knowledge of semantics and the difficult interchanges between words, selves, and things to his subjects in poems which are really more like verse essays: speculative, logical, and refreshingly open-minded in the midst of their intelligent discourse-like approach. They are not by any means the work of a born poet, but rather the productions of a highly intelligent and dedicated bystander who has seen, late in life, that he holds a lifetime of poetic knowledge and information in his hands, and has wished to see what he could do with it on his own. This is understandable and commendable, and the difficult and modest successes of the poems are real successes. Nevertheless, I doubt that I shall give them the second and possibly other readings that they and their notes require, for Dr. Richards's verse is of a kind that I cannot for the life of me like very much. Its overingenuity seems to me just that, and this quality is, I strongly suspect, the main reason for the decline of the audience that Richards deplores in the long essay he appends to the poems. Too many potential readers think that it isn't worth all that trouble. The other few readers, those hardy ones who have their diplomas in the course, spend their time grimacing at each other like gymnasts, saying, "I can get more out of a poem than you can: more meanings, more possibilities of meaning, more extensions, more suggestions, more primary and secondary and tertiary ambiguities than you can." In answer, the poet says, "I can get more in, and some, even, that *none* of you can come at." I can't shake off the conviction that verse so written—verse like Richards's and Empson's—has done much to drive the audience underground, into the beatnik coffeehouses, with its specialized references, its recondite images from physics and semantics, its metaphors requiring knowledge of photons, tensors, and the malfunctioning of the pancreas in diabetes, all things that notes must be required to "fill the reader in" on and without which the meanings—even *one* of them—can't be grasped or even guessed at. It seems to me that the way to the audience Richards wants is through a poetry which makes available not endless subtleties to hash over in graduate seminars but poetry written with what Benn calls "primal vision": not many levels of meaning—though one can, from anything written in words, even advertisements, extract tangential connotations *ad infinitum*—but a single overwhelming one. Of course I don't suggest that verse like Richards's shouldn't be written and printed. It should, both for people like Robert Lowell and Kathleen Raine who like it a lot, and for people like me, who like it only distantly and acknowledgingly. But I do mean that Richards's remarks about poetry and its lamentably small number of subscribers are difficult to take seriously in view of the real reasons that people do not read verse. These reasons should be apparent to Richards more than to anyone else, for his poems *illustrate* as few others do why poetry is little read by others than poets, friends and relatives of poets, and captive audiences such as reviewers. I don't want an intelligent, sensitive, and dedicated man like Richards to come down to the level of the man on the street, who is none of these things and couldn't care less. But I *am* saying that that man, who might conceivably have something to gain from poetry were he to come at it his own way through writers he could comprehend more or less quickly and then, if he wished, read later for their complexities, is likely to be and undoubtedly is repelled by an initial contact with the overrefinement of the intellect in verse, and by poetry written for only the super-intelligent, super-sensitive, and nuance-haunted audience which Richards posits, but which has not yet come into being. For Richards or anyone else to suppose that this is not the case is simply to ignore the facts, and the testimony of the "potential audience" itself.

[1962]

YVOR WINTERS

REGARDLESS of what else may be said of him, Yvor Winters is the best example our time has to show of the poet who writes by *rules*, knows just what he wants to do when he begins to write a poem, and considers himself compelled to stick to his propositions in everything he sets down. He tells us in a note that he regards this book* as "a kind of definition by example of the style I have been trying to achieve for a matter of thirty years." Since his early poems are notably different from his later ones, this must mean, not that the style he mentions is in all the poems, but that the poems are arranged to show how and through what routes the style has been reached. These early poems which Winters has seen fit to supersede are very much influenced by those of William Carlos Williams, but they seem to me better than any poems Williams has ever written. They not only show great spontaneity and imagination—an imagination really working with and in and *through* its subjects—but also a high degree

* *Collected Poems* by Yvor Winters. Denver, Alan Swallow.

of intuitive linguistic perceptiveness; above all, they are wonderfully free of the will, that Medusa-face that turns hearts and poems to stone. They are very much the poems of a man who, though not quite sure of what he is doing, is yet seeing and experiencing newly, freshly, in each poem as if for the first time, his world and the words by which it may be explored and lived. I believe this Winters entirely when he says, "Adventurer in / living fact, the poet / mounts into the spring, / upon his tongue the taste of / air becoming body." Among certain reviewers in the past it has been a commonplace to denigrate Winters's later poems by praising his earlier ones, but these first poems exist, and there are always going to be people like myself who prefer them. Their most surprising characteristic is their wonderful feeling for motion—one somehow thinks of Winters as inert—their feeling for color and light, set down with young uncertainty and eagerness. There are twenty-three of these early poems, arranged in what I take to be chronological order, and a group of excellent translations, before the later style makes its appearance, appropriately enough in a poem called "The Moralists." It begins, "You would extend the mind beyond the act, / Furious, bending, suffering in thin / And unpoetic dicta; you have been / Forced by hypothesis to fiercer fact." Here in full force is the kind of writing by which Winters wishes to be remembered: the strict metrics, the hard, obvious rhymes, the hard-jawed assurance, the familiar humorless badgering tone, the tendency to logic-chop and moralize *about* instead of presenting, the iron-willed determination to come up with conclusions, to "understand" and pass definitive judgments no matter what. As one reads, it gets more and more difficult to believe that a man's *life* is supposed to be contained in these pages, with the warmth, joy and sorrow, the disappointments and revelations that must surely have been parts of it. One can't help being struck by the poverty of Winters's emotional makeup; there are only a few things which seem to have made much of an impression on him. The principal one of these is what he conceives to be the function of the university intellectual, the teacher, whose role it is to instill "precision" in the students' minds. He believes, apparently, that in the arena of the university, the arena that opens out into the world of action, the essential battles of the mind are fought, and its heroes are those who teach "well," discern "the truth" (rather than *a* truth), pass it on, and so condition "the mind" of students to take care of itself, know good from evil, false coin from good, in any circumstances thereafter. In these matters, the teacher must first *know*, and as a result of what he knows, others may come to know, too. These are worthy enough themes, though one is inclined to question whether a teacher of literature, even one like Winters, can really have such a profound influence as all that. Though his thesis is grave and perhaps important, the poems in which he sets it forth are unfortunately Winters's worst, full of his tiresome truculence, his mien of sage and defender of the faith, his dogmatic, hectoring manner, his rhymed belaboring of concepts and abstractions, and in general all the rarification, stiffness, and peculiar dusty dryness of the style he has been "trying to achieve for a matter of thirty years." It seems to me that it is this being "hot for certainties" and the uncompromising insistence that he has got them that has ossified Winters as a poet, cut him off from the early exploratory "accessibility to experience" that promised so much, and actually deprived him of any important or even very interesting subject matter. The tightness and concision of his writing are bought at altogether too high a price: that of deliberately stifling the *élan* and going-beyond that first-rate poets count on blindly and rightly. This results in calcified and unlikely poems, academic and "correct" according to the set of rules one has arrived at, and doubtless from this standpoint capable of being defended logically and/or eloquently, but only in arguments which are, in view of what they come to in the poems themselves, simply beside the point. It is evident that this kind of poem is principally an exercise of the logical faculties, a display of what one has come to deem proper as to method and statement. Even this might be all right if the qualities Winters has chosen were not so drastically limiting, or if his means of embodying them were other than they are. The kind of thinking and writing that Winters fosters is good enough for small poets, and doubtless enables them to concentrate and consolidate their modest gifts in a way which is as good as any they may hope for. But for a big talent, which must go its own way, it is and probably has been ruinous, and I am haunted by the vision of a Yeats or Dylan Thomas or W. S. Graham laboring diligently to get into the same Stanford Parnassus with J. V. Cunningham, Donald Drummond, Howard Baker, and Clayton Stafford. The trouble with verse of this sort is, quite simply, that it is all but dead, not only to the power of giving something of the mystery and fortuitous meaningfulness and immediacy of life to the reader, but dead also, and from conception, to the possibilities of receiving these upon itself.

This is not quite, however, the whole story on Winters's later verse. From poems like "To the Holy Spirit" and "Moonlight Alert," one comes to see that Winters's most enduring and characteristic theme is not really the teacher's part, but Nothingness, and the perhaps illusory stand of the mind against it. The pessimism and stoicism and honesty of his poems about himself, not as laying down the law in the William Dinsmore Briggs Room, but as a solitary night-watching man, are utterly convincing. Though they are not free of the moralizing tendency that ruins so many of the later poems, the occasions for this and his other familiar qualities seem more nearly right, and for that reason, and because of Winters's awesome unflinchingness in the face of approaching old age, they are good poems, and compare favorably with the best of the early ones. Maybe these few pieces are worth all the enforced sterility; I suppose it can be argued that good poems are worth whatever price must be paid, even this one. Yet I am immensely saddened by most of Winters's work, and find the touch of it lifeless and life-destroying. But more than that, I cannot imagine anyone sincerely loving his poems or being changed, illuminated, helped, or even significantly instructed by them. And there it is.

[1962]

ROBERT GRAVES

THERE are some writers who reside permanently in the blind spot in one's eye. For me, that writer *par excellence* is Robert Graves. For all of his inescapable talk about the Muse, I cannot for the life of me think that he has ever had more than a distantly nodding acquaintance with her. His other *idée fixe*, "professionalism in poetry," he does exemplify pretty well, unfortunately. Professionalism in Graves's case seems to mean no more than that one uses men and women, gods and goddesses only as convenient fictions helpful in writing the poems that one feels obligated to write if one has set up shop as a poet. And how Graves has set up shop! His picturesque and irascible personality and his enormous production serve public notice that poets do, even in this century, exist, and will live as they will, but the poems themselves (at least to one reader) never really seem sufficient justification for the writer's posture. Though there may be some kind of large humanity, a mocking masculine force at work here,* it never completely emerges, and one wonders, through the rhetorical questions and mildly surprising solutions, whether it is really there in any significant sense at all: when one follows a tedious paperchase of clues toward something no more

* *New Poems* by Robert Graves. New York, Doubleday and Company.

enlightening that "Woman is mortal woman. She abides" one is reminded of nothing so much as what Edmund Wilson said about reading detective stories: that it is like unpacking a crate by having to eat the excelsior, to find at the bottom only a few bent and rusty nails. Graves's supporters will not be deterred by my cavilling; for those who like his earlier work there is more of the same here.

[1964]

ROBINSON JEFFERS

Now that Robinson Jeffers is dead, his last poems have been issued,* culled from handwritten manuscripts by his sons and his secretary. Though some of the pieces were obviously left unfinished—there are several different ones which have the same passages in them—it is worth noting that they are actually no more or less "finished" than the poems Jeffers published in book after book while he lived. This is typical of Jeffers's approach to poetry, I think; he had, as someone remarked of Charles Ives, "the indifference of greatness." Yet now, in some fashion, we must come to terms with Jeffers, for he somehow cannot be dismissed as lesser men—and no doubt better poets—can. As obviously flawed as he is, Jeffers is cast in a large mold; he fills a position in this country that would simply have been an empty gap without him: that of the poet as prophet, as large-scale philosopher, as

* *The Beginning and the End and Other Poems* by Robinson Jeffers. New York, Random House.

doctrine-giver. This is a very real, very old and honorable function for poets, and carries with it a *tone* that has, but for Jeffers, not been much heard among us, in our prevailing atmosphere of ironic shrugs and never-too-much. Admittedly a great deal of bad poetry in all ages has been written from such a stance, but that does not invalidate the idea, or take from Jeffers the credit that is duly his. Surely he provides us with plenty to carp about: his oracular moralizing, his cruel and thoroughly repellent sexuality, his dreadful lapses of taste when he seems simply to throw back his head and howl, his slovenly diction, the eternal sameness of his themes, the amorphous sprawl of his poems on the page. The sheer power and drama of some of Jeffers's writing, however, still carries the day despite everything, and this is not so much because of the presence of the Truth that Jeffers believes he has got hold of but because of what might be called the embodiment of that Truth: Jeffers's gorgeous panorama of *big* imagery, his galaxies, suns, seas, cliffs, continents, mountains, rivers, flocks of birds, gigantic schools of fish, and so on. His Truth is hard to swallow—try looking at your children and drawing comfort from Jeffers's "inhumanism"—but one cannot shake off Jeffers's vision as one can the carefully prepared surprises of many of the neatly packaged stanzas we call "good poems"; it is too deeply disturbing and too powerfully stated. One thinks, uneasily, that the prophetic tone may be more than just a tone, remembering that Jeffers was telling us long before Hiroshima that the ultimate end of science, of knowledge and tool-using, is not comfort and convenience (how he despises such ideals!) but unrelieved tragedy. It is extraordinarily strange how the more awful and ludicrous aspects of the atomic age have come to resemble Jeffers's poems. In a film like *Mondo Cane*, for example, one sees the dying sea turtles, disoriented by the Bikini blasts until they cannot even find the Pacific Ocean, crawling inland to die in the desert, in the blazing sand they think is water, and the hundreds-of-miles-long trail of dead butterflies, the seabirds trying to hatch atom-sterilized eggs, and one thinks compulsively of Jeffers. Few visions have been more desperate than his, and few lives organized around such austere principles. It seems to me that we must honor these things, each in his own way.

[1964]

RALPH HODGSON

THE reader of Ralph Hodgson's poems* must decide, and rather early in the game, whether the poems are childlike or simply childish. The childish in poetry is, of course, unbearable. The childlike is either whimsical or magical; the only thing that can save it from archness, coyness, (and, in Hodgson's case, old-fangledness) is authentic spell-casting, a poetic persuasiveness that makes the reader's eyes grow round and wide and permits him to forget that there was ever anything called "The New Criticism." Some of this quality exists, I think, in a few of Ralph Hodgson's poems. As it turns out, however, he is done no great service by the issuance of this big retrospective volume; his best poems very plainly *are* the famous anthology pieces "Eve" and "The Bull." Though hardly what John Crowe Ransom says they are—"great, wonderful poems that will live forever"—they are full of lovely cadences and images, full of natural song, like poems written by a man whose native language must rhyme to be understood; they have the unaffected ease as well as the essen-

---

* *Collected Poems* by Ralph Hodgson. Edited by Colin Fenton. New York, St. Martin's Press.

tial innocence that makes beauty more strange and marvelous and evil more inexplicable and evil. In these poems, at least, Hodgson has brought a new music to the trimeter and tetrameter lines; they are like poems barely glimpsed, forgotten sounds that come back to one at odd moments, whispering in the haunting singsong of a preternaturally wise child who, one realizes with an awakening shock, is now dead.

[1964]

VERNON WATKINS

THOUGH influenced to some degree by his friend Dylan Thomas and by Yeats, Vernon Watkins* has his own music, very strict and compressed, with a sense of vast forces being held just as powerfully in order. "There is in our lives," he says, "an exact mystery." The mystery is always present in his beautifully spoken poems; being told of it, you are also continuously reminded of what a lovely flowing language English is, of what music there is in it, what pauses, what returns. These qualities are all gathered to major force whenever Mr. Watkins writes himself into a ballad.

> This music hovered round your soul
> Before you first drew breath,
> And those its caul has covered whole
> Shall never come to death,

* *Affinities* by Vernon Watkins. New York, New Directions.

Long though the murderous seawaves roll
With many and many a wreath.

This authentic feeling for the ballad—its rocking drive and hard-breathing sense of predestiny, the presage of doom, the haunted sense of place where, as Pasternak says, "things smack of soil and fate"—Watkins has in heartening and bewildering plenty; his ballads make most other modern verse, including some of Watkins's own, look neat and dutiful. I'd very much like to see Mr. Watkins collect his ballads and write some new ones. That would be quite a book.

[1964]

WILLIAM CARLOS WILLIAMS

WILLIAM CARLOS WILLIAMS is now dead, and that fact shakes one. Has any other poet in American history been so *actually* useful, usable, and influential? How many beginning writers took Williams as their model: were encouraged to write because . . . Well, if *that's* poetry, I believe I might be able to write it, too! Surely his practice has opened up many people to poetry—to the potential poetry in themselves and in their everyday world—in a wholly exemplary way, converting the commonplace, the trivial, the traditionally "ugly" into poetry of a highly personal and a thoroughly *public* order: who, after all, has not *seen*

> . . . a cylindrical tank fresh silvered
> upended on the sidewalk to advertise
> some plumber's shop . . . ?

Williams's readers will know what to expect in this reissue of
The Collected Later Poems,* and will be glad to have the seventeen previously uncollected poems and good older poems like "A
Unison." Here is all of Williams's later work except for *Paterson*
and the poems gathered in *Pictures from Breughel*. One will find
here, also, Williams's most discouraging qualities, monotony and
arbitrariness, which proceed from what looks suspiciously like
the notion that to *present* were sufficient—were *always* sufficient. If a man will attend Williams closely he will be taught to
see, to fasten on the appearance and the meaning that is for him
in the appearance, on the sensory apprehension and truth of an
object or scene in a way that is perpetually open to him—to any
of us—and has but to be used at any given moment, and he will
write solid and usually short, unrhymed, near-prose poems about
how the concrete particulars of the world look and feel to him.
Whether or not that is *enough*, I suspect we must leave to later
generations to decide. It is, however, a very great deal, and Williams as a kind of large-looming divine average, as a man writing
out of his whole humanity with the sympathetic but unflinching
scrutiny of a responsible doctor, is and will be the authentic
hero of this approach. Surely no poet is more American, and in
that there is reason to hope for us all.

[1964]

* *The Collected Later Poems* by William Carlos Williams. New York,
New Directions.

J. V. CUNNINGHAM

J. V. Cunningham* is looking at the modern world from the standpoint of traditional modes of writing, and principally from those of the eighteenth century. He evidently feels himself pulled together and helped by regular metrical patterns and rhymes, reassured and bolstered by form as it has been defined and exemplified by generations of writers before him; one imagines him as a man who would probably feel dismayed and even terrified if ordered, under pain of death, to write in free verse. He knows his limitations, and often one feels that he concedes entirely too much to them: there is, after all, a poetry of opening-out and going-beyond as well as one of compression and concision. But as a compressor, as a coupleteer, as a fastidious and mordant wit, a man who makes interesting dwellings of the neat cells of the couplet and the quatrain, he is hard to beat.

> It was in Vegas. Celibate and able
> I left the silver dollars on the table
> And tried the show. The black-out, baggy pants,
> Of course, and then this answer to romance:
> Her ass twitching as if it had the fits,
> Her gold crotch grinding, her athletic tits,

* *To What Strangers, What Welcome* by J. V. Cunningham. Denver, Alan Swallow.

One clock, the other counter clockwise twirling.
It was enough to stop a man from girling.

Word placement, the exactitude thereof in rhythm, meaning, and tone, is crucial to the success of such writing. I went through this little poem trying to change things, for if something, anything, can be made better than it is as the poem has it, the method is not fully realizing itself. I tried "five silver dollars" in the second line, thinking the poem would gain by greater specificity (and I am not entirely sure that some such change wouldn't help a little here), I tried (timidly) "switching" in place of "twitching," "starred crotch" for "gold crotch," "whirling" for "twirling," and "keep a man" for "stop a man" in the last line. I still feel that I might—at least to *my* satisfaction—debate a couple of these uses and perhaps one or two more, but it was nonetheless also my feeling that Cunningham pretty much had me checkmated all along the line: that he *had* written a largely irreducible, unchangeable poem, a good poem, although not quite of the same order as that poem under glass in Paris several decades ago: the poem that Paul Valéry, seeing it displayed in the vitrine of a bookstore, tried with increasing vexation to change, until he raised his eyes from the text and saw that it was a page of *Phèdre*.

Cunningham is a good, deliberately small and authentic poet, a man with tight lips, a good education, and his own agonies. His handsome little book should be read, and above all by future Traditionalists and Compressors; he is their man.

[1965]

LOUIS SIMPSON

His *Selected Poems** shows Louis Simpson working, at first tentatively and then with increasing conviction, toward his own version of a national, an American poetry: as one reads, it becomes easier and easier to think of him as a specifically American poet, and one finds oneself more than a little surprised that this is so. For after all, what *is* an American poet? Particularly *now?* At the words, at the *thought* of an American poet, one thinks of several alternative possibilities. The first is of a poet (or nonpoet) like Russell Davenport, twenty-odd years ago, and his much-publicized-in-slick-magazines-but-quickly-and-mercifully-forgotten poem "My Country," and of writers like Stephen Vincent Benét at his worst. One also thinks of Whitman not only at his worst but at his best, and of Hart Crane. One thinks of lesser "epical" writers like Sandburg, Norman Rosten, Norman Corwin, Harry Brown, Winfield Townley Scott. And one also remembers chroniclers of the American *scene*, like Karl Shapiro and John Ciardi, including the finest of them all, John Hollander. Simpson is closer to this last group than to any of the others. He demonstrates that the best service an American poet can do his country is to see it all: not just the promise, not just the loss and the "betrayal of the American ideal," the Whitmanian ideal—although nobody sees this last more penetratingly

* *Selected Poems* by Louis Simpson. New York, Harcourt, Brace and World.

than Simpson does—but the whole "complex fate," the difficult and agonizing *meaning* of being an American, of living as an American at the time in which one chances to live. If it comes out sad, as it does with Simpson despite all his wit and compassion, it is a whole and not a deliberately partial sadness, and this gives the pervasive desperate sadness of this book a terrific weight of honesty and truth. Nothing can be done, although at one time perhaps something might have been. But now the individual has only what he has, only what history has allowed him to be born to.

> There's no way out.
> You were born to waste your life.
> You were born to this middleclass life
>
> As others before you
> Were born to walk in procession
> To the temple, singing.

Through the used-car lots, through the suburbs, through the wars that are only the intensification and temporary catharsis of the life we lead now, Simpson moves in this book, and moves memorably and skillfully. Principally there is the feeling of the great occasions of a man's life being veiled, being kept from him by the soft insulations of his civilization, he being all his life comfortable and miserable, taken care of and baffled. Since there is no primitive singleness of response anywhere, since one cannot hope for spontaneity, one takes it out in wit. Simpson's tone is often much like Randall Jarrell's, although more nervous, irritable, and biting. Jarrell's poems deal with the slow wonder of loss; Simpson's less resigned ones are more bewilderedly angry. If I had any objections to Simpson's work they would tend to group around a knowledgeable glibness, an easy literary propensity to knock off certain obvious sitting ducks. But this is a very good book, a good spread of Simpson's work, and the intensity of his intelligent despair throughout it is harrowing. Although at times a little flip, Simpson is in reality no man for facile answers, and if he is self-consciously more American than most of our other writers, that is our gain, and, whether it wants it or not, our country's as well.

[1965]

WILLIAM MEREDITH

In connection with William Meredith's verse,* the two words that come most often to mind—that is, to *my* mind—are "balance" and "relaxation." He is introspective and a little diffident, grave and perplexedly troubled, particularly when he can't do anything about what is happening, what has happened. He is the kind of poet who stands looking at the ocean where the atomic submarine *Thresher* went down, meditating, speculating, grieving intelligently. Things of this nature hurt him into poetry, but not poetry of great intensity. Instead, it seems muffled and distant, a kind of thin, organized, slightly academic murmur. One keeps listening for Meredith's *voice,* and is baffled at its being, although one is surer and surer it is there, so consistently elusive. It is not at all to be found in those poems imitative of, say, Frost, such as "An Old Field Mowed for Appearances' Sake," but rather in pieces like "For His Father" and, oddly, in the wonderful translations from Apollinaire, which seem, although faithful enough as translations, really more Meredith's than Apollinaire's. It is

* *The Wreck of the Thresher and Other Poems* by William Meredith. New York, Alfred A. Knopf.

better to hear "My glass is filled with a wine that trembles like flame" than to hear, in Meredith's poem *to* Apollinaire, "The day is colorless like Swiss characters in a novel," which presupposes that the reader agrees that Swiss characters in a novel (what novel?) are colorless, that everyone knows they are (I, one shyly thinks, didn't know they are, and keeps one's mouth shut about it), and thereby enters into collusion with a certain ingroup variety of bookish snobbery that is probably Meredith's one outstanding weakness as a writer. But at his best he is a charming poet, cultivated, calm, quietly original, expansive and reflective, moving over wide areas slowly, lightly, mildly and often very memorably.

[1965]

JOHN BERRYMAN

BERRYMAN* is a poet so preoccupied with poetic effects as to be totally in their thrall. If Randall Jarrell's Longinian pitfall is flatness, his is mannerism. His inversions, his personal and often irritatingly cute colloquialisms and deliberate misspellings, his odd references, his basing of lines and whole poems on private allusions, create what must surely be the densest verbal thickets since Empson's. Jarrell's poetry must seem *natural*, and naturally said, to be successful. Berryman has thrown all such techniques out a very high window, and has gone—somewhat like a Hopkins

* 77 *Dream Songs* by John Berryman. New York, Farrar, Straus and Giroux.

drunk on twentieth-century history, culture, and newsprint—for the supreme artificiality, the mannerism that may become with luck an unmistakable Style. Jarrell's is really an anti-style, somewhat in the same fashion as the style Stendhal advocated when he urged young novelists to pattern their prose on the Code Napoléon. But Berryman's is a style beyond style, a constructed and magnificently unnatural style which concedes almost nothing to the reader. Henry and Mr. Bones, the classic figures, eternal opposites, foils, comics, straight men and semblables of minstrel shows, go through such a variety of anguished acts, change into so many costumes and dialects, comment so curiously and deeply on such a wide range of subjects, that the reader feels distinctly that he is having to learn—is, exhilaratingly, learning—a new language, a kind of Berryman Esperanto, through reading the poems.

Berryman, although not a natural poet, although anything but natural-sounding, is sometimes very nearly a great poet. The manipulations are always apparent, the reader's muscles are always tense with the straining of the poem to lift itself by its bootstraps. Yet when the weight is up—at untold cost—it is still up, although dangerously and precariously, and Berryman through sheer will and guts has put it there.

[1965]

ROBERT FROST

"Belovèd" is a term that must always be mistrusted when applied to artists, and particularly to poets. Poets are likely to be belovèd for only a few of the right reasons, and for almost all the wrong ones: for saying things we want to hear, for furnishing us with an image of ourselves that we enjoy believing in, even for living for a long time in the public eye and pronouncing sagely on current affairs. Robert Frost has been long admired for all these things, and is consequently one of the most misread writers in the whole of American literature.

In Frost's case the reputation has come, at least to some extent, from the powerful additive of the Robert Frost Story, a secular myth of surprising power and tenacity: an image that has eaten into the rock of the American psyche and engraved Frost's very engravable face as in a kind of Mount Rushmore of the nation's consciousness. The "Frost Story" would, in fact, make quite an acceptable film script, even allowing for the notorious difficulty Hollywood has in dealing with writers. We enjoy wandering off, mentally, into a scenario of this sort, partly because we know that the main facts of the Frost Story, leaving aside the interpretation that has been put upon them, *are* facts, and also because the Story is and has long been something we believe in with the conviction accorded only to people and events in which we want to believe and will have no other way. Frost is unassailable, a national treasure, a remnant of the frontier and the Thoreauistic virtues of shrewd Yankeedom, the hero of the dozing American daydream of self-reliance and experience-won wisdom we feel guilty about betraying every time we eat a TV dinner or punch a computer. The Frost Story stands over against all that we have become, and hints with mysterious and canny authority that it all might have been otherwise—even that it might yet be so.

It is a dream, of course. To us a dream, surely, but also a kind of dream to Frost, and despite the authenticity of whatever settings the film might choose for its backgrounds, despite the rugged physical presence of Frost himself, any film made of such elements would have to partake of nostalgic visions. It might open, for example, with a sequence showing Frost moving among his Properties—apple trees, birch trees, stone fences, dark woods with snow falling into them, ax handles, shovels, woodpiles, ladders, New England brooks, taciturn neighbors—and then modulate into a conversation with Frost for that cryptic, homely, devious, *delightful* way of making sense out of life— any aspect of it—that the public so loved him for: his way of reducing all generalities to local fact so that they become not only understandable but controllable.

If one wanted to include chronology one might have a little difficulty in making Frost's life in England interesting, for aside from showing some of the places he lived in and visited and photographs of some of the people he knew, like Ezra Pound, Edward Thomas, and Lascelles Abercrombie, it would be hard to do much more than suggest his experiences there. Most of this part would probably have to be carried by voice-over narration, and might deal with Frost manfully being his Own Man, resisting being exploited and misinterpreted by Ezra Pound ("that great intellect abloom in hair"), and with his being a kind of literary Ben Franklin in Georgian England, uncorrupted and wary, delighting the jaded and oversophisticated with, well, his authenticity.

One might then work forward by easy stages into what everybody knows is coming: the great Recognitions of the final years, the readings, the lectures and interviews, the conferences with students and the press—thus affording more time for the Frost Talk—the voyage to Russia and the meeting with Khrushchev, and so on, all culminating in the Ultimate Reading, the Kennedy Inaugural and its little drama of the sunlight, Vice President Johnson's top hat, and the details familiar to those who watch great as well as small events on television. Another poet, Galway Kinnell, has written of this occasion:

> And as the Presidents
> Also on the platform
> Began flashing nervously
> Their Presidential smiles
> For the harmless old guy,
> And poets watching on the TV
> Started thinking, Well that's
> The end of *that* tradition,
>
> And the managers of the event
> Said, Boys this is it,
> This sonofabitch poet
> Is gonna croak,
> Putting the paper aside
> You drew forth
> From your great faithful heart
> The poem.

That drawing forth of the poem from "the great faithful heart" would be the end—how could you top it?—and everyone could leave the theater surer than ever that he had inherited something, some way of responding and speaking as an American, that matters.

To move from this drama of public appearances to Lawrance Thompson's *Robert Frost: The Early Years** is to move, if not wholly out of the myth—for Thompson is very much in its thrall, despite all that he knows of Frost's actual life and personality—then rather into the area of its making, and the reasons for its making. One cannot inhabit Dr. Thompson's book, even under the influence of the Story (or the film, for legends are probably all films of one kind or another), without ceasing to be comfortable in one's prior assumptions. As partial as it is, Dr. Thompson's account is yet the fully documented record of what Frost was like when he was not belovèd: when he was, in fact, a fanatically selfish, egocentric, and at times dangerous man; was, from the evidence, one of the least lovable figures in American literature. What we get from Dr. Thompson is the much less cinematic narrative (and yet, what if someone tried to film *this* Frost Story?) of the construction of a complex mask, a *persona*, an invented personality that the world, following the man, was pleased, was overjoyed, finally, to take as an authentic identity, and whose main interest, biographically and humanly, comes from the fact that the mask is almost the diametrical opposite of the personality that lived in and motivated the man all his life. Most of *Robert Frost: The Early Years*, which takes Frost up through his period in England, is concerned with the twined alternatives of fear and *hubris:* with Frost's desperate efforts to establish and maintain his self-image in the face of every conceivable discouragement, the period when he would quit any job—he quit a good many—go back on any commitment, throw over any trust or personal relationship which did not accord him the deference he persuaded himself he deserved. Dr. Thompson talks persuasively—though not, I think, conclusively—of Frost's need to protect his sensibility from crasser natures and desensitizing work, but one never really believes that this justified

* *Robert Frost: The Early Years* by Lawrance Thompson. New York, Holt, Rinehart and Winston.

Frost's arrogance and callousness on the many occasions when they were the most observable things about him. These were the years of Frost's hating and turning on anyone who helped or cared for him, from his friends like Carl Burell, who worked his poultry farm for him while he nursed his ego, to his grandfather, whose generous legacy Frost insisted on interpreting as a way of "writing off" the poet and "sending him out to die" on a farm that the grandfather actually purchased to give Frost a livelihood and a profession.

The fact that this is the "official" biography keeps coming back to one as one reads, and with this a recognition of the burden that must surely have been on Dr. Thompson's shoulders in writing it: the difficulty in dovetailing the author's bias in favor of his subject—for it is abundantly apparent that Thompson really does deeply care for Frost's work and also for Frost himself—and the necessity to tell what did in reality occur on various occasions. Dr. Thompson has large numbers of facts, and the first task of the biographer is to make facts *seem* facts, stand up as facts before any interpretation is made from them. One of the ways to do this is to be pedestrian, for the world's facts are pedestrian, and most of the time simply sit there saying over and over again, I am here, I am true, I happened, without any particular emphasis. Consequently there is a good deal of material like "at this stage the Frosts had an unexpected visitor, none other than Edmund J. Harwood, from whom Frost's grandfather had bought the Derry farm" and "another acquaintance was made that evening, a burly red-faced country squire named John C. Chase, the modestly well-to-do owner of a local wood-working factory, which turned out a variety of products including tongue-depressors and similarly shaped tags for marking trees and shrubs in nurseries." This makes for a certain monotony, but one is inclined to go along with it partly because it is the truth—the man's name *was* John C. Chase, and he *did* make tongue depressors—but mainly because it is a necessary background for the second and far more important of the biographer's tasks, that of interpretation. That part is primarily psychological, and if the protagonist has not chosen to tell either the biographer or someone else why he said or did something on a given occasion—and one must be constantly wary of taking him at his word—one must surmise. Dr. Thompson is very good at this, most of the time, but also at some points unconsciously funny.

> During her sophomore year, Jeanie [Frost's sister] suffered through moods of depression much like those which had beset her, intermittently, since her childhood days in San Francisco. Her spells of tears, hysteria, ravings, which caused her to miss more and more days of school, puzzled her mother increasingly. In the midst of one spell Jeanie was making so much noise that Mrs. Frost turned desperately to her son for help. Enraged, he stormed into Jeanie's bedroom, found her lying face down on the bed, turned her over, and slapped her across the face with the flat of his hand. Just for a moment the one blow had the desired effect: Jeanie grew silent, stopped crying completely, and sat up. She stared at her brother and then said, scornfully, "You cad, you coward." That was not Rob's only use of violence when trying to help his sister.

When other incidents indicate clearly that brother and sister absolutely detested each other, one has a certain hesitation in identifying "Rob's" motive as helpfulness. Yet it seems to me that Dr. Thompson's deductions are right a great deal more than they are wrong, and that is really all we can ask of a mortal biographer.

Frost was born in San Francisco in 1874. We watch him live through the decline and death of his alcoholic, ambitious father, follow him as he is shunted around New England as a poor relation, supported by his gentle, mystical mother's pathetically inept attempts to be a teacher. We see him develop, as compensation, a fanatical and paranoiac self-esteem with its attendant devils of humiliation, jealousy, and frustration. He considers suicide, tries poultry farming, loses a child, settles on poetry as a way of salvation—something, at last, that he *can* do, at least to some extent—borrows money and fails to pay it back, perseveres with a great deal of tenacity and courage but also with a sullen self-righteousness with which one can have but very little sympathy.

He wanted, and from his early days—Dr. Thompson makes much of his "idealism," learned from his mother—to be "great," distinctive, different, a law unto himself, admired but not restricted by those who admired him. He did well in high school when he found that good marks earned him a distinction he had never had before, but he was continually hampered by his arrogance and his jealousy of others, and after graduation seems to have been able to do little else but insult the people who tried to help him and accept and quit one humiliating job after another with as bad grace as possible.

During all this time, however, his writing developed, and in a remarkably straight line. He had, almost from the beginning, a flair for straightforward, uncomplicated versification of the traditional kind, and a stubborn belief that poetry should sound "like talk." He also apparently fastened very early on the notion that to hint is better than to say, and the idea that there are ways of saying, of seeming to say, both more and less than one seems to be saying.

Determining all questions of technique was his conception of the imaginative faculty as being essentially *protection*, self-protection, armor for the self-image. Looking back on Frost through the lens of Dr. Thompson's book, one finds it obvious that the mode, the manner in which a man lies, and what he lies about—these things, and the *form* of his lies—are the main things to investigate in a poet's life and work. The events of Frost's life, events similar to those experienced by a great many people, are not nearly so important as the interpretation he put upon them. The *persona* of the Frost Story was made year by year, poem by poem, of elements of the actual life Frost lived, reinterpreted by the exigencies of the *persona*. He had, for example, some knowledge of farming, though he was never a farmer by anything but default. Physically he was a lazy man, which is perhaps why images of work figure so strongly in his poems. Through these figures in his most famous pieces, probably his best poems—haying, apple-picking, mowing, cleaning springs, and mending walls—he indulged in what with him was the only effective mode of self-defense he had been able to devise: the capacity to claim competence at the menial tasks he habitually shirked, and to assert, from that claim, authority, "earned truth," and a wisdom elusive, personal, and yet final.

At his simplest, his most rhythmical and cryptic, Frost is a remarkable poet. In deceptively "straight" syntax and in rhymes that are like the first rhymes one thinks of when one thinks of rhymes, Frost found his particular way of making mysteries and moral judgments start up from the ground under the reader's feet, come out of the work one did in order to survive and the environment in which both the work and the survival prolonged themselves, leap into the mind from a tuft of flowers, an ax handle suddenly become sin itself, as when "the snake stood up for evil in the garden." This individualizing and localizing way of getting generalities to reveal themselves—original sin, universal Design, love, death, fate, large meanings of all kinds—is a major factor in Frost's approach, and is his most original and valuable contribution to poetry. Like most procedures, it has both its triumphs and its self-belittlements, and there are both good Frost poems and awful ones, not as dissimilar as one might think, to bear this out.

The trouble, of course, is that Frost had but little idea of when he was in a position to make an effective ("earned") judgment and when he was not. In the beginning he was cautious about this, but when the public spurred him on, he was perfectly willing to pronounce on anything and everything, in poems or out of them. This resulted in the odd mixture of buffoonery and common sense (but hardly ever more than that) of his last years.

And yet at his best, which we must do him the service of identifying as his most characteristic, he is perfectly amazing. We have all harbored at odd times a suspicion that the key to large Significances lay close at hand, could we but find it. Frost understood how this feeling could be made to serve as the backbone of a kind of poetry that was not only profound but humanly convincing as well, as most poetry, panting and sweating to be linguistically interesting, is not. One *believes* the Frost voice. That itself is a technical triumph, and of the highest kind. It enables the poems to come without being challenged into places in the consciousness of the "average" reader that have been very little visited before, and almost never by poems.

Yet it is well to remember, for all the uplifting force that it has legitimately, and illegitimately, been in so many lives, for all the conclusion-drawing and generalizing that the public has esteemed and rewarded it for, that the emotions of pain, fear, and confusion are the roots of Frost's poetry. Lionel Trilling, with his usual perceptiveness, has seen this, and seen it better than anyone else, perhaps even including Frost, ever saw it. Trilling's Frost of darkness and terror is more nearly the real Frost, the Frost permanently valuable as a poet, than any other, and it is in poems where these emotions fuse with his methods—poems like "Design"—that he moves us most.

What he accomplished, in the end, was what he became. Not what he became as a public figure, forgotten as quickly as other public figures are, but what he became as a poet. He survives in what he made his own invented being say. His main achievement, it seems to me, is the creation of a particular kind of poetry-speaking voice. He, as much as any American poet, brought convincingness of tone into poetry, and made of it a gauge against which all poetry would inevitably have to be tried. This voice endures in a few powerful and utterly original poems: "After Apple-Picking," "Provide, Provide," "To Earthward."

Dr. Thompson's authoritative and loving book makes clear that Frost's way was the only one open to him, and also the fact that, among other things, his poems were a tremendous *physical* feat, a lifelong muscular striving after survival. Though tragically hard on the people who loved him, put up with him, and suffered because of him, Frost's courage and stubbornness are plain, and they are impressive. But no one who reads this book will ever again believe in the Frost Story, the Frost myth, which includes the premises that Frost the man was kindly, forebearing, energetic, hardworking, good-neighborly, or anything but the small-minded, vindictive, ill-tempered, egotistic, cruel, and unforgiving man he was until the world deigned to accept at face value his estimate of himself. What price art, indeed? Dr. Thompson's biography has, or should have, the effect of leading us all into a private place—the grave of judgment, or the beginning of it—where we ponder long and long the nature "of life and art," their connections and interconnections, and the appalling risk, the cost in lives and minds not only of putting rhythmical symbols of ink on a white page, but of encountering, of reading them as well.

[1966]

EDWIN ARLINGTON ROBINSON

A REEVALUATION of the work of a poet as established as Edwin Arlington Robinson should involve us in some of the fundamentals we tend to forget when we read any poetry that happens to come to hand—the poetry that is thrust upon us by critics and in courses in literature as well as the poetry that we seek out or return to. As should be true of our encounter with any poetry, reevaluation requires that we rid ourselves of preconceptions and achieve, if we can, a way of reading an established poet as though we had never heard of him and were opening his book for the first time. It requires that we approach him with all our senses open, our intelligence in acute readiness, our critical sense in check but alert for the slightest nuance of falsity, our truth-sensitive needle—the device that measures what the poet says against what we know from having lived it—at its most delicate, and our sense of the poet's "place," as determined by commentary, textbook, and literary fashion, drugged, asleep, or temporarily dead.

Like most ideal conditions, this one cannot be fully attained. But it is certainly true that an approximation of such a state is both an advantage and a condition productive of unsuspected discoveries in reading poets we thought we knew, particularly poets whom we thought we knew as well as Robinson. In Robinson's special case it is even more difficult than usual, for the course of poetry has to a certain extent turned away from him, making his greatest virtues appear mediocre ones and directing public scrutiny from his introspective, intellectual, and ironic verse toward poetry in which more things seem to be taking place in a smaller area—poetry in which the poetic line is compressed and packed to the point of explosion and the bedazzlement of the reader is considered synonymous with his reward.

Robinson achieved unusual popularity in his lifetime. When he died in 1935, at the age of sixty-five, he had won the Pulitzer Prize three times and had gained a distinction rare for a poet—his book-length poem *Tristram* had become a best seller. But in the public mind, Robinson has during recent years been regarded as only his vices of prolixity, irresolution, and occasional dullness would have him. Yet if we could manage to read Robinson as if we did not know him—or at least as if we did not know him quite so well as we had believed—or if we could come to him as if he were worth rereading, not out of duty and obedience to literary history but as a possible experience, we would certainly gain a good deal more than we would lose.

I

Suppose, eager only for the experience of poems, we were to look through this book* before reading it, noting only the shapes of the poems on the page. We would see a good many short, tight-looking poems in different structural forms, all of them severely symmetrical, and page after page containing long vertical rectangles of blank verse. Though this selection leaves out the Arthurian poems on which Robinson's popular reputation was made as well as the other later narratives of his declining years, there are still a number of middling-long poems that no editor interested in Robinson's best work could possibly eliminate. The chances are that we would be inclined to skip these and first read one of the shorter ones. What would we find if it were this one?

> We go no more to Calverly's,
> For there the lights are few and low;
> And who are there to see by them,
> Or what they see, we do not know.
> Poor strangers of another tongue
> May now creep in from anywhere,
> And we, forgotten, be no more
> Than twilight on a ruin there.
>
> We two, the remnant. All the rest
> Are cold and quiet. You nor I,
> Nor fiddle now, nor flagon-lid,

* This essay was first published as the introduction to *Selected Poems of Edwin Arlington Robinson* edited by Morton Dauwen Zabel. New York, The Macmillan Company.

May ring them back from where they lie.
No fame delays oblivion
For them, but something yet survives:
A record written fair, could we
But read the book of scattered lives.

There'll be a page for Leffingwell,
And one for Lingard, the Moon-calf;
And who knows what for Clavering,
Who died because he couldn't laugh?
Who knows or cares? No sign is here,
No face, no voice, no memory;
No Lingard with his eerie joy,
No Clavering, no Calverly.

We cannot have them here with us
To say where their light lives are gone,
Or if they be of other stuff
Than are the moons of Ilion.
So, be their place of one estate
With ashes, echoes, and old wars—
Or ever we be of the night,
Or we be lost among the stars.

It is a poem that opens, conventionally enough, with a reference to a place—one suspects from the beginning that it is one of
those drinking places where men gather against the dark and call
it fellowship—where there were once parties or at least convivi-
ality of some sort; of that company, only two are left, and one
of these is speaking. We feel the conventionality of the theme
because we are aware that the contrast between places formerly
full of animation and merriment with the same places *now* is one
of the most haggard of romantic clichés and the subject of innumerable mediocre verses (though infrequently, as in some of
Hardy, it can be memorable and can serve to remind us that

such contrasts, such places, do in fact exist and *are* melancholy and cautionary). Yet there is a difference, a departure, slight but definitive, from the conventional. This difference begins to become apparent as we read the last two stanzas, which are mainly a roll call of the missing. The Robinsonian departure is in the way in which these dead are characterized. What, for example, are we to make of the reference to "Clavering, / Who died because he couldn't laugh?" Or of "Lingard with his eerie joy"? What of these people, here barely mentioned, but mentioned in connection with tantalizing qualities that are hard to forget, that have in them some of the inexplicably sad individuality that might be—that might as well be—fate? I suspect that one who began as even the most casual reader might wish to know more of these people, and he might then realize that in Robinson's other poems, and only there, he would have a chance of doing so.

A first perusal of "Calverly's" might also lead the perceptive reader to suspect that the poet is more interested in the human personality than he is in, say, nature; that he is interested in people not only for their enigmatic and haunting qualities but also for their mysterious exemplification of some larger entity, some agency that, though it determines both their lives and their deaths, may or may not have any concern for them or knowledge of them. Of these men, the poet cannot say "where their light lives are gone," and because he cannot say—and because there is nothing or no way to tell him—he cannot know, either, what his own fate is, or its meaning; he can know only that he himself was once at Calverly's, that the others who were there are gone, and that he shall follow them in due time. He cannot say what this means or whether, in fact, it means anything. Though he can guess as to what it might mean, all he finally *knows* is what has happened.

This condition of mind is a constant throughout all but a very few of Robinson's poems. It links him in certain curious ways with the Existentialists, but we are aware of such affinities only

tangentially, for Robinson's writings, whatever else they may
be, are dramas that make use of conjecture rather than overt
statements of ideas held and defended. It is the fact that truth is
"so strange in its nakedness" that appalled and intrigued him—
the fact that it takes different forms for different people and
different situations. Robinson believed in the unknowable constants that govern the human being from within; in addition, he
had the sort of mind that sees history as a unity in which these
human constants appear in dramatic form. This explains why he
had no difficulty at all in projecting Welsh kingdoms and biblical encounters out of houses and situations he had known in
New England, much as his own Shakespeare was able to fill
"Ilion, Rome, or any town you like / Of olden time with timeless Englishmen."

The unity of the poet's mind is a quality that is certain to
make its presence felt very early in the reader's acquaintance
with Robinson. One can tell a great deal about him from the
reading of a single poem. All the poems partake of a single view
and a single personality, and one has no trouble in associating the
poems in strict forms with the more irregular ones as the products of the same vision of existence. The sensibility evidenced
by the poems is both devious and tenacious, and it lives most
intensely when unresolved about questions dealing with the
human personality. Robinson is perhaps the greatest master of
the speculative or conjectural approach to the writing of poetry.
Uncertainty was the air he breathed, and speculation was not so
much a device with him—though at its best it is a surpassingly
effective technique—as it was a habit of mind, an integral part of
the self. As with most powerful poets, the writing proceeded
from the way in which Robinson naturally thought, the way he
naturally *was*, and so was inextricably rooted in his reticent,
slightly morbid, profoundly contemplative, solitary, compassionate, and stoical personality and was not the product of a conscious search for a literary "way," an unusual manner of speak-

ing which was invented or discovered and in which the will had a major part.

Robinson's tentative point of view was solidly wedded to a style that has exactly the same characteristics as his mind. It makes an artistic virtue, and often a very great one, of arriving at only provisional answers and solutions, of leaving it up to the reader's personality—also fated—to choose from among them the most likely. Thus a salient quality of Robinson's work is the extraordinary roundness and fullness he obtains from such circumlocutions of his subjects, as though he were indeed turning (in William James's phrase) "the cube of reality." One is left with the belief that in any given situation there are many truths —as many, so to speak, as there are persons involved, as there are witnesses, as there are ways of thinking about it. And encompassing all these is the shadowy probability that none of them is or can be final. What we see in Robinson's work is the unending and obsessional effort to make sense of experience when perhaps there is none to be made. The poet, the reader, all of us are members of humanity in the sense Robinson intended when he characterized the earth as "a kind of vast spiritual kindergarten where millions of people are trying to spell God with the wrong blocks."

It is through people that Robinson found the hints and gleams of the universal condition that he could not help trying to solve. Like other human beings, he was cursed with intelligence and sensibility in a universe made for material objects. "The world is a hell of a place," he once said, "but the universe is a fine thing," and again, "We die of what we eat and drink. / But more we die of what we think." Robinson has been perhaps the only American poet—certainly the only one of major status—interested *exclusively* in human beings as subject matter for poetry—in the psychological, motivational aspects of living, in the inner life as it is projected upon the outer. His work is one vast attempt to tell the stories that no man can really tell, for no man can know their real meaning, their real intention, or even whether such exists, though it persistently appears to do so. In all Robinson's people the Cosmos seems to be brooding in one way or another, so that a man and woman sitting in a garden, as in "Mortmain," are, in *what* they are, exemplars of eternal laws that we may guess at but not know. The laws are present in psychological constitutions as surely as they are in physical materials, in the orbital patterns of stars and planets and atoms, only deeper hid, more tragic and mysterious, "as there might somewhere be veiled / Eternal reasons why the tricks of time / Were played like this."

Robinson wrote an enormous amount of poetry (how one's mind quails at the sheer *weight*, the physical bulk, of his fifteen-hundred-page *Collected Poems*!), but at the center of it and all through it is the Personality, the Mind, conditioned by its accidental placement in time and space—these give the individuations that make drama possible—but also partaking of the hidden universals, the not-to-be-knowns that torment all men. In these poems "The strange and unremembered light / That is in dreams" plays over "The nameless and eternal tragedies / That render hope and hopelessness akin." Like a man speaking under torture—or self-torture—Robinson tells of these things, circling them, painfully shifting from one possible interpretation to another, and the reader circles with him, making, for want of any received, definitive opinion, hesitant, troubling, tentative judgments. The result is an unresolved view, but a view of remarkable richness and suggestibility, opening out in many directions and unsealing many avenues of possibility: a multidimensional view that the reader is left pondering as the poem has pondered, newly aware of his own enigmas, of what he and his own life—its incidents and fatalities—may mean, could mean, and thus he is likely to feel himself linked into the insoluble universal equation, in which nature itself is only a frame of mind, a projection of inwardness, tormenting irresolution, and occasional inexplicable calms.

. . . she could look
Right forward through the years, nor any more
Shrink with a cringing prescience to behold
The glitter of dead summer on the grass,
Or the brown-glimmered crimson of still trees
Across the intervale where flashed along,
Black-silvered, the cold river.

II

As has been said, Robinson's method—which on some fronts
has been labeled anti-poetic—would not amount to as much as it
does were not the modes of thought presented in such powerful
and disturbing dramatic forms. For an "anti-poet," Robinson
was an astonishing craftsman. One has only to read a few of his
better poems in the classic French repetitive forms, such as "The
House on the Hill," to recognize the part that traditional verse
patterns play in his work. This much is demonstrable. It is
among those who believe the poetic essence to lie somewhere
outside or beyond such considerations, somewhere in the image-
making, visual, and visionary realm, that Robinson's position has
been challenged. And it is true that his verse is oddly bare, that
there are few images in it—though, of these, some are very fine
indeed—and that most of it is highly cerebral and often written
in a scholarly or pseudoscholarly manner that is frequently more
than a little pedantic. Many of his poems contain an element of
self-parody, and these carry more than their share of bad, flat,
stuffy writing.

There were slaves who dragged the shackles of a precedent
      unbroken,
Demonstrating the fulfillment of unalterable schemes,
Which had been, before the cradle, Time's inexorable tenants
Of what were now the dusty ruins of their fathers' dreams.

Infrequently there is also a kind of belaboring-beyond-belaboring of the obvious:

> The four square somber things that you see first
> Around you are four walls that go as high
> As to the ceiling.

And now and then one comes on philosophical pronouncements of a remarkable unconvincingness, demonstrating a total failure of idiom, of art:

> Too much of that
> May lead you by and by through gloomy lanes
> To a sad wilderness, where one may grope
> Alone, and always, or until he feels
> Ferocious and invisible animals
> That wait for men and eat them in the dark.

At his worst, Robinson seems to go on writing long after whatever he has had to say about the subject has been exhausted; there is a suspicious look of automatism about his verse instrument. The reader, being made of less stern stuff, will almost always fail before Robinson's blank verse does.

Robinson certainly wrote too much. Like Wordsworth—even more than Wordsworth, if that is possible—he is in need of selective editing. In the present book, this is what the late Morton Dauwen Zabel has done, and I believe with singular success. The Robinson of this book is much more nearly the essential, the permanently valuable Robinson than the Robinson of the *Collected Poems*, though there are unavoidable exclusions—particularly of the good book-length poems, such as *Lancelot* and *Merlin*—which one might legitimately regret and to which it is hoped that the reader will eventually have recourse. Yet even in the present volume one is likely to be put off by the length of many of the pieces. Then, too, if the casual reader skims only a little of a particular poem and finds that nothing much is happening or that event, action, and resolution are taking place only in various persons' minds, he is also likely to shy away. But once *in* the poem, committed to it, with his mind winding among the alternative complexities of Robinson's characters' minds—that is, winding with Robinson's mind—the reader changes slowly, for Robinson hath his will. One is held by the curious dry magic that seems so eminently unmagical, that bears no resemblance to the elfin or purely verbal or native-woodnote magic for which English verse is justly celebrated. It is a magic for which there is very little precedent in all literature. Though external affinities may be asserted and even partially demonstrated with Praed and Browning, though there are occasional distant echoes of Wordsworth, Keats, Hardy, and Rossetti, Robinson is really like none of them in his root qualities; his spell is cast with none of the traditional paraphernalia, but largely through his own reading of character and situation and fate, his adaptation of traditional poetic devices to serve these needs—an adaptation so unexpected, so revolutionary, as to seem not so much adaptation as transformation.

Another odd thing about Robinson is that his best work and his worst are yet remarkably alike. The qualities that make the good poems good are the same qualities that make the bad poems bad; it is only a question of how Robinson's method works out in, "takes to," the situation he is depicting, and often the difference between good, bad, and mediocre is thin indeed. This difficulty is also compounded by the fact that Robinson is equally skilled as a technician in both memorable poems and trivial ones. In the less interesting poems, particularly the longer ones, Robinson's air of portentousness can be tiresome. Reading these, one is tempted to say that Robinson is the most prolific *reticent* poet in history. Though he gives the impression that he is reluctant to write down what he is writing, he often goes on and on, in a kind of intelligent mumbling, a poetical wringing of the hands, until the reader becomes restive and a little irritated. In these passages, Robinson's verse instrument has a certain kinship with the salt maker in the fairy tale, grinding away of its own accord at the bottom of the sea. Then there is the gray, austere landscape of the poems, the lack of background definition. One is accustomed to finding the characters in a poem—particularly a narrative poem—in a *place*, a location with objects and a weather of its own, a world which the reader can enter and in which he can, as it were, live with the characters. But there is very little of the environmental in Robinson's work. What few gestures and concessions he makes to the outside world are token ones; all externality is quickly devoured by the tormented introversion of his personages. In Robinson, the mind eats everything and converts it to part of a conflict with self; one could say with some justification that all Robinson's poems are about people who are unable to endure themselves or to resolve their thoughts into some meaningful, cleansing action. So much introversion is not only harrowing; it can also be boring, particularly when carried on to the enormous lengths in which it appears in "Matthias at the Door" and "Avon's Harvest."

And yet with these strictures, the case against Robinson's poetry has pretty much been stated, and we have on our hands what remains after they have been acknowledged.

III

No poet ever undertood loneliness or separateness better than Robinson or knew the self-consuming furnace that the brain can become in isolation, the suicidal hellishness of it, doomed as it is to feed on itself in answerless frustration, fated to this condition by the accident of human birth, which carries with it the hunger for certainty and the intolerable load of personal recollections. He understood loneliness in all its many forms and depths and was thus less interested in its conventional poetic aspects than he was in the loneliness of the man in the crowd, or alone with his thoughts of the dead, or feeling at some unforseen time the metaphysical loneliness, the *angst*, of being "lost among the stars," or becoming aware of the solitude that resides in comfort and in the affection of friends and family—that desperation at the heart of what is called happiness. It is only the poet and those involved who realize the inevitability and the despair of these situations, "Although, to the serene outsider, / There still would seem to be a way."

The acceptance of the fact that there is no way, that there is nothing to do about the sadness of most human beings when they are alone or speaking to others as if to themselves, that there is nothing to offer them but recognition, sympathy, compassion, deepens Robinson's best poems until we sense in them something other than art. A thing inside us is likely to shift from where it was, and our world view to change, though perhaps only slightly, toward a darker, deeper perspective. Robinson has been called a laureate of failure and has even been accused (if that is the word) of making a cult and a virtue of failure, but that assessment is not quite accurate. His subject was "the slow tragedy of haunted men," those whose "eyes are lit with a wrong light," those who believe that some earthly occurrence in the past (and now forever impossible) could have made all the difference, that some person dead or otherwise beyond reach, some life unlived and now unlivable, could have been the answer to everything. But these longings were seen by Robinson to be the delusions necessary to sustain life, for human beings, though they can live without hope, cannot live believing that no hope ever could have existed. For this reason, many of the poems deal with the unlived life, the man kept by his own nature or by circumstance from "what might have been his," but there is always the ironic Robinsonian overtone that what might have been would not have been much better than what is—and, indeed, might well have been worse; the failure would only have had its development and setting altered somewhat, but not its pain or its inevitability.

Though Robinson's dramatic sense was powerful and often profound, his narrative sense was not. His narrative devices are few, and they are used again and again. The poet is always, for example, running into somebody in the street whom he knew under other circumstances and who is now a bum, a "slowly-freezing Santa Claus," a street-corner revivalist, or something equally comical-pathetic and cut off. The story of the person's passing from his former state to this one then becomes the poem, sometimes told by the derelict, the "ruin who meant well," and sometimes puzzled out by the poet himself, either with his deep, painful probing or, as in some of the later long poems, such as "The Man Who Died Twice," with an intolerable amount of poetical hemming and hawing, backing and filling.

And yet Robinson's peculiar elliptical vision, even when it is boring, is worth the reader's time. The tone of his voice is so distinctive, his technique so varied and resourceful, and his compassion so intense that something valuable comes through even the most wasteful of his productions. Not nearly enough has been made of Robinson's skill, the chief thing about which is that it is able to create, through an astonishing number of forms and subjects, the tone of a single voice, achieving variety within a tonal unity. And it is largely in this tone, the product of outlook (or, if I may be forgiven, inlook), technique, and personality, that Robinson's particular excellence lies; thus the tone is worth examining.

Robinson's mind was not sensuously rich, if by that is meant a Keatsian or Hopkinsian outgoingness into nature as a bodily experience and the trust and delight in nature that this attitude implies. His poetic interests are psychological and philosophical; he examines the splits between what is and what might have been, what must be and what cannot be. That Robinson sees these differences to matter very little, finally, does not mean that they do not matter to the people who suffer from them; it is, in fact, in this realm of delusionary and obsessive suffering that Robinson's poems take place. Though his mind was not rich in a sensuous way, it was both powerful and hesitant, as though suspended between strong magnets. This gives his work an unparalleled sensitivity in balance; and from this balance, this desperately poised uncertainty, emanates a compassion both very personal and cosmic—a compassion that one might well see as a substitute for the compassion that God failed to supply. It is ironic at times, it is bitter and self-mocking, but it is always compassion unalloyed by sentimentality; it has been earned, as it is the burden of the poems themselves to show. This attitude, this tone, runs from gentle, rueful humor—though based, even so, on stark constants of human fate such as the aging process and death—to the most terrible hopelessness. It may appear in the tortuous working out of a long passage, or it may gleam forth for an instant in surroundings not seen until its appearance to be frightening, as in the poem below.

"Isaac and Archibald" is a New England pastoral in which a twelve-year-old boy takes a long walk with an old man, Isaac, to visit another old man at his farm. Nothing much happens, except that both Isaac and Archibald manage to reveal to the boy the signs of mental decline and approaching death in the other. The two men drink cider; the boy sits and reflects, prefiguring as he does the mature man and poet he will become. The boy's awareness of death is built up by small, affectionate touches, some of them so swift and light that they are almost sure to be passed over by the hurried reader.

> Hardly had we turned in from the main road
> When Archibald, with one hand on his back
> And the other clutching his huge-headed cane,
> Came limping down to meet us.—"Well! well! well!"
> Said he; and then he looked at my red face,
> All streaked with dust and sweat, and shook my hand,
> And said it must have been a right smart walk
> That we had had that day from Tilbury Town.—
> "Magnificent," said Isaac; and he told
> About the beautiful west wind there was
> Which cooled and clarified the atmosphere.
> "You must have made it with your legs, I guess,"

Said Archibald; and Isaac humored him
With one of those infrequent smiles of his
Which he kept in reserve, apparently,
For Archibald alone. "But why," said he,
"Should Providence have cider in the world
If not for such an afternoon as this?"
And Archibald, with a soft light in his eyes,
Replied that if he chose to go down cellar,
There he would find eight barrels—one of which
Was newly tapped, he said, and to his taste
An honor to the fruit. Isaac approved
Most heartily of that, and guided us
Forthwith, as if his venerable feet
Were measuring the turf in his own door-yard,
Straight to the open rollway. Down we went,
Out of the fiery sunshine to the gloom,
Grateful and half sepulchral, where we found
The barrels, like eight potent sentinels,
Close ranged along the wall. From one of them
A bright pine spile stuck out alluringly,
And on the black flat stone, just under it,
Glimmered a late-spilled proof that Archibald
Had spoken from unfeigned experience.
There was a fluted antique water-glass
Close by, and in it, prisoned, or at rest,
There was a cricket, of the soft brown sort
That feeds on darkness. Isaac turned him out,
And touched him with his thumb to make him jump

Until the introduction of the cricket and the few words that
typify it, there is nothing startling in the passage, though it is
quite good Robinson, with the judicious adverb "alluringly" attached to the protrusion of the pine spile and the lovely affectionate irony of Archibald's "unfeigned experience" with the
cider. But the cricket, of the *sort* that feeds on darkness, changes

the poem and brings it into the central Robinsonian orbit. Here, the insect is a more terrifying and mysterious creature—a better symbol for the context—than a maggot or dead louse would be, for it is normally a benign spirit of household and hearth. This simple way of referring to it, as though the supposition that it "feeds on darkness" were the most obvious and natural thing in the world to say about it, produces a haunting effect when encountered along with the gentle old farmers' proximity to death and the boy's budding awareness of it.

It may be inferred from the above passages that Robinson is not a writer of unremitting brilliance or a master of the more obvious technical virtuosities. He is, rather, a poet of quick, tangential thrusts, of sallies and withdrawals, of fleeting hints and glimpsed implications. In his longer poems, particularly, the impacts build up slowly, and it is only to those who have not the sensitivity to catch the sudden, baffling, half-revealing gleams—those who are "annoyed by no such evil whim / As death, or time, or truth"—that Robinson's poems are heavy and dull. Though he has a way, particularly in the later poems, of burying his glints of meaning pretty deeply in the material that makes them possible, Robinson at his best manages to use the massiveness of discourse and the swift, elusive gleam of illumination—the momentary flashing into the open of a stark, tragic hint, a fleeting generalization—as complementaries. And when the balance between these elements is right, the effect is unforgettable.

At times it appears that Robinson not only did not seek to avoid dullness but courted it and actually used it as a device, setting up his major points by means of it and making them doubly effective by contrast, without in the least violating the unity of tone or the huge, heavy drift of the poem toward its conclusion. He is a slow and patient poet; taking his time to say a thing as he wishes to say it is one of his fundamental qualities. This has worked against him, particularly since his work has survived into an age of anything but slow and patient readers. The pedestrian movement of much of his work has made him unpopular in an era when the piling on of startling effects, the cramming of the poetic line with all the spoils it can carry, is regarded not so much as a criterion of good or superior verse of a certain kind, but as poetry itself, other kinds being relegated to inferior categories yet to be defined. But Robinson's considered, unhurried lines, as uncomplicated in syntax as they are difficult in thought, in reality are, by virtue of their enormous sincerity, conviction, and quiet originality, a constant rebuke to those who conceive of poetry as verbal legerdemain or as the "superior amusement" that the late T. S. Eliot would have had it be.

The Robinson line is simple in the way that straightforward English prose is simple; the declarative sentence is made to do most of the work. His questions, though comparatively rare, are weighted with the agony of concern, involvement, and uncertainty. It is the thought, rather than the expression of the thought, that makes some of Robinson difficult, for he was almost always at pains to write simply, and his skills were everywhere subservient to this ideal. My personal favorite of Robinson's effects is his extremely subtle use of the line as a means of changing the meaning of the sentence that forms the line, the whole poem changing direction slightly but unmistakably with each such shift.

> What is it in me that you like so much,
> And love so little?

And yet for all his skill, Robinson's technical equipment is never obvious or obtrusive, as Hopkins's, say, is. This is, of course, a tribute to his resourcefulness, for in his best pieces the manner of the poem is absorbed into its matter, and we focus not on the mode of saying but on the situations and characters into whose presence we have come.

IV

Robinson's favorite words, because they embody his favorite way of getting at any subject, are "may" and "might." The whole of the once-celebrated "The Man Against the Sky," for example, is built upon their use. When the poet sees a man climbing Mount Monadnock, it is, for the purposes of his poem, important that he *not* know who the man is or what he is doing there, so that the poem can string together a long series of conjectural possibilities as to who he might be, what might happen to him, and what he might conceivably represent.

> Even he, who stood where I had found him,
> On high with fire all round him,
> Who moved along the molten west,
> And over the round hill's crest
> That seemed half ready with him to go down,
> Flame-bitten and flame-cleft,
> As if there were to be no last thing left
> Of a nameless unimaginable town—
> Even he who climbed and vanished may have taken
> Down to the perils of a depth not known

When he reaches the words "may have," the reader is in true Robinson country; he lives among alternatives, possibilities, doubts, and delusionary gleams of hope. This particular poem, which not only uses this approach but virtually hounds it to death, is not successful mainly because Robinson insists on being overtly philosophical and, at the end, on committing himself to a final view. Another shortcoming is that he is not sufficiently close to the man, for his poems are much better when he knows *something* of the circumstances of a human life, tells what he knows, and *then* speculates, for the unresolved quality of his ratiocinations, coupled with the usually terrible *facts*, enables him to make powerful and haunting use of conjecture and of his typical "may have" or "might not have" presentations of alternative possibilities.

It is also true of this poem that it has very little of the leavening of Robinson's irony, and this lack is detrimental to it. This irony has been widely commented upon, but not, I think, quite as accurately as it might have been. Though it infrequently has the appearance of callousness or even cruelty, a closer examination, a more receptive *feeling* of its effect, will usually show that it is neither. It is, rather, a product of a detachment based on helplessness, on the saving grace of humor that is called into play because nothing practical can be done and because the spectator of tragedy must find some way in which to save himself emotionally from the effects of what he has witnessed.

> No, no—forget your Cricket and your Ant,
> For I shall never set my name to theirs
> That now bespeak the very sons and heirs
> Incarnate of Queen Gossip and King Cant.
> The case of Leffingwell is mixed, I grant,
> And futile seems the burden that he bears;
> But are we sounding his forlorn affairs
> Who brand him parasite and sycophant?
>
> I tell you, Leffingwell was more than these;
> And if he prove a rather sorry knight,
> What quiverings in the distance of what light
> May not have lured him with high promises,
> And then gone down?—He may have been deceived;
> He may have lied—he did; and he believed.

The irony here is not based on showing in what ridiculous and humiliating ways the self-delusion of Leffingwell made of him a parasite and sycophant; it works through and past these things to the much larger proposition that such delusion is necessary to life, that, in fact, it is the condition that enables us to function at all. The manufacture and protection of the self-image is really the one constant, the one obsessive concern, of our existence. This idea was, of course, not new with Robinson, though it may be worth mentioning that many psychiatrists, among them Alfred Adler and Harry Stack Sullivan, place a primary emphasis on such interpretations of the human mentality. What should be noted is that the lies of Leffingwell and of Uncle Ananias are in their way truths, for they have in them that portion of the truth that comes not from fact but from the ideal.

> All summer long we loved him for the same
> Perennial inspiration of his lies

There is something more here, something more positive, than there is in the gloomy and one-dimensional use of similar themes in, say, Eugene O'Neill's *The Iceman Cometh,* for in Robinson's poems the necessity to lie (and, with luck, sublimely) is connected to the desire to remake the world by remaking that portion of it that is oneself. Robinson shows the relation between such lies and the realities they must struggle to stay alive among, and he shows them with the shrewdness and humor of a man who has told such lies to himself but sadly knows them for what they are. The reader is likely to smile at the absurdity—but also to be left with a new kind of admiration for certain human traits that he had theretofore believed pathetic or contemptible.

V

These, then, are Robinson's kinds of originality, of poetic value—all of them subtle and half hidden, muffled and disturbing, answering little but asking those questions that are unpardonable, unforgettable, and necessary.

It is curious and wonderful that this scholarly, intelligent, childlike, tormented New England stoic, "always hungry for the nameless," always putting in the reader's mouth "some word that hurts your tongue," useless for anything but his art, protected by hardier friends all his life, but enormously courageous and utterly dedicated (he once told Chard Powers Smith at the very end of his life, "I could never have done *anything* but write poetry"), should have brought off what in its quiet, searching, laborious way is one of the most remarkable accomplishments of modern poetry. Far from indulging, as his detractors have maintained, in a kind of poetical know-nothingism, he actually brought to poetry a new kind of approach, making of a refusal to pronounce definitively on his subjects a virtue and of speculation upon possibilities an instrument that allows an unparalleled fullness to his presentations, as well as endowing them with some of the mysteriousness, futility, and proneness to multiple interpretation that incidents and lives possess in the actual world.

Robinson's best poetry is exactly that kind of communication that "tells the more the more it is not told." In creating a body of major poetry with devices usually thought to be unfruitful for the creative act—irresolution, abstraction, conjecture, a dry, nearly imageless mode of address that tends always toward the general without ever supplying the resolving judgment that we expect of generalization—Robinson has done what good poets have always done: by means of his "cumulative silences" as well as by his actual lines, he has forced us to reexamine and finally to redefine what poetry is—or our notion of it—and so has enabled poetry itself to include more, to *be* more, than it was before he wrote.

[1965]

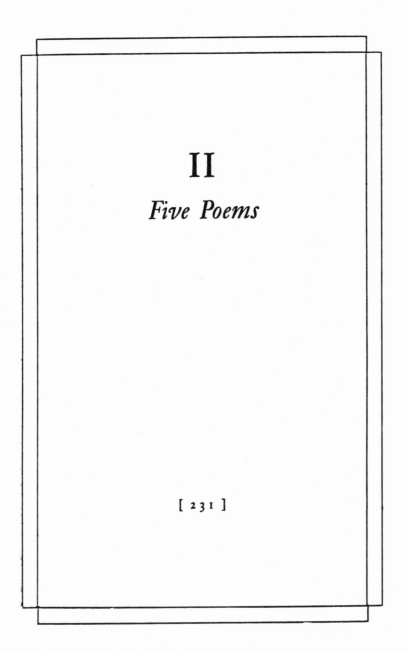

II

Five Poems

Christopher Smart

A SONG TO DAVID

How shall we deal with the mad in their perfect disguises? From the beginning we have suspected them of magic and have wanted what they have, the revelations. But how may we come by these and still retain our own sanity? What must *we* do in order to connect safely with the insane at their clairvoyant and dangerous levels? One may have heard "A Song to David" referred to, for example, as "the great mad song of Smart," and may perhaps also have heard in a twentieth-century dream that verses of it were inscribed on the walls of eighteenth-century Bedlam. What happens, then, when one goes into the poem, clutching sanity like an amulet but with the mind apprehensively and avidly trembling for the lightning of another man's self-destructive revelations?

At first there is simple disappointment. There seems little magic to it, little madness. There is only the rhyme scheme A-A-B-C-C-B with all but the three-beat B lines regular four-beat English tetrameter, surely the strictest and unlikeliest of corsets for the dancing of biblical frenzy that one has heard the poem is. At first one may be reminded of another poet's—Robert Lowell's —reference to madness, to "its hackneyed speech, its homicidal eye," and may reflect that, though the hackneyed speech is pretty much in evidence here, the flash of true madness, the homicidal angel-seeing eye, is not. And yet, and yet. . . .

It is a poem about the musician David, whom Smart sees as a

kind of Old Testament Orpheus. And, as one imagines was true of the Orphic song, the effect of the poem is really in the rapt continuation rather than in the first notes. Slowly begun, the ecstasy and wildness grow, the weird and wonderful and yet natural-seeming comparisons pile tirelessly on each other, the tempo keeps pushing up and up, the certitude increases, the poem rises from plateau to plateau of affirmation, and the control over the stanza is as complete at the end as it was at the unpromising beginning. It may very well be that "A Song to David" *is* the ultimate mad song, combining reason and unreason, inspiration and the strictest of forms, wedding the impossible and the mundane, the visionary and the prosaic in hardheaded English raised to the unlikely altitude of prophecy. Yet, odd as it is, it is not the *practicality* of Smart's obsessed, obsessive vision that we keep holding our breaths over, but rather what seems at every moment to be showing through the form: the possibility that this poem, so obviously and historically and certifiably mad, may indeed, could we but grasp it whole, give us what we have always wanted from the insane: the life-extending, life-deepening insight, the ultimate symbolic sanity.

The poem is made of genius-flashes full of the concealing-cunning of the lunatic: madness dictating the pious, predictable rhymes to which, because of genius, something unpredictable has happened. It is this wild freshness, the fanatical shrewdness, the God's-idiot mysterious confidence and clearness of it, that makes it the marvelous poem it is. Note, for instance, the peculiar and superb use of the Greek alphabet as a system which includes anything and everything there is, subsumed in the days of the week, the days of God's creation of the world, and so on. Look at the unforgettable phrases that Smart seems able to throw in anywhere without traducing his meters or his meaning: phrases like "look upward to the past," and "the Lord is just and glad." Long as it is, the poem is filled with marvels, and they seem to engender each other as effortlessly as the stanzas fulfill their rhymes. It is one of the most joyous and inventive prayers ever prayed, one of the most individual and mysterious, and probably one of the most Godlike. One hopes fervently that Dr. Johnson sensed something or all of this when he said "I'd as lief pray with Kit Smart as with any man"; a prayer with Kit Smart is likely to lift you straight off the floor, or off the London pavements where he frequently knelt.

Smart is a more commonsensical or madder Blake. "A Song to David" is "a glorious hosannah from the den," a wild, well-ordered rereading of part of the Bible as though it were a pagan sun-myth, and it leaves us with an uneasy and exalted feeling: that there is nothing in any poetry to match the madman who rhymes; that poetic forms, for so long worn threadbare by the empty rehearsal of their mere conventions, are renewable only under such perilous conditions; that it takes this, madness, but that once the thing is shown—determined, dared, and done— then both strict poetic forms and the language that uses them have a new chance, a new breathing space under heaven.

[1966]

Matthew Arnold

DOVER BEACH

"DOVER BEACH" has been called the first modern poem. If this is true, it is modern not so much in diction and technique—for its phrasing and its Miltonic inversions are obvious carryovers from a much older poetry—but in psychological orientation. Behind the troubled man standing at the lover's conventional moon-filled window looking on the sea, we sense—more powerfully because our hindsight confirms what Arnold only began to intuit—the shift in the human viewpoint from the Christian tradition to the impersonal world of Darwin and the nineteenth-century scientists. The way the world is seen, and thus the way men live, is conditioned by what men know about it, and they know more now than they ever have before. Things themselves —the sea, stars, darkness, wind—have not changed; it is the perplexed anxiety and helplessness of the newly dispossessed human being that now come forth from his mind and transmute the sea, the night air, the French coast, and charge them with the sinister implications of the entirely alien. What begins as a rather conventional—but very good—description of scenery turns slowly into quite another thing: a recognition of where the beholder stands in relation to these things; where he *really* stands. It is this new and comfortless knowledge as it overwhelms for all time the old and does away with the place where he thought he stood, where his tradition told him he stood, that creates the powerful and melancholy force of the poem.

In statement, "Dover Beach" goes very easily and gravely, near prose and yet not too near. It has something of the effect of overheard musing, though it is addressed, or half-addressed, to someone present. Its greatest technical virtue, to my mind, is its employment of sound-imagery, particularly in the deep, sustained vowels of lines like "Its melancholy, long, withdrawing roar." The lines also seem to me to *break* beautifully: ". . . on the French coast, the light / Gleams, and is gone." I have tried many times to rearrange Arnold's lines, and have never succeeded in doing anything but diminish their subtlety, force, and conviction.

The one difficulty of the poem, it seems to me, is in the famous third strophe wherein the actual sea is compared to the Sea of Faith. If Arnold means that the Sea of Faith was formerly at high tide, and he hears now only the sound of the tide going out, one cannot help thinking also of the cyclic nature of tides, and the consequent coming of another high tide only a few hours after the present ebb. In other words, the figure of speech appears valid only on one level of the comparison; the symbolic half fails to sustain itself. Despite the magnificence of the writing in this section, I cannot help believing that it is the weakest part of the poem when it should be the strongest; the explicitness of the comparison seems too ready-made. Yet I have the poem as it is so deeply in memory that I cannot imagine it changed, and would not have it changed even if I knew it would be a better poem thereby.

In the sound of waves rolling pebbles, an eternal senseless motion, unignorable and meaningless, Arnold hears—as we ever afterwards must hear—human sadness, the tears of things. It links us to Sophocles and to all men at all times who have discovered in such a sound an expression of their own unrest, and have therefore made of it "the eternal note of sadness." Yet our sadness has a depth that no other era has faced: a certainty of despair based upon our own examination of empirical evidence and the conclusions drawn by our rational faculty. These have revealed not God but the horror and emptiness of things, including those that we cannot help thinking beautiful: that *are* beautiful. By its direct, slow-speaking means, the poem builds toward its last nine lines, when the general resolves into the particular, divulging where *we* stand, what these things mean to *us*. The implication is that if love, morality, constancy, and the other traditional Western virtues are not maintained without supernatural sanction, there is nothing. The world that lies before us in such beauty that it seems to have come instantaneously from God's hand does not include, guarantee, or symbolize the qualities that men have assumed were also part of it. It is beautiful and impersonal, but we must experience it—and now suffer it—as persons. Human affection is revealed as a completely different thing than what we believed it to be; as different, in fact, as the world we were mistaken about. It is a different thing but also a new thing, with new possibilities of terror, choice, and meaning. The moment between

the lovers thus takes on the qualities of a new expulsion from
Eden: they tremble with fear but also with terrible freedom;
they look eastward. The intense vulnerability of the emotional
life takes place in an imperiled darkness among the sounds of
the sea and against the imminence of violence, wars, armies
blundering blindly into each other for no reason. Yet there is a
new, fragile center to things: a man and a woman. In a word, it
is love in what we have come to call the existential predicament.
Nearly a hundred years ago, Arnold fixed unerringly and profoundly on the quality that more than any other was to characterize the emotion of love in our own century: desperation.
[1966]

Gerard Manley Hopkins

THE WRECK OF THE DEUTSCHLAND

HOPKINS'S "Wreck of the Deutschland" represented a new direction, an entire new set of possibilities and techniques for English poetry. From the standpoint of influence—that is, considering what poetry after Hopkins really did become—it is probably
the most important poem of the nineteenth century. Though he
had been a fine traditional poet and an interesting and cautiously
experimental writer before "The Wreck of the Deutschland," it
is with this poem that he is first seen completely in the curious,
breathtakingly original form which has since come to be identi-
fied as "Hopkinsian." Here for the first time came fully together
his linguistic and prosodic experiments—of which the most fa-

mous and influential is the conscious employment of what the poet called "sprung rhythm," wherein only the stresses of a line are counted, and the line is allowed to have any number of unstressed syllables—the piety and agony of his Jesuitical faith, his personal suffering over the actuality and meaning of pain and death, and his intensely personal researches into nature, his "inscapes," his capacity to look at things as though time did not exist: as though he and that flower, that leaf, that formation of ice on a pond, that sunset or that drift of cloud were the only things in existence: as though he and the object were both placed in the world exclusively to meet and understand each other's essences.

Because these qualities came together in this way and were forged in Hopkins's mind as they were, the whole concept of what can be done with the English verse line, the English language, was changed. Hopkins is a poet of extremes, of the pushing of vision, the pushing of poetic devices beyond themselves, to a point one degree farther than the *reductio ad absurdum,* one degree higher than the ludicrous, which is in some cases the degree of sublimity. In no other poet, not even Shakespeare or Donne, is it quite so obvious to the unwarned reader that a new *dimension* has been added to poetry. All other poems, even some of those commonly called "great," are likely to seem linguistically thin, a little prosaic and easily satisfied with themselves, compared with Hopkins. On first encountering Hopkins's intense, peculiar, rapid idiom, a great many people have said to themselves that here, at long last, is a *complete* poetry, working powerfully at all levels, at once both wild and swift beyond all other wildness and swiftness and stringently, savagely disciplined: a language *worked* for all it can give.

It is a poem about death at sea: a death that has to be *imagined* rather than suffered by a poet whose being, himself, at the time that "they fought with God's cold" "Away in the loveable west, / On a pastoral forehead of Wales" adds to the delirious guilt of the tone. In a fearsome and nearly miraculous metamorphosis, this guilt becomes a furious affirmation of the role of suffering in life. The sea itself, the sea into which the *Deutschland* founders with its five nuns, is the most powerfully real and *active* sea in English literature, not surpassed even by the sea of *Beowulf*, *The Seafarer*, or any of the bardic poets who would seem able to render water, spray, and pain with a great deal more authority than could a withdrawn, scholarly, nineteenth-century teaching Jesuit. And yet, through labors that made the writing of poetry so horrendously difficult as almost, but not quite, to make it impossible, Hopkins was able to catch the rhythms and terrors of the sea at its most murderous, as it surrounds the human spirit at its most hopeless. Hopkins's triumphant cry in the nun's "O Christ, Christ, come quickly" is a point from which English religious poetry has never risen. Christ is with the hopeless, even those *this* hopeless, even when they are blinded with snow and spray and their voice swallowed by the wind. The snow, the killing wind, are all God's: it is all part of the Way.

This assumption, this affirmation, is where some readers, as it were, "hang up." One cannot deny Hopkins the power and originality of his verse; these are too evident, too overwhelming. Yet the continual recourse to the figure of Christ, not only in this poem but in most of Hopkins's others, to solve the problems of conflict implicit in the action of the poem, comes, after so much of it, to seem a calling of the god from the machine. Hopkins's repairing to Jesus and to God as the solution not only of every human problem but of every poem strikes some readers as predictable and even a little complacent.

But the language, the rhythms, the desperate originality of vision, the curious recklessness coupled with the marvelously wrought prosody, the sense of a disciplined outpour that is still, in every syllable, an outpour: these are Hopkins. His world, his work, are tight and compressed like a spring; they are feverish and a little hysterical. One cannot read too much of Hopkins at a time, for one cannot match his intensity. But "The Wreck of the Deutschland" introduced into the English literary tradition the idea of a *total* poetry. Consequently it represents a renewal of the language: a renewal from the region of the unforeseen, the unforeseeable, the triumphantly personal, the theoretically worked-out that works.

[1966]

Francis Thompson

THE HOUND OF HEAVEN

THOUGH a poet in the latter half of the twentieth century might write a poem with the same theme as "The Hound of Heaven" —the estrangement of the sinner from God's love and the devious and paradoxical ways in which he comes back to it—he would not be likely to conceive and write it in the way Thompson has done. If the mythological content has not entirely gone out of Christianity, at least it has greatly changed, and rhetoric of this particular grand, robed-seer kind has tended to disappear as well. There is a built-in hollowness in latter-day attempts at the sublime tone; many a swelling period has exploded in the face of the "Aw, come off it" that is one of our era's unique contributions to literary and other judgments. We welcome irony, indirection, a cool, ingroup knowingness. But ecstasy? Well, no.

And yet the first thing to be noted about "The Hound of Heaven" is that it *is* grand: intentionally and grandly grand. It is also *curiously* grand. And though it is unashamedly baroque it is also in part very daring linguistically; Hopkins or Joyce would have liked a coinage like "lustihead," and Hart Crane would surely have been excited by "the long savannahs of the blue." Yet it is the conception even more than the details that is daring, inspiring; it is the conception that takes the all-or-nothing chances, running the risk of toppling the whole poem into the frigidity and bombast that Longinus describes as being the pitfalls of the noble style that fails its intentions. Moreoever, "The Hound" is not only grand, but *cosmically* grand. It is as if Thompson had taken the metaphysical conceit of Donne and Marvell literally, expanding it beyond all foreseeable bounds by inventing the most thrilling and monstrous figure of speech he could, and then not only come to believe it but leapt into it bodily. The poem is spectacularly far-fetched, but far-fetched with the excessiveness and total commitment that one feels instantly to be either the qualities of genuine inspiration or those of lunacy. Be this as it may, it is plain that Thompson has one characteristic that visionary and mystical poets—certain kinds of religious poets—must have: rapture. In its grip, he shows no fear whatever of employing a scheme of imagery that involves, literally, the whole universe, with its star systems, winds, moons, clouds, suns, seas: he is not only unafraid of his own conception but plunges triumphantly and gigantically into it, for, though the sinner whose pursuit by the celestial Hound is terrified, fleeing beautifully through sunsets, "wild sea-snortings" and the eyes of children, the poet who writes of all this is gorgeously at home, reveling in the metaphysical flight very much as if it were a physical one: the cosmic and foredoomed paperchase of a sinner who has angelic powers. Since the universe is apprehended as the sinner experiences it, and so in a sense is *in* him, "The Hound" can also be read as a psychological poem, a study in religious guilt-hysteria. But it is first and last a great—or near great—poem.

The structure of "The Hound" is superb, and the recklessness of its rushing imagery and rhetoric—things that start fast and *cannot* slacken—will not fail to enthrall any reader who will truly submit to them. Its pitch is high, nearly shrill, but pure and beautifully modulated. Though its form is that of the irregular Cowleyan ode, its dramatic force depends mainly on its central paradox, which is that the pursued flees as if damned, when capture would in fact be his salvation. The "Hound" (and who but a man of Thompson's peculiar baroque-mystic orientation would have used *this* as the figure of God?) pursues simply by being the creator of and in-dweller in everything that is, imbuing all things with His essential quality of love. His gentle pursuit, which seems the most dreadful possible one to the sinner desperate to keep his youth and powers intact, does, however, take on something of the truly ominous—pursuit, itself, is terrifying—and there is something particularly terrible in the conviction that grows in both sinner and reader that there is literally no escape. The sinner flees, not through Kafka's dingy offices and bad telephone connections, but through the world, God being where He has always been, in the stones and trees and grasses and waves of the sea. It has always seemed to me to be indicative of the angelic potential in the sinner himself that he can fly upon winds, court stars, put his heart against that of the sunset and swing the earth a trinket at his wrist. This is in part the reason that the flight is the most beautiful portion of the poem, and fortunately it constitutes most of it. The capture and reconciliation—the explanation—is, as it would almost have to be, disappointing. And it is a measure of Thompson's accomplishment that the speech of God at the end disappoints us as much as it does, for one may have come to think that Thompson is a poet who might actually know—or guess—what God would say under these circumstances: that Thompson could speak with the tongues of angels as well as those of men, as he seems always about to do.

No matter; Thompson has entered, as well as created, his vision of the sinner-as-quarry, and turned the cosmos into a ritual hunt in some of the most frankly gorgeous imagery, some of the most resounding and yet curiously individual rhetoric, since

Milton. For these reasons, "The Hound of Heaven" is a memorable poem, a poem like a theological nightmare, a Freudian or
narcotic dream of excessive guilt where Existence itself, the
ground of the flight, is really the protagonist of the poem, being
in the sinner's and Thompson's hysterically heightened vision as
excessive, unbelievable, haunted, and magnificent as it is whenever we choose or are compelled to bear the full brunt of its
beauty and terror.

[1966]

William Carlos Williams

THE YACHTS

In the daily lives of all human beings—as well as in the lives of
poets—occur what might be called "instant symbols": moments
when a commonplace event or object is transfigured without
warning, as though by common consent of observed and observer, and becomes for the perceiver both itself and its meaning. Williams's "The Yachts" is that kind of vision, that kind of
poem: a scene whose symbolic possibilities burst in upon—or
out of—the observer. The poem dramatizes rather than insists
on this condition, but everywhere implicit in its matter-of-fact
lines is the possibility that any of us in any situation may see not
only the surface but the depth, the whole *intent* of the actions
and people we live among: that at any moment anything we experience is likely to become more than what we had comfort-
ably agreed with ourselves it is content to be, and that the world

is perpetually capable of concretizing and *presenting* its most powerful, disturbing, and profound symbols in an instant, and in ways known only to the private beholder.

In this case, the scene is a yacht race. The poet speaks of it matter-of-factly, in a sympathetic but curt, slightly impatient tone. Williams's voice, with its American bluntness, its imagistic concreteness, its dislike of rhetorical shows, is a convincing medium through which to feel the significance—the lightning flash of import—that hits the poem about midway in its length. The first feeling that the reader has is one of vague unrest: it may be that the yachts are too perfect in their graceful appointments and movements, more perfect than their crews. They are like life on a greeting card, a life that no real human being has ever been able to live up to, though many have tried. Or it may be that poet and reader are troubled by the social implications that yachts usually carry: money, snobbery, privilege. Even so, none of these associations is *quite* enough to account for the feeling of unrest and dissatisfaction conveyed by the first lines of the poem. After all, why should someone so matter-of-fact as *this* poet be disturbed by an event as charming, exciting, and graceful as a yacht race? And then—though no one explanation can account for it—the sea over which the yachts pass without seeming to be touched by it has suddenly changed into a sea of bodies terribly and uselessly beseeching the yachts for help, or even for notice; it has become a watery hell like something in Dante. The perfection of the yachts has something profound to do with all the loss, all the death and irrevocability in the world. It is the *cost* of this kind of perfection that makes the poet recoil in horror, as the meaning the yachts have for *him*, breaks free of the first troubling but vague connotations, and "the horror of the race dawns staggering the mind." And yet it is only the poet who sees the horror, only he whose mind is staggered by what, now that he *sees* it, the race suggests.

"The Yachts" is a symbolic rather than an allegorical poem, for the vessels do not mean *just* social and economic privilege,

the exploitation of the working classes who made the yachts for
the enjoyment of those who race them, but rather serve as an
image that catches and binds in a central figure all human situations that have to do with these things, with oppression, greed,
sloth, with perfection that human creatures can create but cannot attain in themselves, but also—on the other side of the figure
—with rejection, with the demise of the body, with death, with
the abject yearning of the dead to possess a *significance* once
more, even if only for the one instant of a watery hand grasping
the prow of an inhumanly beautiful hull and making an impression on it, having some effect, mattering. As Randall Jarrell has
finely said, "The Yachts" is "a paradigm of all the unjust beauty,
the necessary and unnecessary injustice of the world." To that I
would add that it is also a wonderful and terrible witness to the
fact that the things we see every day, the things we think we
know, are at any moment likely to explode in our faces with
meaning, and thence to *exist* for us most obsessively and necessarily in that connection: in that system of meaning that only we
have discovered, and that we must exorcise, deal with or learn
from in ways equally private, equally haunting, equally difficult.
[1966]

III

The Poet Turns on Himself

BARNSTORMING FOR POETRY

I⊤ is a winter night in the Midwest, and a man is lying alone in a strange room. On the dresser, beside the complicated clock-radio that is supposed to wake him, there is an untidy bundle of railroad, bus, and airline schedules marked with a red pencil, and various notes to himself about how to get to bus and train stations and airports. He keeps opening his eyes in his sleep—or what amounts to it—and looking at his watch, turning it one way and another so that its thin hands can catch the cold light coming in across the snowy campus from the chapel tower. There is only one bus out of town, and it leaves at 4:30 in the morning.

It is time. He gets out of bed and stumbles toward the alarm; just as he reaches it, rock-and-roll music bursts into his face. Rather than fool with trying to shut it off, he pulls out the plug, feeling that he has had his revenge. He turns on the light and dresses, not quite able to believe he is where he is: some place in Wisconsin, where he has given a poetry reading at a small college; he is, in fact, in the middle of a tour of such readings.

So far—considering he is not Robert Frost or Dylan Thomas —he has had nothing to complain of as to the size and response of his audiences. Actually, they have been responsive to a degree he has come to think of as excessive and even manic, but he suspects that attendance at these affairs may be mandatory in some cases. Then, too, many of the schools, like this one, are far back in the country and there is nothing much to do. Still, he is pleasantly gratified at the turnouts, at the students who gather round him afterward, asking questions, pressing their manuscripts into his hands, telling him what is wrong with such and such a poem he has read, such and such a line, such and such a concept. He has never been lionized by anyone, not even his immediate family; but these small, repeated tastes of local notoriety are definitely agreeable, and he does his best to live up to them.

That, in fact, is his problem: the living-up-to, the giving them what they want, or might be expected to feel entitled to from a poet aside from the poems themselves. "Just be yourself," he told himself in the beginning. Ah, but *what* self? The self he has become on this trip bears but little relation to the self he left at home in the mind, say, of his wife. He has taken to doing some curious things. For example, he has acquired a guitar, which he carries about with him as though he were Carl Sandburg. He has not played the guitar for years, but he feels immediately all sorts of new and presumably poetic things happen to him each time he carries it to another campus. At the inevitable parties given after his readings, he plays one or two songs and then scuttles back into conversation, satisfied that he has done the something idiosyncratic that people are expecting and that, much more dangerous to psychological stability, he expects of himself.

He has several disadvantages to overcome. He is middle-aged, beginning to lose teeth and hair. He is ordinarily mild-mannered and agreeable, and secretly thinks of himself as rather colorless and uninteresting. He has written poems for years because he liked to write them, but he has never thought of them as participating in a public act, a kind of literary vaudeville. At the outset of the trip he had thought that the poems themselves would be enough; if they were good, and he read them well, he could collect his money at each stop with a clear conscience. But it is he who is not satisfied with *just* reading; it is not only poetry that is involved: it is the poet as well.

A strange madness took hold of him when he discovered at

the first reading that everything he said was noted and commented upon. Too, he *thinks* he heard a bearded student mutter
something discontented about "lack of fire" (or was it lack of
flair?), and at that moment the image of his great predecessor, the
only predecessor, Dylan Thomas, blazed up humiliatingly in the
front of his mind. The result of this was that he deliberately drank
twice as much liquor as he is accustomed to at the party after the
reading, waved his arms wildly about, said anything and everything that came into his head, insulted somebody—merciful
heavens, who on earth was it?—and had a terrible hangover the
next day.

Yet he has in some obscure way been a good deal better satisfied with himself, has drunk very nearly as much at all the six or
eight schools following that one, and is now looking forward to
acquiring the courage to get drunk *before* the reading. He is
exhausted and exalted as he has never been, and now, standing in
the center of a new reality—in this case a cold, sleepless room—
he looks at these things for the last time, picks up his bag and
manuscripts and his symbolic guitar, and goes out into the white
darkness.

There are few lights on the campus, and he is uncertain about
the instructions designed to get him to the bus station. Crossing
the campus on the one path he knows, he keeps reminding himself of what he is doing in this hamlet, lost somewhere in the
snows of northern Wisconsin: he is—eternal strangeness!—a
wandering singer, an American poet. When at last he reaches the
station, he discovers he is too early by twenty minutes. He sits
down, closes his eyes. Time is annihilated; the bus driver opens
the door. He stumbles aboard the panting bus and collapses.

When he wakes up, the bus is in the terminal in the next city.
He gets out and looks around for whoever is supposed to meet
him. There is no one but a priest, and finally it dawns on him
that the college he is to read at that night is denominational. He
goes up to the priest, who has in fact been sent to drive him out

to the college. "I couldn't believe you'd be the one I was looking for," the poet says in his new frankness. "I couldn't believe that you were, either," says the priest with equal candor.

In a station wagon they drive forty miles into the forest. At the college he is given a room in a cavernous building and told that he has an hour or two before dinner. He lies down on the bed, then gets up and paces back and forth. There is a skull on the table, and suddenly, at the sight of this *memento mori,* the great themes of poetry hit him squarely: the possibility of love and the inevitability of death. He has tried for years to formulate his relationship to these things and to say something about them. He takes out his three volumes of poetry and his manuscript of a fourth book, and, ever cognizant of his bodiless, staring audience and of the skull beneath his own skin, rearranges his evening's program around the themes of love and death.

He gives the best reading of his life, the one that all subsequent performances will have to be judged by. Realizing that all role-playing is shameful beside the feeling he experiences now, he has the sensation that his words are being received almost as things, and toward the end he comes to think that the things have the quality of gifts: disturbing gifts, perhaps, inept, inadequate gifts, but gifts just the same: he feels that he is giving something. And the grave, slightly puzzled, sympathetic faces take on expressions he is grateful for, indicating a particular favor conferred upon a stranger they will never see again, one who last night was not gracefully but disgracefully drunk and out of his element, and who now is half in another world with fatigue; one who has spent the most satisfying part of a long trip alone in a room with a skull.

In this reading, for once in his life, he *feels* a correct balance between what is on the page, put there by him at odd, beyond-himself moments, and . . . and the faces. In the middle of a phrase the losses endured by everyone every day—the negation of possibility that occurs each time we pass another human being in the street, in a bar (ah yes, he needs a drink badly), on the stairs of a building and never know him—come home. Who is that thin, serious boy with the crew cut? What is his life like? Where will he die? Who is the nun giving him a calm sense of purposeful life through her thick glasses? He finishes, stands staring for a moment, establishing them in his mind, and steps down.

The next morning he catches the bus at a reasonable hour and rides calmly back to the city. With a certain flair, now, he pulls out the packet of schedules. Something is wrong: he has forgotten that his one afternoon reading of the tour is to take place that day, and he has four hours to go seventy-five miles. The college seems to be all but inaccessible, there being no buses or trains until after the time of the reading. From the airless, close-packed, winter bus station he tries to call his contact at the college, but cannot reach him. He hails a cab and asks the fare to the town he is going to. It is more than he wants to pay, and, caught up by a daring all-or-nothing plan, he tells the driver to take him to the highway. He pays and gets out, scarcely knowing what he is doing, but feeling a little better at being pointed in the right direction. He is standing alone in the snow in a strange state, hitchhiking at the age of forty-five.

An hour goes by. He considers various alternatives, but they are all as absurd as the wish to grow wings. Besides, another kind of exhilaration has come over him, and he sings with white breath to the passing cars, thinking of the open road, the dear love of comrades, the hoboes of Hart Crane's *The Bridge.* Finally someone stops, a farmer, and takes him twenty miles down the road. The farmer turns off the highway and leaves him, and this time he really is in a deserted landscape, with dead corn in the fields, an inept scarecrow, and a few big birds hunched and puffed on the telephone wires. He is happy and grinning; he feels resourceful, foolish, and lucky. "America," he says aloud with powerful vagueness. "Poetry." A car stops. It is driven by a student at the college he is going to.

At the college he reads, sleeps. The next morning he takes a walk around the campus with a young student who is interested in Yeats's occult preoccupations, a curious subject to discuss in the healthy, farmerish atmosphere of this particular college.

Much rested, he gets on a train and rides a deserted parlor car to his next stop, where he is met as arranged and housed with a young professor who writes poems himself and is enthusiastic and companionable. He reads, has a drink at a faculty party, and goes to bed. He dreams he is a scarecrow in a field, and writes poems in his head all night. Some few phrases stay with him when he wakes. He notes them down and moves on to his next stop via local airline.

This is a girls' college, also far off in the country. He finds it a little ominous that the only other large institution in the town is the state insane asylum. Since he has forgotten to telegraph his arrival, no one meets him at the airport. He phones the head of the English department, is picked up. He is taken to a room in one of the girls' dormitories, which gives him an odd sensation indeed, only partially alleviated when he learns that he is next door to the house mother.

He eats dinner with the English department and the Writing Club in the student dining hall, in an unwearying, pulsing tide of female voices. There are many furtive amused glances at him, and he replies in kind. But he is uncomfortable, even desperate; he is sure he has not written any poetry that would appeal to girls, and he even entertains the idea of sneaking back to his room and dashing off a couple of things modeled on Walter Benton's *This Is My Belovèd*.

Perhaps, though, some recent poems about his children will do. He reads these quietly and has a distinct sense of quitting while he is ahead. The applause is long and loud, and when he steps down from the stage into a wave of feathery, sweatered girls, a memorable thing happens to him. One of them, not the one he would have picked to do such a thing, or picked at all, asks suddenly, "May I kiss you?" He agrees without thinking, and she does it with startling ardor.

The next place is a branch of a state university located in the industrial district of a large city. Though he is met at the bus station, it is plain that no one is much interested in his being there. Walking across campus, he hears a loud continuous noise as of revolutions and student demonstrations combined with assembly lines and riveting. To his astonishment, directly in front of the auditorium a lanky student is standing on the hood of a 1953 Buick with a John-Henry-type hammer in his hands, and, having bashed out the windows, is now engaged in beating in the top of the car with inaccurate gusto and many loud grunts. A crowd of muffled students cheers him on; it is a fund-raising scheme for some club or other.

All through the reading the hammering goes on. When an especially loud cheer comes in from outside he looks up, thinking momentarily that it is for him, but no: it is for an exhausted hammerer, or for a new one relieving him. He learns to time his words and lines to the hammer-strokes, and before he is finished he finds his poems, usually rather loose in rhythm, taking on a thumping, thundering kind of metric as he adjusts his delivery more and more to the inevitable banging. Privately he resolves to see if he can work something out in his poetry on this basis later on. What the hell, he thinks, this may be a major technical breakthrough for me. The accompaniment continues, he bellows louder and louder, and the flinching audience is with him to the end. In all, it is a strangely good occasion.

He leaves that night for another city where he has a friend he can stay with for a day or so. He flies in, watching the lights of the city.

The friend will drive him to the next engagement, which is the last. They start out, and take a wrong turn somewhere. On a highway complex as big as this one it is hard to get turned around. It begins to snow: traffic slows all around them for miles. Finally a lucky turn gets them off the freeway; they are not so far from the college as they thought, but he is already half an hour late for the reading. They reach the college, then the building. A crowd of students just coming from the auditorium sees him approaching with his ragged books and manuscripts. One whispers to another. Though he is a little afraid to, he admits who he is, and is instantly surrounded. Someone points him in a direction and he begins walking with students trailing him as though he were a messiah or a Beatle. He reaches a stage, mounts, looks at the last of all clocks with a certain condescending benevolence, and begins.

It is over. He relaxes with the friend in the city for a day and a night before flying home. He sees the people who sponsored his tour—editors of a venerable poetry magazine—has dinner with them, recounts some of his adventures. Everyone seems pleased by the way things have gone; there have even been some letters of appreciation from the schools. But he is still bothered by the difference between his touring self and his usual self. He has definitely been another person on this trip: more excitable and emotional, more harried, more impulsive. Yet he knows that these qualities will die out upon his arrival home and he is more than a little glad of it; they are too wearing, too hard on the nerves. He might live more vividly in this condition, but he cannot write in it. He must calm down and work. But on the aircraft aimed at last at his home, he feels also that such nervous excitement, such over-responsiveness to things, is probably the poet's part. Intensity, he murmurs, where have you been all my life.

He settles down for the sleep that will annihilate the miles, becoming an older and more dependable self, yet remembering the skull in the room, a plain girl's unexpected kiss, the student with the nine-pound hammer. For better or worse, he has been moving and speaking among his kind.

[1965]

NOTES ON THE
DECLINE OF OUTRAGE

I

To be a white Southerner in the mid-twentieth century is to realize the full bafflement and complexity of the human condition. It is not only to see parts of one's world fall irrevocably away, but to feel some of them, tenaciously remaining, take on an accusing cast that one would not have thought possible, and long-familiar situations assume a fathomless, symbolic, and threatening weight. It is also to feel the resentment, the old sense of outrage rise up again toward all those who are not Southerners—against those who would change the world which one's people have made, insisting that it conform to a number of principles with which no one could possibly argue, but which the social situation as it exists must be radically altered to fit. To the "average" Southerner, who, like the average person anywhere, does not think much about issues in the abstract—though abstractions are everywhere implicit in his conduct—the continuing and increasing pressure being brought upon the white South to "do something" about the Negro is felt simply as a return of the indignation that attended Reconstruction—a resolve that the white Southerner shall continue to exercise autonomy in his own affairs and shall resist conforming to the dictates (for that is how he conceives them) of others living in other parts of the country.

This resolve is indicated by any number of private and public rationalizations, but these in themselves are not as important as what they connote: the Southerner's belief that his self-determination is being sapped and bled away by forces that have neither his interests in mind nor an adequate knowledge of his basic situation in its day-to-day reality. Negroes, who heretofore had seemed to occupy a place in the social structure which was, as far as many white Southerners were concerned, as good as ordained by God, have now taken on an entirely new dimension, and it is especially troubling that this new dimension is simply that of their ordinary humanity, long deferred by a series of historical circumstances reaching back for hundreds of years and rooted in the greed and callousness of men long dead. It is also beginning to be shockingly apparent that, in the simplest, easiest, and most obvious way in the world, generations of men later than the slave traders and plantation owners have kept human beings essentially like themselves in a state of economic and social bondage scarcely to be believed, and have done so with absolutely no qualms or even any notice of what was in fact taking place, lulled within a kind of suspended judgment with respect to the Negro's humanity, which allowed him to exist only in a special way, limiting his experience and even his being to areas where they conformed, not only to the ideas about Negroes most congenial to the white Southerner's preconceptions about race, but to the white man's opinion of himself.

It is an even more terrible paradox that the very quality that has been obscured all this time—the Negro's ordinary, everyday humanness—is obscured even more thoroughly, now that he has become a symbol which concretizes the historical uneasiness of an entire people, pointing up, as nothing else in this country has ever done before, the fearful consequences of systematic and heedless oppression for both the oppressed and the oppressor, who cannot continue to bear such a burden without becoming himself diminished, and in the end debased, by such secret and cruel ways that he is never really sure of what is happening. No act of redress is possible for the thousands who have been spiritually maimed, to say nothing of the countless lives wasted on the hardest and most unrewarding kind of labor, amidst the most degrading and soul-breaking life situations that have ever existed in America.

All these things are now in the minds of Southerners; they are charged with hidden significance whose true import comes from history's inadvertent and almost poetic power of revelation; and they in turn charge innumerable personal relations—thousands of them each day—with the chagrin, the helplessness, and the indwelling terror that come from centuries of wrongdoing that those who began and fostered them never, incredibly, conceived as wrong, or at least not wrong enough to do anything about. This is absurd, one thinks. How could anyone fail to see the Southern Negro's situation as wrong, as completely, blindingly, hauntingly wrong? The point is that Southerners did not, or that they refused to see the life the Negro has been given for what it actually is, pleading historical causes, jackleg theories of race, economic considerations, and a good many other things— none of which, not even the cotton empire or the age-old power of money to purchase labor, has any permanent meaning before the fact that millions of people have served in utter hopelessness through no fault but that of their birth, and for no reason but that others, differently born, should benefit.

It is a problem which, to many, admits of no solution, but toward a solution of either a merely painful or a starkly terrible kind it appears to be moving. It is not too much to say that in the "Negro problem" lies the problem of the South itself. Because of it, people are wondering now, as never since the 1860's, "What does it mean to be a Southerner? What does the social and economic and cultural history of this part of the country mean to *me*, to my life?" Above all they ask, "What will happen now, and *how* will it happen?" Rather than deal in generalities, it is better to go back to the individual as he exists in a predicament in which these questions come implicitly into play, and to attempt to understand the manner in which he asks them, not of others, but of himself.

II

On a downtown corner of a Southern city in midsummer, a man, a youngish though not quite young man, is waiting for a bus. He is not used to riding on buses, as he has his own car: in truth, he dislikes buses now more than ever, for he is aware that they have recently become a great deal more than the groaning, clumsy vehicles they have always seemed to be. They have been transformed into small, uncomfortable rolling arenas wherein the forces hidden for a hundred years in the structure of his society threaten to break loose and play themselves out each time a bus pulls away from a corner. Here, a city injunction has just been passed permitting Negroes to occupy any empty seat they prefer. The bus that appears, however, is not tossing with conflict or running blood from the windows. As usual, the Negroes are sitting well toward the back, and, as usual, our man prepares to pick a seat toward the front, as much toward the front as possible, perhaps next to a thin man in a flowered sports shirt and steel-rimmed glasses.

But suddenly he realizes that quite another thing is now possible. Seized by a desperate logic and a daring he cannot and does not want to account for, he walks past this man and on into the section occupied by Negroes. As he passes the last of the whites he has a powerful sense of pure transgression which gives way immediately to a kind of guilty, clandestine joy even more powerful. It is the sense of crossing a boundary beyond which there will be no going back, and it has all the exhilaration and fear, all the intimations of possibility and danger that might be occasioned by passing a real frontier into a strange land, perhaps even into the country of an enemy.

But *what* enemy? And why an enemy? He sees only two immense Negro women, a man in overalls and a painter's cap, a mulatto girl in a white uniform, ten or twelve others of both sexes, so familiar as to be indistinguishable from each other, and a plump, tea-colored young man who holds a small, even lighter colored boy on his lap. None of these people seems to wish him ill, or to hold anything against him; yet he is more conscious of his own color at this moment than he ever remembers being, for he recognizes it in the light in which he is told the rest of the world regards it: the color of the unjust man, more damning than the whiteness of the leper. In spite of this, or more likely because of it, he takes a firm grip on the rail of the lurching bus and slides into the seat beside the plump man and his son. After all, has not the city edict, has not the Emancipation Proclamation, freed *him* as well as the Negro? He realizes only too well his intense self-consciousness about the meaning of his gesture; for it is purely that. At the same time, through an awesome silence, he hears his mind repeat every cliché about Negroes he has ever heard: "Would you want one living next door to you?" Or, coming not so much from himself as out of the very air he breathes, out of the tremendous sunlight itself: "Would you want your sister to marry one?"

Though he has heard these questions asked rhetorically all his life, he has never before entertained them at any real depth of interest. His sister has not married "one," and it is highly unlikely that a Negro will move in next door to him, for thus far zoning laws in his neighborhood have been rigidly maintained. Yet over and above the information asked for and the responses demanded by these questions, he is aware of a far more signficant thing: the spirit of outrage that surrounds the words, the assumption that even to *ask* the questions is outrageous, and that such a transgression is to be set right only with the collaboration of the questioned, whose most violent denial is needed to place things in their customary perspective again. He cannot imagine answering such questions in the affirmative; or, if he can barely imagine it, he is at the same time conscious of the withering climate of indignation that would attend the answers, an indignation more killing than any other he can think of, because it would include, in addition to that of his contemporaries, the infinitely more terrible condemnation of his own past.

At this moment he is very much aware of himself as a Southerner, and that he is in some way betraying someone or something, even though the impulse which brought him to his present seat on the bus may have been completely laudable, *sub specie aeternitatis.* Oddly enough, he cannot help feeling also a sharp upswing of defiant joy at remembering that he *is* a Southerner, a joy that in no way wishes to distinguish approval from disapproval, right from wrong, good from evil. He is of the people from whom the Army of the Confederacy was drawn, and this is and has always been a source of intimate personal strength to him. The lives of both his grandfathers are with him, he believes, whenever they need to be, and help him understand what men may mean to each other in a common cause, regardless of whether or not history labels the cause worthy of their effort. Yet nothing like Pickett's Charge, nothing like the Shenandoah campaigns of Stonewall Jackson exists, any longer, to give Southernness an atmosphere of accomplishment, destiny, and glory. Of the spirit that caught up the Confederate Army and made Jackson, Lee, and Jeb Stuart the demigods of his people, almost none remains, and what of it does still exist has no adequate channel through which to flow. Southern autonomy, qua Southern, now tends instead to come out in petty, vindictive acts of ill will toward the Negro, and he wants no part of that.

All this he knows, but at the same time he recognizes the fact that the South still stands for . . . for something. He has read W. J. Cash, and so has been told the "truth" about the much-advertised codes of Southern honor, the cult of Southern womanhood, the Southerner's characteristic extroversion and his "habit of command," the cultural shallowness of the nineteenth-century South, and so on. He knows the verdict of history on his people. He knows one more thing about history too: that it has trapped the Southern white just as securely in his complex of racial attitudes as it has trapped the Southern Negro in his deplorable social, physical, and psychological environment. And he knows that with the increase of industry and "business," with their attendant influx of thousands of people each month from other parts of the country, the "solidarity" of the South, in manners as well as in attitudes about race, is breaking down more and more rapidly, and that when the older patterns of behavior are gone, there will be nothing to put in their place save the empty money-grubbing and soul-killing competitive drives of the Northern industrial concerns. He knows that, as a Southerner, he has only a few things left to him: the intonation of his voice, an appetite for certain kinds of cooking, a vague familiarity with a few quaint folkways far off in the mountains, and his received attitude toward the Negro; and that of these the only one important as a rallying point for his Southernness, as an effective factor in producing sectional assent, as a motivating force in political action, is the last.

It is abundantly apparent that his people do not want their sense of being Southerners to die. This may be the reason that there is, all around him, a tremendous, futile yearning back toward the time of the Civil War, when something concrete could be done, when a man could pick up a gun and *shoot* at something, in a setting of purpose and meaning. In the light of the Supreme Court ruling on segregation, the Civil War has come to seem no longer a defense of slavery and of states' rights, as Southerners had reluctantly begun to admit, but of the South against the encroachment of Others, and so heroic—the battle for one's home and one's mind against the invaders. Perhaps because of this his own brother is obsessed by the Civil War in a particularly curious way. He is a collector of relics. Accompanying his brother to the battlefield sites that surround the city, as well as to some others farther off in the country, he has walked slowly through farms, climbed over breastworks, waded through stream beds in the fraught, stammering heat of August, swinging the flat metal plate of his brother's mine detector over acres of weeds and brush in search of the war buried here for a hundred years a few inches beneath the pine straw. He has heard the lifeless and desperate cry of rusted metal, and dug with a totally inexplicable enthusiasm and dread, perhaps unearthing a piece of a parrot shell, a Minié ball, part of a canister container, a belt buckle, a branding iron, a corroded mess tin, and once even a sword transformed by the earth and time into a long, warped shape like a huge burned matchstick, whose brass handle, under polishing, later took on its soft, fiery, original sheen. But looking at the decrepit guns on the walls of his brother's house, at the golden, breadlike patina of rust on the thousand fragmentary metals of destruction, and pondering on the unearthly, leper-white Minié balls and canister shot, he knows that the continuing power of the Civil War is not in these things but in its ability to dramatize and perpetuate a feeling about a way of life. It is actually a symbol of his people's defense of their right to be Southerners, and as such is more effective now than it has been at any other time during his own life.

As he sits at the present moment, however, he is not a Confederate soldier in whose hands these weapons are new and bright. He is merely a man moving slowly in a public conveyance through a heat-shimmering city built on land where such swords and bayonets have lain underground for a century. May he not take this fact itself as a new beginning place for self-definition? Why may he not simply be a man, like and unlike others, living from day to day as best he can? Yet as he asks this question he is struck by a peculiarly terrifying thought. Can the past so easily be denied? Whether the past has been right or wrong, intelligent or mindless, good or evil, it is still the past, the only one, and it cannot change. Because of it, he is who he is; of the subjects occasioned by his reverie, every one wells up out of history— the history of his people as Southerners. Yet may there not be feelings, states of being which underlie and do not depend exclusively upon the past?

On the pretext of looking out the window, he glances at his

companions. The young Negro father has got over his initial self-consciousness, which, to tell the truth, was not even in the beginning very pronounced. He has set his light porkpie hat on the back of his head and is playing with his tiny son, who, to the other man in the seat, looks exactly like every other small Negro boy he has ever seen, except for being dressed in a white shirt and short, dark blue wool pants with halters, and very bright black shoes. The man is now sticking out his wide pink tongue at his son, who swipes at it. They are both laughing. Well, what does one do next, if one is obviously looking, not out the window at all, but at another person no more than a foot away? "That's a fine boy you've got there," the young man does in fact say, and for the first time the Negro looks at him, a little shyly but squarely. In his gaze there is, thank God, no real mistrust, though he ends his reply with "sir." And there the conversation ends.

But something has happened, and it brings with it a new flood of questions more demanding than any others the young man has asked himself. What, actually, is his attitude toward Negroes, over and above gestures, over and above received opinions? And how does he really feel about the South—the actual South he lives in, that is, stand as it may in the shadow of that other, dead, undead, imagined, magnificent, and tragic South? And how are these questions related? For it is certain that they *are* related in some profound and fundamental way. He must admit immediately that he has always concurred, or as good as concurred, in the assumptions about Negroes that his forebears and contemporaries have had, and have. The unspoken rationale underlying these assumptions is that, inexplicably but in perfect keeping with the natural order of things, Negroes have been endowed with human shape and certain rudimentary approximations of human attitudes, but that they possess these only in a kind of secondary or inferior way, and, to the end of having this be readily recognizable, have also been given a skin pigmentation and a facial bone structure which make their entire status apparent at a glance, and even from a very great distance. Spoken or unspoken, these are the beliefs that have assigned every Negro, from the lowest hod carrier up through the ministry and the medical profession, his place in the Southern scheme of things.

The notion that the Negro must be "acclimated" slowly to the Caucasian world, now advanced among some Southerners as a genteel refinement on the above idea, is in reality not nearly so honest an appraisal of an actual state of mind as the more fundamental assumption from which it proceeds. As a result of the practices rather than the "theories" concerning the Negro, the worst possibility, the most fearful dream the white Southerner can have—or at least that the young man can imagine himself as having—is to have been born a Southern Negro. As he is, as he has existed among the circumstances of his life, he has always rather liked Negroes, in an offhand, noncommittal way, though it is certain that he has never formed a deep man-to-man (or, for that matter, man-to-woman) relation with one. Yet he realizes that he has just as surely always participated in the popular belief that the Negro is more or less a child, happy and easily diverted, or, more properly, somewhere between a child, a pet, and a beast of burden, but prone to flare up, especially among his own kind, into a terrible jungle violence. The Negro is also commonly thought to be the victim of a lust so powerful that before it all laws, all social codes and restrictions are as nothing, and during these seizures may leap from a sheltering fringe of bushes, like a wild shadow cast from Africa, and attack a solitary white woman working in a field, a girl on her way home from high school. He knows that there is enough misconstruction placed upon certain aspects of the Negro's life in his past and present environment to give these assumptions the outward cast or appearance of an entire truth, and that any isolated instance of Negro-white rape, for example, is enough to corroborate and intensify this feeling, and the others which attend it, all over the South, and to bring halfway to the surface disturbing dreams of all-out racial conflict and an intolerable sense of impending anarchy which must at all costs be put down.

But where does he, the questioner, stand in these matters? What *does* he believe? Does he believe that Negroes are essentially children? No; he does not. He believes that the Negro is a man like any other, woefully stunted and crippled by his circumstances but with amazing reserves of tolerance and humor, and a resilience that should eventually take its place among the most remarkable shows of human adaptability in history. Does he then believe in denying the Negro the social and economic concomitants of his humanity? No; he does not. There is no possible justification of such a denial. Yet why then does he *act* as if he believed, exactly to the extent that the veriest redneck or country politician rabble-rouser believes, *all* these admittedly indefensible ideas? Well, because . . . because he is a Southerner, and these attitudes are part of his past, of his "heritage" as a Southerner, and he suspects that if he relinquishes them, he also gives up his ancestry, to say nothing of severing an essential bond between himself and his contemporaries, all of whom are struggling in various ways to preserve segregation.

At present, with an impersonal materialism visiting its final ravages on the only place on earth he has ever really belonged, he does not want the *sense* of this place, the continuity of time as it has been lived, the capacity of the past to influence and if possible to assist him in thought and action, to disappear entirely. With others of his generation, he has wandered a great deal, and now, staring forward into the comfortable abyss of middle age, he wants, *really* wants, to regrow his roots, if such a thing is yet possible, in the soil from which he sprang. He does not believe the South to be merely a matter of climate and fried chicken; he understands it as a place where certain modes of thought are mutually held without the necessity of constant analysis and definition. One of these, and increasingly the main one, is the white Southerner's attitude toward the Negro, as the

Negro exists in *his* "place." What that place is, however, he does not yet want to examine. Setting aside momentarily the "Negro question," what of the South itself, the South that he remembers? In what ways has it made him what he is?

Of the world in which he grew up, he can honestly recall only a very few things which he would identify as characteristically Southern, but these are powerfully centered in his consciousness. He has lived elsewhere in the United States, for example, and he can think of no other region where the family, on out through distant cousins, nephews, great-uncles and aunts, has such actual solidity and warmth as it does in the South. It is not that members of Northern and Midwestern families care for each other any the less, so much as it is that there seems to be in the South (or seemed in those years to be) a more vivid and significant belief that blood ties underlie and bolster the human affections in a way not to be explained by either logic or environment. There seemed, there still seems to him, something indisputably right about this. Though he has many relatives for whom he does not greatly care, he has always valued even those as part of the family association, the great chain of being that attached him truly, by ties surpassing in power anything the mere mind of man can invent, to other human beings in a group.

Something of this feeling extends outside the circle of kinship, also. A good deal of snobbery notwithstanding, it is hard for a Southerner to feel anything but a sense of basic comradeship with other Southerners, regardless of their relative social status. And this too seems valuable. To be told, with all the authority of the United States Supreme Court, that some of the beliefs proceeding from this community are wrong, and have been wrong from the beginning, for all the time the community has been alive, seems not only monstrous but preposterous as well, and appears to have more than a tinge of the *hubris* of man trying to set himself up against the existing nature of things, and to dictate by abstractions rather than by the realities in which people live. The sense of community and belonging is probably the most important single good that a society can bestow; it has been strong in the South, though including, as it manifestly does, a number of grievous injustices; it has been strong, and now it is fast disappearing; and he is dismayed and even frightened to see it go. He remembers something, long since thought forgotten, he once read in a book in France, laboriously puzzling out the sentences with the aid of a glossary. Perhaps it was in one of the *Journals* of Julien Green, himself of American Southern parentage: "The South did not really lose the Civil War until around 1920, when it consented to follow the lead of the North." With this statement he heartily concurs. That is, he concurs emotionally. As soon as he examines what might have happened, and probably would have happened, if the South had *not* consented to follow the lead of the North, he sees that the present trend of industrialism and business was not only more or less inevitable, but probably even for the best, dreadful as some of its results have been.

Could the South, in fact, have remained a farming region? With machines doing more and more of the farm labor and consequently decreasing the number of agrarian jobs, how could a population consisting entirely of farmers have been supported? Or should the South deliberately have turned its back on the machine, and insisted upon using the modes of labor, transportation, and distribution of a hundred, of a hundred and fifty years ago? Can one forget that a machine, the cotton gin, helped to create and maintain the infinitely rich cotton empire of the Old South? How then have the machine and not have it? How change and not change? How in all conscientiousness deny advances in medicine, public health, education, to say nothing of agriculture? Should the South have willfully turned itself into an enclave of clannish, half-educated farmers, hopelessly outmoded in every phase of contemporary life, even in the one profession which they knew and lived by?

Obviously not. To insist upon such artificial means to preserve a few admittedly desirable features of family and community life is to ignore everything in the human makeup that moves and wants to improve itself and the conditions among which it exists. There is no compromise between the old modes of Southern life and "progress," a word which no one likes, but which one must inevitably use. With the machine, and the shifting and mixing of populations it encourages, the sense of place is attenuated, and with it the sense of belonging by right to a given segment of the earth, held in common with other human beings to whom one is tied by the immense force of the past, by the lives of forebears who knew and in their time lived on the same part of the earth, who fought for it, who are buried in it, and who, somehow, seem still to be brooding over and watching the ground which they possessed in a profundity now become unattainable to their heirs.

Nowhere else in this country, not even in New England, is the ancestor held in so much real reverence as he is in the South—his opinions, his acts, his idiosyncrasies, his *being*. Consequently, nowhere else is his spirit, his ghost, so powerful, disturbing, and influential. "Why, your grandfather Tom would turn over in his grave if he thought . . ." or, "What would your dead mother think, if she could see you now?" Questions like this, perhaps more than any the living could ask, require answers. Well, what *would* his dead mother—or, worse still—what would his grandfather Swift think if he *could* see him now, sitting in the same seat in a bus with a Negro? His grandfather's first reaction would be, he is sure, incredulity, and then . . . and then . . . outrage. "What in the world has happened to you, boy?" he would no doubt ask, in a rising, irresistible, and particularly terrible tide of resentment, and a bewilderment even more terrible. He feels a quick, deep flush of shame thinking of this; he has loved and honored his grandfather; he loves and honors him still.

Of the old man he retains several images of tremendous depth and authority. The most important of these is simply a recollection of sitting on the porch of a house in the country, listening to his grandfather tell of his experiences in the troop of General

John B. Gordon. For a moment, in speaking of a battle, he had rested his steady and very old hand on the child's shoulder and said, "I wish you could have been there with me." He can still feel the touch of his grandfather's hand. And he has always liked to think that in some way he *was* with his grandfather that day, and that he did not falter, but acted with the unhesitating courage and authority he is sure his grandfather must have displayed, not because the situation required it, but because his life did. Never has he had so much reverence for anyone else as for his grandfather Swift, the kindest, gravest old man he can remember, or would ever want to remember, whose manners proceeded from the most scrupulous consideration for others with whom he came in contact, but even more from a kind of climate of courtesy which belonged to the world that had created him. He remembers also his grandfather's behavior with Negroes: considerate, but admitting of no argument and no redress. So far as he had been able to tell, the Negroes accepted and even welcomed these conditions, and he recalls the uncontrollable grief of many of them as they stood by his grandfather's coffin.

These memories are now intolerably confused. He asks himself if the good of his grandfather's life, and of the kind of life which produced his grandfather's character, were not inextricably entangled with attitudes which, rightly seen, are and have always been indefensible, inhuman, corrupt, and corrupting. It hardly matters that such attitudes have been implicit in human affairs ever since the first primitive man realized that it would be more profitable and considerably easier for him if he could get another to perform certain tasks instead of having to do them himself; he is occupied at the moment mainly with the knowledge that his grandfather's indignation, his *outrage*, could he see his grandson now (and in this land of powerful and eternal ghosts, does he not see?), would be limitless, and would include a betrayed, bewildered, and unbearable sadness. The young man understands himself as the victim of a cruel and fathomless paradox, a dilemma between the horns of which only a god could survive and still retain his identity. But perhaps he has led himself into an absurd train of logic. Is it in fact true that he cannot really be the grandson he wishes to be without seeing Negroes as his grandfather saw them? Can he truly be his grandfather's kinsman, torn as he is by a thousand doubts that never would have troubled those of his grandfather's generation?

To state the issues in this way is undoubtedly to insist upon their extremes, but he knows that sooner or later the public fruit of what is now opinion must ripen, and that in the end he will have to go on record as being of a certain mind, having taken a stand. After the Supreme Court decision on segregation, and with the admission of Negroes to buses and streetcars on an equal footing with whites, with their entry into white residential areas and private clubs and eating places, and, above all, into the public schools, he knows he will have to assert himself one way or the other on the Question. He needs no one to remind him of the consequences of the position he may take; if he sides with Negroes instead of against them, he will have helped as effectively as he could ever hope to do to kill the South and lay it in its grave.

Yet he is, after all, not his grandfather. He recognizes only too well the distance of his fall, the gulf between his grandfather's character and his own. Still, he does not in all honesty believe that he can by an effort of will, even for the sake of retaining his identity as a "Southerner," take opinions and attitudes for his own which are not his, and against which his whole nature as a sentient and rational man rebels. He cannot, either, regard himself as a "neutral," to be which is an ultimate impossibility. Then where, exactly, *does* he belong?

As nearly as he can tell, he sees his position, and the South's, more in terms of an image, a vision or daydream, than in a logical formulation. It is a banal image, but for him at least it is endowed with the capacity to define the situation in just such a set of clear-cut and dramatic opposites as a subtler, more considered approach might fail to furnish. It is the image of a wall, an old, high, crumbling but still massive wall along the top of which are set sharp, rusty spikes and broken bottles. He has actually seen such a wall, not in the southern United States, but somewhere in Europe. However, in his mind he sees himself, his family, and his ancestors living on one side of the wall. He lives on the side he does because his forebears have lived there, because he has been joined to them by the divine accident of birth, and because they built the wall. On the other side, there because they were once brought and purchased like beasts, in indescribable poverty and humiliation which they have learned by their own means to turn into a kind of virtue accessible to none but them, live Negroes. This is the Negro's "place," the place in which he must stay to be allowed his identity by those who determine the forms and limits which that identity may take.

Through the closely guarded door in the wall come certain Negroes, under all but constant surveillance of whites. Through it, in point of fact, and under this constant scrutiny, come very nearly all Negroes at one time or another, and most of them every day—the men to work at menial, badly paid jobs, tearing up and laying down railroad track, driving trucks, lifting heavy weights, running elevators, digging, piling, sweating, grunting, and heaving, with amazing musculature and unquestioning patience; the women to wash clothes, to look after white children, to serve the tables and clean the houses of the whites. At night they return through the wall, and the door is closed. Behind the wall, what happens, when the Negro is once again inside the one poor world he can call his: when he is "in his place"?

The young man has never had more than a fragmentary and inadequate notion of what lay behind the wall, in the easily violated world of the American Southern Negro, but he feels continually the human force trapped and maimed there. He knows that the Negro's place is squalid, dark, and huddled, and he suspects it is filled with an undercurrent of violence scarcely to be borne. When in high school, and drawn there by some obscure, compulsive reason, he spent part of a Saturday night in the emergency ward of a city hospital, and watched the attendants bring in the victims of that violence, shot in the belly at close range with shotguns, slashed with razors, gored and spitted and gouged with ice picks and pocketknives, beaten with pokers, bleeding, unconscious, or moaning slowly and hopelessly, accompanied by women, relatives, and even children. Somewhere among this background, among the locked-together, filthy shacks and the unseen menace of Saturday night and its duels with straight razors and bread knives, the man sitting next to him is attempting to raise a family in decency, and, yes, in love.

Upon what tremendous power does this man draw, to be able to play with his child here in perfect unselfconsciousness, with no apparent resentment toward anyone, content in his own being and in the small fact of his son? Or is the Negro, in this light, simply the victim of another's self-abasing sentimentality? Is there and has there been at the very heart of the South, all these years, such a source of unused intelligence, unwanted friendship, thwarted and never-defeated affection as would make one catch one's breath even to think of? Yes; and nothing has thwarted these possibilities so much as the zealous guardianship of Southern uniqueness and identity, admittedly in some ways a good, but not *the* good. The South, once crippled beyond humiliation and now clinging to its prejudices as the last vestige of its autonomy, its irreplaceable sense of destiny and glory, is a South he does not believe should be preserved at all costs—that is, at the cost of condemning millions more like the man beside him to lives of the most brutal and hopeless degradation.

For all these reflections, he himself is not any the less a Southerner than he has always been. He is by no means sure that traces of what he has been raised to look upon as his "natural" advantages over Negroes will not remain with him for the rest of his life, do what he will to get rid of them. Not for a moment does he entertain the notion that these prejudices are just, fitting, or reasonable. But neither can he deny that they belong to him by inheritance, as they belong to other Southerners. Yet this does not mean that they cannot be seen for what they are, that they cannot be appraised and understood. The greatest danger, he believes, resides in the assumption that there is no reason to struggle against such prejudices, since they have been closely woven into the very fabric of Southern reality for at least a hundred and seventy-five years. Again, where does this leave him? He is quite convinced that it is just as wrong to love a man solely because he is black as it is to hate him solely because he is black. If there is a solution to the South's dilemma it must come from the individual, or rather from a number of personal relationships, each composed of a Negro and a white who have discovered (the Negro as well as the white, for he has much to learn of the white in any role other than that of master) the common basis for their lives as men, a thing more fundamental than any environment or set of social customs could supply.

With the practical means by which this kind of relationship might be fostered he is as yet unconcerned. It may begin with as simple a thing as a conversation on a bus. In order for this to come about, of course, it is first necessary that it be made possible for the Negro and white in question to sit together on a bus. The basis for such legislation as would bring this about, it is to be hoped, is that by such means both Negro and white can begin to comprehend their likenesses as men more readily, and that their differences may begin to lose the importance that they have had. Yet legislation is completely self-defeating if such is not the outcome, and if "civil rights" simply set the Negro up as an out-and-out enemy, to be despised, flouted, and openly disdained, where hitherto he had been tolerated, so long as he remained "in his place." Legislation is undoubtedly involved in the answer, but legislation is of no value whatever without goodwill and the part that must be played by the real and not the advertised heart.

He is glad that he is not amazed by his own feelings at this moment, and that the thought of his grandfather's outrage is not so saddening and terrible as it had seemed at first. He is glad that he has communicated on a human level, though briefly and as though across an immense gulf, with the young Negro man and his son. To extend his private emotions into a social panacea is not within his strength, and he has no wish to do so, especially since such an attempt might well destroy the personal and so the only value of those emotions. He believes, however, that if such feelings are possible to him, they are to others also. He laughs a little ruefully as he discovers that all the time he has been thinking he has been murmuring to himself, as a semi-unconscious accompaniment, "The past is dead, the past is dead."

But even as he realizes what he is saying, he knows that it is not true. The past is never entirely dead, nor should it be disowned or forgotten. His powerful and perhaps foolish pride in the military effort of the Confederacy is not dead, nor is the memory of his grandfather. The human insufficiency of the Southern "cause" in no way diminishes the steady courage and devotion to each other of his forebears, nor do the racial beliefs of his grandfather destroy his kindness, his seriousness, his quaint and marvelous honesty, courtesy, and directness. Perhaps his grandfather would have been an even better man had he gone among the Negro slaves like Christ, preaching the gospel of freedom, but as it is, he has been good enough; he has been a far better man than his grandson in every way but this. And is the grandson's behavior, even here, superior? If so, how? It is probably true that he will retain at least to some degree some of the attitudes he has inherited with his way of life. But he can now separate them and attain a partial objectivity, and so a partial mastery over them, which his grandfather had never seen any reason to do. If he cannot quite envision a cocktail party composed of Southern Negroes and whites, all enjoying each other's company as if they were all white, or all Negro, and if he still flinches at the idea of Negro-white intermarriage, he can at least begin to recognize the common humanity of himself and the young man sitting beside him, though their differences, both as to racial heritage and countenance, may still appear, and be, enormous.

When the Negro and his son get up to leave the bus, the young man, no more self-consciously than might be expected, raises his hand in good-bye, and the Negro smiles, no more self-consciously than might be expected. A few blocks farther on, the young man gets off and enters his office building, harboring a bargain with himself that he knows he cannot possibly keep in all its implications. But the core of what he has come to believe is not an illusion, he suspects. He tells no one about it, for he correctly assumes that such things must be entirely personal and freely arrived at to be valuable. He goes in to work for a firm almost all of whom are Northerners, the products of forces other than those which have shaped him and brought about his reverie. He knows in a way they do not even suspect that most of the uniquely Southern traditions and characteristics he loves (and that they, occasionally, joke with him about in a vague, uninvolved fashion) cannot continue to exist without the social milieu, the entire complex of attitudes and mutually held opinions that nourished them, since social customs are not subject to the tampering of sociologists in their efforts to promote the desirable aspect of mores and eliminate the undesirable. The best he can do, he reflects, is to go outward toward persons whom he respects, admires, and likes, "regardless of race, color, or creed."

In his case, given his time, his background, and the temper of unrest that exists in the South, this may well be as destructive a thing as he could do, for whatever Negroes he may wish to know as well as for himself. But he must believe that in the end it will not be destructive, and so he must take the consequences, also, of believing that in this place where he was born and where he will probably die, where the Negro must become either a permanent enemy or an equal, where in one form, one body, unsteadily balanced, live the ex-slave, the possible foe, and the unknown brother, it can be a greater thing than the South has ever done to see that the last of these does not die without showing his face.

[1961]

THE POET TURNS ON HIMSELF

WHEN I was in high school thirty years ago, I had courses in literature and memorized a number of poems, parts of which I can still remember, although I seldom do. From the class in poetry I went to another class in the basement of the high school, which was called Manual Training and purported to teach us how to work wood lathes, do a little light carpentry, weld, pour metals, and perform other similar tasks which I have not had occasion to repeat since that time. Then, however, I could not help being struck by the contrast between what we had been doing in the poetry class and the materials and skills—the means and the tangible results—of our work in Manual Training and, like every other American boy, I developed a strong bias in favor of learning how to *do* something, of being able to make something, of having at least in some degree a skill that paid off in "measurable entities."

To a certain extent I still have this prejudice, as I believe many American poets do: we are such a thoroughly pragmatic people that intangibles, such as spirit, "soul," or even good taste, are always a little embarrassing to acknowledge or discuss. Yet even in my high school days I also began to be aware of a connection

—a very disturbing and apparently necessary one—between words in a certain order and the events of my own life. When I was in the Service in the South Pacific shortly thereafter and first heard the phrase "sweat it out" applied in a context where I *was* sweating it out—an artillery barrage—there blazed up in my mind, for the first time fully there, the idea of perfectly expressive language, for sweating it out was exactly what we were doing under those palm logs: there was nothing else we could do. I believe I responded to this phrase neither more nor less strongly than the other men in that hole with me; it was a phrase all of us understood equally well, each with his own temperament, without the need for commentary.

From this incident and a few others like it stems my interest in language and in its peculiar use which we—or at least I—call poetry. Occasionally, very occasionally, I would hear another phrase in popular speech, in the argot of the army, in a fortunate sentence in a newspaper (sometimes even in a misprint) that seemed to me to have this same unforeseeable but *right* correlation between lived time—experience—and words, but it was only years later that I recognized, very slowly, that this quality I was seeking more and more was poetry. The realization came to me that the highest concentration of language employed in this way was in the work of those very writers who had seemed so utterly useless to me when I was forced to study them in high school.

I eased into poetry, over a course of many years, by some such route. As a writer of poetry I began comparatively late, around my twenty-fourth year. I came to poetry with no particular qualifications. I had begun to suspect, however, that there is a poet—or a kind of poet—buried in every human being like Ariel in his tree, and that the people whom we are pleased to call poets are only those who have felt the need and contrived the means to release this spirit from its prison. As soon as I began writing I knew that I had the need, but that the means were not immediately forthcoming. I knew nothing whatever of poetic technique, of metrics, prosody, stanzaic construction, and to a certain extent I still consider those things—all the things that Herbert Read calls "the bag of monkey-tricks of English poetry"—as secondary to something else which I can only define, using one of the words I most despised in my younger days, as the spirit of poetry: the individually imaginative or visionary quality.

The first poem I wrote that had anything good in it—anything that I had seen for myself—was, I think, a description of football players dressing in a locker room. It seemed to me that their body-hair was *dry*—very dry-looking—and I put this into the poem, although against my better judgment, since it was a decidedly unbeautiful detail and at that time I wanted very much to write "beautiful" poems. When I looked at what I had put down on paper, I could see immediately that this line, poor as it was, had a quality of observation and of immediacy not to be found in the rest of the poem, which was derived from half a dozen other poets I had been reading. At that unlikely time I began to see what poetry would have to be for me and came by the idea that words, once placed in a certain order, will stay where they have been put and say what one tells them to say.

But what did I want to tell them to say? Very slowly I gravitated toward another idea which, like the other, has never left me: the belief in the inexhaustible fecundity of individual memory. When I examined my own memory, I found that certain images stood out in my mind and recurred to me at odd times, as if seeking something, perhaps some act of understanding, from me. Some recollections seemed more important than others, without my being able to tell why. Later, I saw that these incidents, the more important ones, not only were potential raw material for the kind of poetry I wanted to write, but were in fact the principal incidents in my life: those times when I felt most strongly and was most aware of the intense reality of the objects and people I moved among.

Recently I was delighted to read, in the work of a French

poet, Patrice de la Tour du Pin, an account of this poet's similar conclusions. La Tour du Pin confirms in me the belief that the isolated episodes and incidents of a human life make up, in the end, a kind of sum, a continuous story with different episodes, and that these moments of natural responsiveness show what he is and in a sense explain him; in the case of a poet they are not so much what he writes but what he *is*. If I were to arrange my own poems in some such scheme, chronologizing them, they would form a sort of story of this kind, leading from childhood in the north of Georgia through high school with its athletics and wild motorcycle riding, through a beginning attempt at education in an agricultural college, through World War II and the Korean War as a flyer in a night-fighter squadron, through another beginning at college, this time completed, through various attempts at a valid love affair culminating in the single successful one known as "marriage," through two children, several deaths in the family, travels, reflections, and so on.

The poet as well as the man is always a little shocked—though he hopes that at forty-five his story is not near its conclusion—to find that his story will most likely never be told in any other way than that in which he is telling it, and that when he is gone it is the only story he will ever have. In the end, however, he will settle for that, for just those conditions: underlying everything he writes is the dual sense of being glad to be alive to write that particular poem and of outrage at the possibility of the loss of all the things that have meant much to him—outrage that these personal, valuable things could ever be definitively lost for anyone. Beneath his words is this sense of battling against universal dissolution, of the loss of all he and other men have been given as human beings, of all they have loved and been moved by.

All this I felt, though very dimly at the beginning. I had some things that I wanted to write about; I had certain ways of feeling about them: about war, about love and sex, about athletics, about being a Southerner, about hunting and flying and canoeing, about the flight of birds and the movement of animals and the feeling of swimming in the presence of fish. But there seemed to be no language for writing about these things in any way which would do them the kind of justice I believed they deserved. I read a lot of poets, trying to find something I could use. Though I responded strongly to many of these poems, there were a great many that I did not respond to at all, even though I felt I should. I responded to these, in fact, no more than I had done in high school; no more than I do now.

I was distressed at the license that many poets claimed for themselves and which, I thought, allowed a great deal of highly dubious material to be brought into poems. For the live feel and delivered personality of one good phrase there seemed to be hundreds of poems built out of literary lumber: hundreds of dead, period-style poems indistinguishable from one another, the fodder of classrooms. Very early in the game I knew I wanted to avoid writing like that, like those poems. I was then, without knowing it, involved in the question of style and with that I wrestled for a long time—am still wrestling.

I had in the beginning a strong dislike of rhyming poems, for the element of artificiality is one of the characteristics of poetry I most distrust, and I have always had trouble distinguishing between artificiality and the traditional modes and methods of verse; for a time I was convinced that craft and artifice were the same thing. At the same time I also had a secret suspicion that Whitman, Lawrence, the Imagists, and others were cheating, absolving themselves from the standing problems and difficulties of verse. But I found, unlike so many others, that the qualities of poems which seemed to me poetic—*essentially* poetic—were not in the least dependent on whether or not they occurred in poems which rhymed. I also discovered that the restrictions imposed by rhyme led me away from what I had intended to say. Other writers have since told me—citing Valéry and others—that significant discoveries are made through the attempt to satisfy such restrictions and that as often as not one ends up as a result with a better poem than one anticipated. Doubtless this is true, and it is also true that certain poets, certain kinds of creative minds, are helped enormously by the support they receive from such sources. Nevertheless, such a practice did not seem right for me; I felt continually carried past my subject, carried around it, sometimes close to it but never in it in the way I wished to be in it.

I saw that I was faced with a kind of choice and that it was an important choice: should I continue to try to satisfy the conditions of rhyming English verse, or should I sacrifice rhyme and try to come to terms with my subjects in some other way? I decided to do the latter and have used rhyme in very few poems since. Although I didn't care for rhyme and the "packaged" quality which it gives even the best poems, I did care very much for meter, or at least rhythm. I have always liked strongly cadenced language and the sound of words in a line of verse is to me a very important part of its appeal. I read a good many manuals and textbooks and treatises on prosody, some of which were interesting, but none of them helped me to get the sound I wanted. Most of the material I read on metrics concluded that the systematic use of anapests and dactyls tends to monotony, and I accepted this judgment on faith and continued to try to work with the customary English iambic line.

Yet now and then I began to hear lines of verse, lines without words to them, that had what was to me a very compelling sound: an unusual sound of urgency and passion, of grave conviction, of inevitability, of the same kind of drive and excitement that one hears in a good passage of slow jazz. I thought that perhaps if I kept listening to those sounds and found satisfactory words for them, this strong carrying rhythm might help restore to the poems something of the feeling of formal completeness that I had sacrificed when I decided against using rhyme, and at the same time it might allow the poems a certain sense of self-determination which the straitjacket of rhyme did not seem to me to allow. It was not until later that I thought to analyze the metrical basis of the sounds I kept hearing at odd times—when stopped at traffic lights, when walking in the early morning, when playing tennis or hunting in the woods of north Georgia—and discovered that they were anapestic.

I sat down at the typewriter one afternoon in an American business office and wrote:

> All dark is now no more.
> This forest is drawing a light.
> All Presences change into trees.
> One eye opens slowly without me.
> My sight is the same as the sun's

I was very much excited by this, for it had something of what I wanted: a strange, incantatory sound, a simplicity that was direct without being thin, and a sense of imaginative urgency that I had never been able to get into verse before. It was something new for me; it satisfied and excited me at the same time and I abandoned work on everything else I was doing, including office work, to finish it. When I completed it I began to write other poems in the same way, starting with a subject—often very vaguely defined—and letting rhythms develop out of it, aided, no doubt, by years of guitar playing, and then supplying what I thought were the right words to inject the subject into the cadences that now seemed to be running in my mind endlessly, not stopping even when I was asleep. I saw at once—or rather I *heard* at once—when I began to have this kind of relationship to sound, language, and subject, that the anapest needn't always result in the monotonous, slugging, obtrusive singsong that it has in the poems of Edgar Allan Poe, Robert Service, Kipling, and others. I found that the anapest was as capable of interesting variation as any other kind of line; in fact, as the iamb itself.

Along with the rhythmical experiments, I also found that what I was working toward was a very stripped kind of simplicity in verse; what I really wanted to be able to do was to make effective *statements*. I began to use short lines, usually having three accents or beats, because I wanted to say one thing—hopefully, one memorable thing—in each line: one thing that would make its own kind of impression and would also connect with other single things, one per line, and so form a whole poem. In the poem I have been talking about, "Sleeping Out at Easter," I used this approach and used also a kind of refrain technique that, so far as I know, I invented for the occasion. In this, the last or refrain lines of the stanzas unite to make, themselves, a last stanza which sums up the attitude and action of the poem. It is a poem about Easter and a man who is sleeping in the back yard of his home the night before Easter. He wakes in a small grove of pine trees and finds that he is thinking of resurrection.

Sleeping Out at Easter

All dark is now no more.
This forest is drawing a light.
All Presences change into trees.
One eye opens slowly without me.
My sight is the same as the sun's,
For this is the grave of the king,
Where the earth turns, waking a choir.
   All dark is now no more.

Birds speak, their voices beyond them.
A light has told them their song.
My animal eyes become human
As the Word rises out of the darkness
Where my right hand, buried beneath me,
Hoveringly tingles, with grasping
The source of all song at the root.
   Birds sing, their voices beyond them.

Put down those seeds in your hand.
These trees have not yet been planted.
A light should come round the world,
Yet my army blanket is dark,
That shall sparkle with dew in the sun.
My magical shepherd's cloak
Is not yet alive on my flesh.
 Put down those seeds in your hand.

 In your palm is the secret of waking.
 Unclasp your purple-nailed fingers
 And the wood and the sunlight together
 Shall spring, and make good the world.
 The sounds in the air shall find bodies,
 And a feather shall drift from the pine-top
 You shall feel, with your long-buried hand.
 In your palm is the secret of waking,

For the king's grave turns him to light.
A woman shall look through the window
And see me here, huddled and blazing.
My child, mouth open, still sleeping,
Hears the song in the egg of a bird.
The sun shall have told him that song
Of a father returning from darkness,
 For the king's grave turns you to light.

 All dark is now no more.
 In your palm is the secret of waking.
 Put down those seeds in your hand;
 All Presences change into trees.
 A feather shall drift from the pine-top.
 The sun shall have told you this song,
 For this is the grave of the king;
 For the king's grave turns you to light.

Through this method and largely through this poem, I discovered that the simple declarative sentence, under certain circumstances and in certain contexts, had exactly the qualities I wanted my lines of poetry to have. As I wrote more poems of this kind, I was increasingly aware of two things. The first was that I liked poems which had a basis of narrative, that described or depicted an action, that moved through a period of time—usually short—and allowed the reader to bring into play his simple and fundamental interest in "what happens next," a curiosity that only narrative can supply and satisfy. I also discovered that I worked most fruitfully in cases in which there was no clear-cut distinction between what was actually happening and what was happening in the mind of a character in the poem. I meant to try to get a fusion of inner and outer states, of dream, fantasy, and illusion where everything partakes of the protagonist's mental processes and creates a single impression.

It was with some such intention as this that I wrote "The Lifeguard," in which a lifeguard at a summer camp for boys, after failing to rescue one of the children from drowning, hides in the boathouse and, in his delirium of grief and helplessness, comes to believe that he can walk out upon the water of the lake where the child drowned and raise him back up into life: that he can accomplish the most impossible of all human feats and the most desirable: undo what has been done.

The Lifeguard

In a stable of boats I lie still,
From all sleeping children hidden.
The leap of a fish from its shadow
Makes the whole lake instantly tremble.
With my foot on the water, I feel
The moon outside

Take on the utmost of its power.
I rise and go out through the boats.
I set my broad sole upon silver,
On the skin of the sky, on the moonlight,
Stepping outward from earth onto water
In quest of the miracle

This village of children believed
That I could perform as I dived
For one who had sunk from my sight.
I saw his cropped haircut go under.
I leapt, and my steep body flashed
Once, in the sun.

Dark drew all the light from my eyes.
Like a man who explores his death
By the pull of his slow-moving shoulders,
I hung head down in the cold,
Wide-eyed, contained, and alone
Among the weeds,

And my fingertips turned into stone
From clutching immovable blackness.
Time after time I leapt upward
Exploding in breath, and fell back
From the change in the children's faces
At my defeat.

Beneath them I swam to the boathouse
With only my life in my arms
To wait for the lake to shine back
At the risen moon with such power
That my steps on the light of the ripples
Might be sustained.

Beneath me is nothing but brightness
Like the ghost of a snowfield in summer.
As I move toward the center of the lake,
Which is also the center of the moon,
I am thinking of how I may be
The savior of one

Who has already died in my care.
The dark trees fade from around me.
The moon's dust hovers together.
I call softly out, and the child's
Voice answers through blinding water.
Patiently, slowly,

He rises, dilating to break
The surface of stone with his forehead.
He is one I do not remember
Having ever seen in his life.
The ground I stand on is trembling
Upon his smile.

I wash the black mud from my hands.
On a light given off by the grave
I kneel in the quick of the moon
At the heart of a distant forest
And hold in my arms a child
Of water, water, water.

My second book, *Drowning with Others,* is made up of poems written in this manner: poems with a predominantly anapestic rhythm and dealing often with dream, hallucination, fantasy, the interaction of illusion and reality. My third book, *Helmets,* employed many of these same themes and approaches, but was less pronouncedly rhythmical and less hallucinatory. By this time I had begun to grow a little restive at the limitations of my method and was beginning also to dislike the way I had been handling the narrative elements. All my old reservations about the vitiating effects of artifice began to trouble me once more; I was afraid that I had simply substituted another set of conventions—of artifices—for those I had congratulated myself on discarding earlier. Although I still felt I had chosen rightly in aiming for simplicity of diction and the other qualities that attracted me, I felt in addition that I needed to move beyond these qualities as I had employed them, into other areas of diction, image, and subject matter.

I began to conceive of something I called—doubtless misleadingly—the "open" poem: a poem which would have none of the neatness of most of those poems we call "works of art" but would have the capacity to involve the reader in it, in all its imperfections and impurities, rather than offering him a (supposedly) perfected and perfect work for contemplation, judgment, and evaluation. I was interested most of all in getting an optimum "presentational immediacy," a compulsiveness in the presentation of the matter of the poem that would cause the reader to forget literary judgments entirely and simply experience. I experimented with short lines some more and, eventually, with putting several of these together on the same physical plane to make up what I called the "split line," in which spaces between the word groups would take the place of punctuation. I wrote two longish poems using the split line; they were published as *Two Poems of the Air*. The first is "The Firebombing," and includes a section which attempts to depict the sensations of a pilot in an aircraft at night over the enemy's home country, in this case Japan.

> There is then this re-entry
> Into cloud, for the engines to ponder their sound.
> In white dark the aircraft shrinks; Japan
>
> Dilates around it like a thought.
> Coming out, the one who is here is over

Land, passing over the all-night grainfields,
In dark paint over
The woods with one silver side,
Rice-water calm at all levels
Of the terraced hill.
                              Enemy rivers and trees
Sliding off me like snakeskin,
Strips of vapor spooled from the wingtips
Going   invisible   passing   over   on
Over   bridges   roads for nightwalkers
Sunday night in the enemy's country   absolute
Calm   the moon's face   coming   slowly
About
              the inland sea
Slants   is woven with wire thread
Levels out   holds together like a quilt
Off the starboard wing   cloud flickers
At my glassed-off forehead   the moon's now and again
Uninterrupted face going forward
Over the waves in a glide-path
Lost into land.

Going: going with it . . .

Of late my interest has been mainly in the conclusionless poem,
the open or ungeneralizing poem, the un-well-made poem. I hope
in the future to get the reader more and more into the actions
and happenings of the lines and require him less and less to stand
off and draw either aesthetic or moral judgments. If I am successful in this, my themes will stand forth clearly enough: the
continuity of the human family, the necessity of both caused
and causeless joy, and the permanent interest of what the painter
John Marin called "the big basic forms"—rivers, mountains,
woods, clouds, oceans, and the creatures that live naturally
among them. The forfeited animal grace of human beings, occa-

sionally redeemed by athletes, interests me also, and the hunter's sense of understanding with the hunted animal.

All poetry, I suspect, is nothing more or less than an attempt to discover or invent conditions under which one can live with oneself. I have been called a mystic, a vitalist, a pantheist, an anti-rationalist, and a good many other things. I have not been conscious of the applicability of any of these labels, although they very well may all apply. At any rate, what I have always striven for is to find some way to incarnate my best moments—those which in memory are most persistent and obessive. I find that most of these moments have an element of danger, an element of repose, and an element of joy. I should like now to develop a writing instrument which would be capable of embodying these moments and their attendant states of mind, and I would be most pleased if readers came away from my poems not at all sure as to where the danger and the repose separate, where joy ends and longing begins. Strongly mixed emotions are what I usually have and what I usually remember from the events of my life. Strongly mixed, but giving the impression of being one emotion, impure and overwhelming—that is the condition I am seeking to impose on my readers, whoever they may be. The doing, of course, is another thing.

AFTERWORD
to the New Ecco Edition

MOST of the criticism I have written is in this book, and was done originally as reviews for various magazines. It is interesting and a little shocking to reencounter some of the things I said, some of the opinions I made public at those times, in those places, and any effort to make my judgments at the present time dovetail with those of my younger self must necessarily be foredoomed. In fourteen years I have set, settled, changed, changed around, changed back, changed again. Yet I have not varied from the opinion that if a critic locks himself into fixed positions on a writer and on works, positions he considers it a moral necessity to maintain, he thereby surrenders his openness, his accessibility to experience, the moment-to-moment responsiveness of his life-situation, and indeed part of himself. I realize that these assumptions are hopelessly vague as the basis for any sort of permanently valuable criticism, and yet change is a part of my or anyone else's makeup, do what anyone will.

I now feel that I was partially wrong in some of these judgments, partially right in others, totally wrong in a few, and exactly right in an equal few. The rightest assessment I made, I think, was that of W. S. Graham. Everything I said about the poems is in the poems, and is just as I said it was. In fact, if I had it to do over again, I would write a whole article on Graham's work and focus on the extraordinary new approach to prosody he has made possible. I would quote a lot more, particularly from poems like "The Thermal Stair," his elegy for the painter-pilot Peter Lanyon, killed in a gliding accident in 1964. As it is, I can quote a little of this now, from the part where the poet and the artist, dead in a thermal climb, drink, listening to the sea, in a pub.

> Climb here where the hand
> Will not grasp on air.
> And that dark-suited man
> Has set the dominoes out
> On the Queen's table.
> Peter, we'll sit and drink
> And go in the sea's roar
> To Labrador with wallis
> Or rise on Lanyon's stair.

I was wrongest in my grotesque overestimation of the work of Nikos Katzanzakis, and I feel that the essay on him was more an exercise in effusiveness on my part than responsible criticism. And yet I still like what I say about existence, about the creative mind, using Katzanzakis as a pretext, better than almost anything I have written about poetry, and I am grateful that Katzanzakis's *Odyssey* gave me the opportunity to say it. I must conclude that there is some imaginary poet named Katzanzakis who exemplifies this effusion on my part, but the real one doesn't. *That* one now strikes me as a rather tiresomely obvious, self-serving and humorless man, pompous and somewhat unpleasant in the self-aggrandizing and pseudo-philosophical manner of the worst of Nietzsche.

Regrettably perhaps, I no longer feel it necessary to pay any sort of lip-service to William Carlos Williams, who in my opinion is a poet of no merit whatsoever. A good doctor, I am sure, a reasonably good observer of some aspects of American life, a good human being, generous and well-intentioned, but as a writer flat, obvious and uninteresting beyond the telling.

I would stand by my remarks on Yvor Winters, and on his school, exemplified here by Ellen Kay and Donald Drummond. If asked I would say the same thing again, except that I would be even harsher, I expect. Even so, I have come around on Thom Gunn, whose approach is essentially the same as theirs. The difference is talent; Gunn has it and they do not. I think now that the best case that can be made for neoclassical verse in our time is made by Gunn. I should have seen the possibilities of this in my review, and this failure is probably the most flagrant in the book, if my section on Katzanzakis or my absurd overestimation of Hayden Carruth is not.

On two of these writers I am still as divided, as uncertain, as before. These are Robinson Jeffers and Randall Jarrell. Since writing these pieces I have read almost all of both writers over again, and I don't believe I will ever be able to make up my mind, so glaring and extreme are the defects and virtues. For example, the sweep of Jeffers is impressive, as I noted. As the world dwindles, computerizes and plasticizes, it is even more impressive; one looks through Jeffers's dark, long lines at the Carmel coastal hills as though at the Lost Paradise itself. And yet his metaphors, his actual linguistic insights, are second-rate, almost invariably. If a defense could be made for poetic technique that ignores or cannot command the actual essence of poetry, which is the highly individual apprehension of some aspect of reality or fantasy fixed in disturbing, inimitable and releasing words, then Jeffers would be worth defending. But this will have to be done by somebody else. I am finished with Jeffers, except in classrooms, or alone, late at night.

To me, Randall Jarrell is one of the most curious cases in all literature. I have a provisional pantheon of three never-fail poet-critics by whom I measure others. These are John Peale Bishop, Conrad Aiken, and Delmore Schwartz. To these, and at that level (though they are not practicing poets), I would be inclined to add Dwight Macdonald and Stanley Edgar Hyman. But far above that reliable professional class is Randall Jarrell; he is in a class by himself; he is something *else*, as they say in the South. Both when he is wrong (or when *I* think he is wrong) and when he is right he is full of so much intelligence, so much ebullience and involvement and concern that he makes other critics, even those I have cited, appear to be suffering from some unnecessary terminal illness, compared to his superb, open-minded, bright, resourceful, enthusiastic, healthy example. But the poems . . . the poems.

It is impossible for me to understand how a person like Randall Jarrell, with the gifts of intellect and discretion and daring and wit that he had, with his devotion to the life of art and especially of poetry, with the leisure and the will to write as voluminously and at the same time as carefully as he wished, could not, for all these bestowings, write truly memorable poetry. It may be that he gave away too much to the situation itself, to each of the dramatic episodes he wrote about, to the "human situation" in which he was so deeply involved. That may have been it; I don't know. But the fact is that Jarrell's language does not truly and deeply live for me. I can't remember any of his *lines*, or the actual words in which he says a thing. I can remember some of his situations, and almost all of his attitudes, but not his words. The essay, the dialogue, I wrote about Jarrell was the first critical article I ever published in a national magazine, and between then and now I met and corresponded with Jarrell, and came to prize his example and his life, his wit, his commitment and enthusiasm, more than ever, and consequently I have strange and mixed feelings about what I said a long, sincere, confused, stupid time ago; I feel now that I overrated the poetry and underrated him. And there the matter rests. For now, anyway.

As a kind of free-ranging hindsight, an inventory of changed and unchanged opinion, here are some other self-critiques, regrets and assertions.

I wish I had had more to say about John Berryman and the poetry of the will, and about affectation and mannerism as it pertains to this, for I think that the inventive use of the will is important in Berryman's approach to composition, and is perhaps more important, generally, than we might have thought.

To Robert Frost I was not unkind enough. What I said in favor of his poetry I said by an extreme effort of self-delusion, and under what I must have felt as the heavy pressure of critical—rather than popular—opinion. In reality I have never been able to abide Frost's work, with its dreadful meeching self-righteousness, his attitude of sullen cringing, of a kind of triumphant skulking. To finish off New England, I can also say that I overrated Edwin Arlington Robinson, whom I now find unreadable, though in the penance of the long introduction I did for a *Selected Poems* I discovered something in Robinson's enormous doorstop of a *Collected Poems* that I would not forego: one line: "And Lingard, with his eerie joy."

On Cummings I would say exactly the same thing, though less raptly; on Roethke the same, and on Wilbur.

There are smaller figures than these that I seem to have taken wrongly in one way or another. Though in the main I was favorable to Winfield Scott's long poem *The Dark Sister*, I no longer care much for it; it is not nearly up to the best of Scott's work. On the other hand I have since read Scott Donaldson's biography, *Poet in America*, and as a result came to read most of Winfield Scott's verse and whatever of his prose I could find. I now think Scott one of the better poets of our time, and if Donaldson had not already done so—and if the late George P. Elliott, a likewise neglected and good poet, also had not—I would be tempted to say why. Of the self-ruinations of American poets, Scott's is the most typical, and the saddest, and he deserves the recognition for the lack of which he quite literally died.

Charles Olson is like William Carlos Williams, whom he very much resembles: well-meaning and congenitally unable to say one memorable thing. However, someone put me on to Paul Christensen's book about Olson, *Call Him Ishmael*, which turns out to be far more interesting than Olson is, and valuable.

William Stafford is even better than I said he was, and if I had more room I should like to talk about the wonderfully individual, off-beat and convincing tone he brings into poetry.

I like Robert Penn Warren's work and Edwin Muir's more than

I did, and Marianne Moore's and Louis Simpson's less. I can still see no merit in Robert Graves, for all his bluster, except for one or two poems that seem to have been written by someone else, or by mistake.

On Allan Ginsberg I wish I had not wasted even one sentence. The opinion reprinted here was one of the first reviews of *Howl*, and in my overcompensatory and mistaken wish to be "fair" I gave too much ground. Now, however, at the age of almost sixty, I can state with some certainty that I like real poetry, not joke-poetry. Ginsberg's influence has been disastrous, and has enabled anyone in sight to announce himself a "poet" with talentless brashness and contribute to filling the air and innumerable small magazines with forgettable maunderings, all of this resulting in a disregard for real imagination, real originality, real poetry, real being. The critics who have taken Ginsberg's kind of thing seriously are as much to blame as Ginsberg for such deprivation; all these will pass into the great compost heap of social history, and a few good poets and poems will be left, whether they are those I select or others.

As to the writers dealt with in these pages, I invite the reader to find whatever truth and permanence they may have somewhere between my extremes, or in extremes even more drastic, either way.

James Dickey

Columbia, South Carolina
March, 1981

INDEX

of Principal Poets Discussed